ROCKMAN
POB 332
rockman@netvision.net.il
MEVESSERET,ISRAEL/90805

None of Them Were Heroes

Letters Between the Lines
1938–1942

Chaim Rockman

PUBLISHING
JERUSALEM ◆ NEW YORK

NONE OF THEM WERE HEROES
Letters Between the Lines 1938–1945
Published by DEVORA PUBLISHING COMPANY
Text Copyright © 2003 by Chaim Rockman

Cover and Book Design: S. Kim Glassman
Editor: Sorelle Weinstein

All rights reserved. No part of this book may be reproduced or transmitted in any form or by any means, electronic or mechanical, including photocopying, recording, or by any information storage and retrieval system, without permission in writing from the publisher.

ISBN: 1-930143-74-5

Email: sales@devorapublishing.com
Web Site: www.devorapublishing.com

Printed in Israel

Contents

Acknowledgements 5
Background 6
Introduction 7
Main Characters 13
Newspapers Referenced 14

1. The Schmulewitsches' First Years in England 17
2. Surviving Krystalnacht 33
3. Adolf Rochman Plans His Escape 43
4. Dina Thorn – A Friend or Foe? 53
5. Uncle Zelig Secures a Visa for Adolf 65
6. Hitler Plans First Stages of War 71
7. Freedom Around the Corner – Adolf Sets Off for England ... 81
8. Adjusting to Life in England – Adolf Becomes Peter 93
9. Blood is Thicker than Water – a Testing Time for Family Loyalties 105
10. Trapped in Leipzig – Lina Cries for Help 119
11. Britain Prepares for War 135
12. Peter Faces Dilemma As Time is Running Out for Lina ... 145
13. Life for Jews in Leipzig Going from Bad to Worse 155
14. Peter Discovers Newfound Freedom in Leeds 167

15. Lotti Pursues Romance with Peter 179

16. Winter of Discontent – Desperation Sweeps Europe 195

17. Schmulewitsch Family Wedding 201

18. Peter Presents Ultimatum to Dina 215

19. Berta Desperate to Leave Rumania 239

20. Zelig Writes in Protest Against Mosley 253

21. Max Detained in Refugee Prison Camp in Isle of Man ... 265

22. Hitler Invades Soviet Union 275

23. Peter Regrets Not Joining Friends in Palestine 285

24. Liquidation of Cetata Alba – Berta and Judith
    Meet a Tragic Death 295

25. Peter Announces Marriage 303

26. Too Little, Too Late – Peter Finally Receives Visa for Lina ... 315

Family Photos 325

Acknowledgements

I would first and foremost like to thank my wife, Eva, who had the patience to listen to me read each chapter, and tirelessly gave her insights and comments.

I would also like to thank Jackie Dack from Guisborough for helping me collect and edit the material on Guisborough Shirt and Underwear Factory.

I would like to thank Goeffrey Young from Guisborough for putting me in contact with the Guisborough Museum.

In particular, I would like to thank Dr. Katrin Keller from Leipzig University for helping me in the translation of the letters and finding contacts within the archives of the University. I also would like to thank Solvejg Hoppner in helping me find relevant material from the former Gestapo archives in Leipzig.

I would like to express my gratitude to the staff of the Jewish Museum in Leipzig who helped me map out the residence of Lina Rochman in her final years in Leipzig and the train schedules with their passenger lists of those that were sent to Riga Concentration Camp.

I would like to thank the Barnet, Katz and Fishbine families for inviting me into their homes and giving me as much information and photos as they possibly could in order to complete the family tree.

I would also like to acknowledge the Yad Vashem and the Leo Baeck institutions for giving me access to their archives and libraries. At the same time, I would like to thank the Colindale Library and their staff.

Finally, I would like to thank my sister Zilila for sharing with me the first letter that she found, and to my mother for helping me fill in the gaps of my family's history.

Chaim Rockman

Background

NONE OF THEM WERE HEROES is based upon letters that were sent between family members as they were scattered around the world during World War II. The Oberman and Schmulewitsch families, who originated from Leipzig, left Germany as the Nazi regime seized power in 1933. The first couple to leave was Berta (Rochman) and Siyoma Grusman, who fled to Cetata Alba in Rumania. Following them, the Schmulewitsch family moved to Guisborough in England in 1935. Following the November 1938 *Krystalnacht* pogrom, Adolf Rochman, who later changed his name to Peter Rockman, arrived in England in 1939. Other friends and family members escaped to Palestine, Kenya and the U.S.A. Adolf's mother, Lina Rochman, remained in Leipzig throughout the war, and was deported in 1942 to a death camp in Riga.

The only way the family members could keep in contact was through letters. Phones and other means of communication that we know of today were not available to the wide public, and most definitely not to Jews. The letters tell a story of simple people from simple backgrounds from a simple neighborhood in Leipzig. Their main aim was survival, survival in a changing world with new situations that they had not known before and for which they were totally unprepared.

As the title of the book indicates, none of the characters were heroes and did not leave their mark in history. Their names do not appear on street signs or in history books. However, the fact that their story is published today is proof of the legacy they left behind – generations of children who not only survived to tell their story, but also built a future for themselves and for generations to come. This, more than anything, is evidence that these "non-heroes" triumphed over those who tried to destroy them.

Introduction

I was born in Manchester, England in the mid-1940s. My father was a German refugee, who had escaped the tentacles of the Nazi regime, and my mother is a native Mancunian, who was the daughter of Jewish immigrants who arrived in England at the end of the 19th century.

When I was five years old, my parents decided to leave behind the relatively comfortable lifestyle of a middle-class Jewish family in Manchester, and, with the most basic of belongings, boarded a boat in Southampton, which took my parents, my sister and I to the newly-born State of Israel.

It seemed that my sister and I adjusted more easily to the Middle Eastern climate than my parents did. The language, difference in climate, mentality and way of life in Israel were all alien to Peter and Mike (Myrtle) Rockman, and they had a hard time building their lives anew in this strange country. But for us children, it was great fun. Due to the lack of housing, we lived in a tent on the beach in a small town not far from Lebanon. Like most people, we did not have electricity, running water or a telephone, but this did nothing to dampen our spirits. My sister and I were away from the stuffy, rigid way of life in England, and that was all that mattered. We would walk barebacked, and sometimes barefooted, in the sun, free to explore our new surroundings, and swim in the sea whenever we pleased.

Life in Israel was particularly challenging for my father. Reserved and self-contained, he did not talk to us about his feelings, or even his past as a German refugee. No sooner had he finally adjusted to life in England, which was drastically different from his previous life in Germany, did he pick up and move to yet another country with a new language and a different set of values. His history and background were shrouded in mystery, and we were never admitted entrance into his secret world of thoughts. One must remember that it wasn't until the Eichmann Trials in 1961 that people started to openly discuss the Holocaust. Israel was a country that was building its future, and did not want to look back at the past. The Second World War and the Holocaust remained strictly taboo subjects to be avoided at all costs.

My father passed away in 1964, and took his secrets and feelings with him to the grave. All my sister and I were aware of was that he had arrived in England from Leipzig sometime between 1930 and 1940. The rest of his life story, and all that had happened to him before, was completely unknown to us, and as time passed, it became less important for us to find out more about this deeply introspective man who was our father.

By the early nineties, I had completed my military duty in the Navy, earned a History Degree from Hebrew University in Jerusalem, worked as a tour guide, and had lived in three countries – France, England and New Zealand. I married twice and bore five children. After years of travelling and self-searching, I found myself back in Israel, the country that I had been brought to at the age of five years; the country I call home.

As the river of life continued to flow, with its unpredictable ups and downs along the way, the picture of my father became increasingly blurred. Apart from my mother and my sister, I was aware of no other family who could help keep the memory of my father alive. This was compounded by the fact that he was buried far away in a different town. I was not yet eighteen years old at the time of his death, and had only a photo to hold onto, which was brought out at the birth of each of my children, when we would search for family resemblances. I decided to name my first child Petra, in his memory.

The memory of my father was soon to revitalize itself in our consciousness, one early morning in 1991, as my family and I were sitting in the basement of our Jerusalem house, taking the

INTRODUCTION

necessary precautions against the chemical bombs that might be launched by Iraq during the first Gulf War. A phone call from my sister abruptly woke me up from my slumber. She asked me if I had known that our father's name was not Peter, as we had always known him, but Adolf. She went on to ask me if I was also aware that his mother, our grandmother, was most likely liquidated in one of the concentration camps in the Holocaust. What's more, she told me, he had a sister and a niece who lived in some small town in Rumania, where they had perished. I told her that this was all news to me, and the only vivid memory that I could summon up was that of my father avidly listening to the wireless, once a week, when they would announce names of lost friends and relatives dispersed during the war. I recalled that the names of the sought-out survivors sounded Yiddish, Hebrew and Polish. The person searching for his family or friends would inform listeners of the lost person's nickname, town of residence, and where they had last been seen. Anyone having any further information was asked to please send a letter to such and such address. My father would gingerly note down the address, and I clearly remember him sending me to the post office the following day to buy stamps and sometimes send up to 15 letters. As a child, I obeyed my father's instructions – I did not know what and how to ask, and my father did not volunteer the information. Until the day he passed away, he did not know what became of his sister, brother-in-law and niece.

I asked my sister if her sudden interest had anything to do with the letters he used to send. Not at all, she said. While searching through her cupboards for her gas mask that had been distributed some months before, in preparation for the up-and-coming gas bombs that were due to come our way from Iraq, she fell upon a box of old letters, photos and documents from the thirties and forties, that were addressed to Adolf, and were written in German, Yiddish, and sometimes English. She asked my mother who this

Adolf person was, and what these letters were doing in her house. My mother informed her that Adolf was the name of our father prior to his move to England. Although my sister was not at all conversant in Yiddish or German, she managed to work out that some of the letters came from his sister in Rumania.

Unable to imagine what importance or secrets these letters carried, I told her that I would pick up the box after the war with Iraq was over. Once the letters came into my possession, I started to translate and decipher them. This in itself was no easy task. Many of the letters were written in phonetic Yiddish, on bits of old cardboard and toilet paper, as well as torn pieces of wallpaper. Blunt pencils were used, and every inch of space on the "paper" was taken advantage of. When the writer reached the end of the page, he/she would write in the margins, at the top and bottom of the page, and on the other side. The letters had no beginnings and no endings. The photos, which by this time were yellow and fading, were of people and places I did not know or recognize.

Trying to organize the pictures and letters into some kind of order was a task that took me over five years to complete, with the help of a history expert from Yad Vashem and a cryobiologist from Leipzig University. Suddenly, a window to a whole new world had been opened before my eyes. Relatives from England, Rumania, Russia, Israel, Canada and Africa, whom I had never heard of, appeared on the horizon – a family history that went back to fur traders and gold merchants in Poland at the end of the 19th century. Leipzig, which until then had no meaning to me except as a name, became familiar, as I learnt of its neighborhoods, streets, synagogues and institutions, before, during and after the war.

With the help of the letters and the Zionist Archives, I managed to interview over 80 people who knew the characters mentioned in the letters. The interviews took place in crumbling houses and apartments, old age homes, by the side of deathbeds, in different countries all over the world. Trying to juggle my quest

INTRODUCTION

to unravel my family history with my family responsibilities was a challenge, but definitely worthwhile. It gave me a whole new perspective of who my father was: who were his friends and family, and what were his experiences. I began to see him not just as a father, but as a person. I felt a deep bond, and an unusual sort of friendship, with this man who had passed away while I was still a teenager. I began to see him with different eyes, and could relate to his experiences as a youth and young man.

If I have any regrets, it is that these letters did not fall into my hands many years before, when most of the people mentioned in the letters were still alive and lucid. I also regret not being able to ask my father hundreds, or maybe thousands, of questions, which could shed some light on events that, until today, are still a mystery to me. Now that I am older than he was when he passed away, I regret not being able to put my arms around him, and tell him I love him so much more now that I know who he was and what enormous difficulties he went through in the latter part of his life.

In 1996 I was injured in a work accident, and broke my leg. I was hospitalized in Soroka hospital in Be'er Sheva. The young doctor who was tending to me after my surgery introduced himself as Lieutenant Grusman. I could hear very clearly from his accent that he came from one of the inner parts of Russia. After getting to know him better, I asked him if he was related in any way to Siyoma Grusman, my father's brother-in-law from Cetata Alba on the Black Sea, whom I never knew. I was astonished and excited to hear that my Uncle Siyoma was this young man's grandfather. He went on to tell me that after joining the Kerch Army Group, that was part of the 62nd Red Army under Lt. Gen. Kozlov, as a horse veterinarian, Siyoma was engaged in battle against the 11th German Army, which was under the command of the famous Field Marshal von Manstein. After the defeat of the Battle of Kerch in October 1941, he was badly wounded and taken over the straits of Azov to mainland Russia, where he was admitted to the military hospital in Rostov. After Rostov was occupied, and the hospital destroyed, Siyoma left, with thousands of other refugees, on a journey eastwards. They sometimes travelled on cargo trains that were transporting the U.S.S.R.'s heavy industry east out of the range of the Wermacht or by horse or mule. During this time, he made his living by tending to animals, drawing from his experience in husbandry. After close to a year of wandering, he arrived at a farmhouse just outside the city of Gurjev in Kazakhstan, not far from the Caspian Sea.

A widow, whose husband never returned from Stalingrad, took him into the farmhouse. Although they never married, they had children, one of them being this young doctor's father. Grusman stayed in the town and became the main doctor of the local hospital. The doctor told me that his father and grandfather influenced him to study medicine. He studied at the medical school of Stalingrad and became a doctor in 1985. Although he is only half Jewish, and from the "wrong side," as he put it, he decided to move to Israel and make it his home. He arrived here in the early nineties. By the time our paths crossed in the hospital, he was a medical officer in the Bark Brigade of the Armored Core and was taking part in some sort of advanced research in Soroka Hospital. By finding this young man, I felt as if I had come full circle. And suddenly, as I was lying in Soroka Hospital, with one foot raised in the air, it dawned on me that maybe it was more than just a coincidence that I had been injured and ended up being under this doctor's care. So here we are, readers. What started as an ignited interest in my family history became a legacy that could be passed on to future generations, through this book.

Main Characters

Moritz Oberman, *wife's name is unknown*
David Oberman, *Moritz's oldest child. Married to Lily*
Sarah Oberman, *Moritz's oldest daughter. Married to Zelig Schmulewitsch*
Lina Oberman, *Moritz's daughter. Married to Zallel Rochman*

* * *

Berta Schmulewitsch, oldest child of Sarah and Zelig Schmulewitsch. Married to Jack Fishburn
Max Schmulewitsch, *son of Sarah and Zelig Schmulewitsch. Married to Jane*
Herman Schmulewitsch, *son of Sarah and Zelig Schmulewitsch. Married to Ray*
Dora Schmulewitsch, *daughter of Sarah and Zelig Schmulewitsch. Married to Josef Menashe*
Shnoki Schmulewitsch, *daughter of Sarah and Zelig Schmulewitsch. Married to Carol Katz, brother of Lotti*

* * *

Berta Rochman, *oldest child of Lina and Zallel Rochman, Married to Siyoma Grusman*
Esther Rochman, *daughter of Lina and Zallel Rochman.*
Adolf Rochman, *son of Lina and Zallel Rochman. Changes his name to Peter Rockman in England. Married to Myrtle*
Regina, Yoachim, and Ignis, *children from Zallel's first marriage*

* * *

Judith Grusman, daughter of Berta and Siyoma
Gizella, daughter of Regina, granddaughter of Zallel

Newspaper and Other Media Sources

- *Baltimore News-Post* (US)
- BBC (UK)
- *Brest Litovsk Byelorussia* (USSR)
- *Call Bulletin, The* (US)
- *Cleveland Standard, The* (US)
- *Daily Standard, The* (US)
- *Daily Record, The* (US)
- *Daily Worker, The* (UK)
- *Davar* (Palestine)
- *Der Angriff* (Germany)
- *Der Judische Rundschau* (Germany)
- *Die Rote Fahne (The Underground German Communist Newspaper)* (Germany)
- *Evening Press,* (UK)
- *Gainsborough Times, The* (UK)
- *Hebrew Press* (Palestine)
- *Herald Express* (US)
- *Honolulu Star Bulletin* (US)
- *Jewish Chronicle* (UK)
- *Jewish Gazette, The* (UK)
- *Jewish Press, The* (US)
- *Juedisches Nachrenblatt,* (Germany)
- *Leipzig Rundschau* (Germany)
- *London Times* (UK)
- *Los Angeles Examiner* (US)
- *Manchester Daily* (UK)
- *Middlesbrough Gazette* (UK)
- *News Bulletin* (Canada)
- *News Dispatch,* (US)
- *News Paper Dispatch* (US)
- *Portage Lake Gazette* (US)
- *Pravda* (USSR)
- *St. Paul Pioneer Press* (US)
- *Sunday Star, The* (US)
- *Telegraph, The* (UK)
- *Times, The* (UK)
- *Tri-Cities Daily, The* (US)
- *Victoria Daily Times* (US)
- *Views of the World* (Australia)
- *Volkischer Beobachter* (Germany)
- *Washington Daily News* (US)

And

- Press extracts from correspondents in the USSR
- *The Kindertransport (Encyclopedia of the Holocaust)*

To my beloved father, Peter,
who never knew,
and to my beloved son, Daniel,
who died too young to know

Chapter One

The Schmulewitsches' First Years in England

Friday, October 28, 1938
Middlesbrough, England

ZELIG SCHMULEWITSCH CAME IN LATE that day from the factory. He was tired, nervous and distressed. Apparently, learning English was more difficult than he had originally thought. The working standard among employees was not what he was used to back home in Leipzig. He was homesick for the language, culture and friends he had left behind. In addition, the news coming from home was not encouraging. He was worried about his sister-in-law Lina, and his nephew Adolf. His daughter's parents-in-law were also in trouble, and were doing the best they could to get themselves and their property out of Germany. He was expected to help.

They were not the only ones who were seeking assistance. Most of Zelig's friends and family, who, five years ago, did everything they could to discourage him from leaving – arguing that the emergence of the Nazi government would improve matters – had now changed their tune. Apparently, matters had deteriorated, and his friends required urgent help. Although he had managed to establish himself in England quite successfully over the last three years, he was still considered stateless, or, as they called him here, a "Russian Citizen." Since he was not considered to be a "British National," he could not put his signature on the guarantee documents for those refugees arriving from Germany. Zelig was sorry about that, as he would have liked to have been hailed a savior among his family and friends back home. What they did not understand was that he was also a newcomer and still did not know the ropes, the language or understand the culture. What he could do at home with a flick of a finger was so much more complicated here. After all, he could not provide work and be a guarantor to every Tom, Dick and Harry who wanted to come over to England, even if they were Jews.

When Zelig and his wife Sarah first arrived in England, they were worried that they were depriving their children of the culture and activity of the big world that they had left behind. But they soon came to understand, first-hand, exactly what the German culture stood for, a culture that had once captivated them with its splendor. Zelig's eyes were opened to the monstrosities that this "civilization" was capable of perpetrating. Zelig realized that it was preferable to live in a country where there were no music halls, concerts or theater, and where he could not speak the language, than to live among a barbaric people that systematically burned synagogues without batting an eye.

He thought back to how he and his sons, Max and Herman, made the decision, just in time, to leave Leipzig, despite what people around them were saying: that they should wait awhile, and they would see that things were not as bad as they seemed. He recalled a conversation with Adolf and Lina when he informed them of his plan to leave Leipzig and live in Guisborough. They

THE SCHMULEWITSCHES' FIRST YEARS IN ENGLAND

laughed at him and his family, saying, "Do you think they have electricity in the town? Will you need to bring electricity with you?" And now, look at them. They are both begging him to do something, anything, to secure them a permit to come and live in this town that "has no electricity."

It is true, he thought, it did take some big decision-making to pick up the whole family, take the girls out of school and move here. What gave Zelig the final push to leave Leipzig was an incident that occurred on April 1, 1933, as he was on his way home to his house on Menek Strasse. On that day, the Nazi Party had declared, for the first time since it came to power, an official boycott of Jewish shops. He saw the Brownshirts standing outside his friend's shop *Kaufhaus Gebrüder Held* on Merseburger Strasse. He noticed one of his old workers, whom he had not long ago fired, shouting to his hooligan friends, "Here is one of those delinquent Jews going by. Let's get him, and teach him a lesson as the Beloved Füehrer told us to do." Zelig was beaten and knocked down to the ground. When he got up, ten of the hooligans surrounded him, shouting, "Death to the Jews, death to the Jews." Zelig believed them; he did not need any more convincing. It was clear to him that from then on, Jewish blood would be cheap in Nazi Germany. He knew there was no point in seeking police assistance as he would only be beaten for filing a complaint against an Aryan. Right there and then, he resolved that it was time to leave.

It was Zelig's two older sons, Max and Herman, who first came to London in 1933 under the camouflage of exchange students wishing to study English. In the meantime, they explored the possibility of moving their family textile business and manufacturing facilities from Fishbine Strasse in Leipzig to England. At the same time, Max and Herman were to transfer the earnings from their business in Leipzig to Barclay's Bank in London without the Nazi authorities laying their hands on the money. It was then that Herman met his future wife, Ray, who was the oldest daughter of

Mrs. Greensin, the woman he and Max lodged with when they first arrived in England. Ray was only sixteen when they got married, and although Zelig and Sarah came over for the wedding in 1934, they disapproved of the union in the belief that Herman was marrying beneath himself. Ray's mother was not only a divorcee, but earned her living by running a stall in the market.

It was also during this trip that Max met his wife-to-be Jane. Jane was the sister-in-law of Isaac Bellow, the general manager and owner of Bellow Engineering Leeds, which was the main supplier of sewing machines to the textile factory that the Schmulewitsch family had opened in Guisborough, when they came over from Leipzig in 1935–36. Jane was ugly and overweight. It was well known amongst the family that it was a marriage of convenience between a textile manufacturer and a sewing machine supplier. In September 1933, Isaac Bellow was to see to it that the Schmulewitsch family would obtain the necessary permits to reopen their manufacturing facilities in North England. He also arranged for their business to be transferred to one of the small towns in Yorkshire, in North East England. By doing so, they would receive government subsidies to reopen their manufacturing plant, as the towns in this region were considered by Neville Chamberlain's government to be a deprived area. That is how it came to be that Zelig, together with his wife, two sons, three daughters, one grandchild and a son-in-law, found themselves in Guisborough.

Bellow had come through with his promise, but he had a problem with the new laws of the National Socialist Government in Germany, better known as the Nazi party, laws that stated: "Non-Aryans cannot not leave the Fatherland Germany with any of their property or capital." As the Schmulewitsch family had at that time some big Jewish clients in England who would buy their linen, he decided to send Max and Herman over to London. Zelig instructed them to advise these clients to only transfer some of their money to Germany in order to show some income. The remainder should be deposited into a London Barclay's Bank account. This caused them a credit problem when paying for materials and labor, but they could pay for this with Reich Marks, which they took out of their savings.

Zelig also knew that today that this would no longer be possible, since the Deutsche Reich's Bank, together with the *"Zollamt"* (customs department), had closed this loop in the net, catching almost everyone who tried this trick. Once they had sufficient capital in London, Max applied to the Trade Commission, and with the help of Bellow, managed to get a permit to enter Great Britain and reopen their factory there. Obviously, all this had to be done in great secrecy because most of their clerical staff were Nazi supporters, and he had no doubt that they would not hesitate to inform on them to the authorities, feeling like great German patriots. The next stage was to try and coordinate the move of capital and machines in such a way that it would confuse the Nazi authorities.

Herman had an Aryan schoolfriend working for the Reich's Trade Commission. At the time, the friend was active in the Leipzig Communist cell. The friend informed Herman about the new law that that had just been passed, which would allow foreign passport holders who came from former German colonies, such as East Prussia, to transfer some of their manufacturing capital to those former colonies. Zelig originally came from Koenigsberg, which was the capital of East Prussia. This loophole enabled Zelig to transfer his assets out of Germany.

It was clear that from then on, they would have to operate quickly and with greater secrecy. In London, Herman and Max were told to prepare all the papers so they could start moving the family to England.

Zelig was sorry to leave his house in the suburb of Gohlis, right opposite the Rosenthal Park. It had taken them so many years to acquire sufficient status and money to move to a more prestigious area in Leipzig. Gohlis was a concentrated neighborhood reserved for German Jews, not for the stateless Russian or Polish Jews like the Schmulewitsches. Even after they did move, they were never fully accepted into these circles. Zelig often heard them say in the synagogue, *"Der sein nicht von uns"* (they are not one of us). These comments continued for some time until they restored their old membership in the Brody synagogue, which was located on the other side of the park. There, Zelig felt much more among his own people.

With the help of Herman's friend, they collected all the necessary permits to move their factory to Koenigsburg, which was at that time the capital of Eastern Prussia. In 1933–34, this was relatively easy. The Nazi party administration was in its infant stage, and did not have such a concerted idea of what it wanted to do with Jewish property. The officials' only wish was for the Jews to leave, and when they did so, the Nazi officials saw this as a triumph.

The Schmulewitsch family started to arrive in Koenigsberg on December 5, 1934. From there, the journey to Newcastle was short and easy. By the New Year of 1935, the entire Schmulewitsch family found themselves in England. Herman and Max were the first there. The girls were next: Shnoki and Dora, followed by his wife, Sarah. Berta was only prepared to leave Germany if Jack, her husband, could come with her. The family settled in the Gray House in Middlesbrough. Looking back, Zelig regretted two things: One was that Adolf did not want to come with them, excusing himself by saying he must stay with his mother in Leipzig. The second was that he had never taken the time to learn English, thinking it would never be needed since Germany was the trade center of the world.

It took the family a long time to resume the whole operation, since in England everything was measured in inches, feet and yards. Zelig only knew meters and centimeters. This problem was something that took him time to get used to. But today, he knew and understood it well.

Zelig reflected on the risk he had taken in leaving Leipzig, but it had worked out well. Today, he had all his family around him, and Berta had given birth to a son. Max and Herman were married, and they all lived close by. No one called them dirty Jews, and most important of all, they were free people, able to come and go as they wished. They were a respected family in the community. The Schmulewitsch family was respected in Guisborough and Middlesbrough, even among the *goyim* (non-Jews), for providing honorable work and a good income for some 500 women who otherwise would never have found employment. He reminded himself that nowhere in Germany, and most certainly not in Leipzig, would a Jew be a welcome guest in the mayor's office.

He was glad to see that a letter had arrived from his beautiful, favorite niece, Berta, who was living in a small harbor town on the Black Sea, bordering the Soviet Republic of the Ukraine. He had to admit that Middlesbrough was no Paris, not even Leipzig, but it was England, a part of the great British Empire. Where Berta was living with her Communist husband was in Rumania, and how could one compare the two?

As Zelig was about to open the letter from his niece, his wife asked him if he would like "tea," using the English expression for "*Abendessen*." She had lately begun to insert more and more English words into their conversations. He was jealous that she seemed to pick up the language so much faster than him. While eating, he read Berta's letter. At least it was written in a language he could understand. He looked at her neat handwriting on the envelope, which had the likeness of the Rumanian king on its stamp. It was addressed to:

Mr. and Mrs. Schmulewitsch,
The Gray House,
79 Cambridge Road, Middlesbrough, England.

Letter Translated from German:
Friday, September 30, 1938
Trayan St. 50, Cetata Alba, Rumania

Dear Uncle Zelig,

    I was so glad to receive your letter. It arrived here with the mail from Bucharest last week. I was happy to hear how well you and the family have adapted to the new country. I am astonished that you managed to reopen the factory in such a short time, in a place whose language and custom are so strange and foreign to us.

    As for the Jewish community you were asking me about: We have here some 6,000 Jews. We also have two synagogues, one for the Turkish Jews who are called Spanish here (I do not know why the Turkish are named Spanish and the European Jews, like us, are known here as "Galicianers"). There is not much else to tell, but I would say that in spite of the big distance between the two towns, it does seem much the same as you describe Middlesbrough. If I would have to guess, I would say that you had never heard of our town before we came to live here, but I could say the same about where you live. It would be difficult for me to describe Cetata Alba to you. It often reminds me of Murnaw in Bavaria, where we used to go on holiday, in the good old days when Jews were still allowed in hotels. It has a main street with a river flowing in the middle, and on both sides small cafés, that look so much like the fur trade center, Bruel, back home. The cafés, owned by descendants of German families that came in Bismarck's time, offer good German coffee and pastries.

    Although the official language is Rumanian, more Russian is spoken here on a day-to-day basis. I have many friends who speak

THE SCHMULEWITSCHES' FIRST YEARS IN ENGLAND

German, and we even have a literary society and theater company. We meet once a week in the same house that Pushkin lodged in when he came to visit the place about 116 years ago.

We also have a music hall in which I have the opportunity to give a few concerts.

My friends in Leipzig ask me if we still live in caves here, but I can tell you that the town has quite an international flavor. I must say for us Jews, it's not so good. We were forced to sell the tavern, the one that was owned by my husband and his brothers. It was our main outlet for the wine we produced on the farm. Interesting that on the same week that we sold, or should I say, gave up, the tavern, the same "*shaliach*" [an emissary who would travel across Europe trying to recruit Jews to emigrate to Palestine] from the Jewish Zionist Party was passing through town, and tried for the tenth time, maybe, to convince Siyoma to buy land in Palestine. The land is in a small Jewish colony called Rishon Le'ziyyon. He said they have vineyards and a winery that is owned by the Rothschild family, so he can continue to do there what he does here. But Siyoma told him that the situation is not as bad as it looks, and once the Communists will take over, like in the Ukraine, things will only get better for the Jews. I say that it will be too difficult for us at this point in life to change and give up all we have – servants, friends, the European way of life, and the life I have built for myself here – only to go to Argentine or Palestine, or any other "Tine" in the world, just because some Fascist hooligan in Bucharest goes around the streets shouting, "Death to the Jews."

I must say that our life is not so bad, especially if I compare it to life at home in Leipzig. Mama and my friends describe things over there as not being so good.

We still have this big house that Siyoma's parents bought for us when we came, the farm, which is the biggest in the region. Siyoma is the only farmer who owns one of these plowing machines that can pull a plow and do work in one day that take a team of horses a whole week. It has steel wheels and works from steam.

We still manage to sell our wine and meat to all the German villagers within a radius of 100 KM around. "Landsmen," we call them. They still appreciate quality products that remind them of home. They are our best customers. Recently Siyoma bought a summerhouse not far from "the Castle," so during vacation time we can be closer to the beach. I will tell you all about the Castle shortly. Siyoma's family is very respected in town. The oldest brother, the one I told you converted, is the town's mayor. I have friends here. One of them is my seamstress, a cultured Russian woman from Odessa. She escaped the Bolsheviks; her daughter happens to be Judith's best friend. I get along very well with Siyoma's sister, who also owns a farm with her husband. They live not far from us on Shevchebko St. We are one of the few families who own a carriage, the same one we travelled in to Leipzig, just before Hitler (may Satan take him) and his hooligans came to power. I can say that I have built a life for my family and myself, and I would not like to leave. The other day, we got a letter from Lionel Simoom's younger brother, who immigrated to Canada, telling us to come and live there. But I say, what do we need all this for? The way he describes it, his life is very difficult, and certainly not better than our life here. It is true, I do miss Mama. I have asked her many times to come live with us, but she always says she is too old to change and go to live so far away, in a place where they do not speak Yiddish or any other language she can understand.

News from home is very distressing. I hear from Adolf and Mama that every day there are new restrictions, limitations and curtailments on the Jews. My friend Naumi Witerlis, the one who lives on Lonrtzig Strasse just around the corner from Mama's place, tells me she cannot teach any longer in a German school. Her father had to sell his business for close to nothing to any Aryan.

THE SCHMULEWITSCHES' FIRST YEARS IN ENGLAND

With the money he got, he will try to get a certificate to go to Haifa in Palestine, where her sister is already living, but that may also take time. Worse, she told me that there are rumors going around that they are going to throw out all the Polish and stateless Jews if they will not leave of their own free will. There is talk about people that have been sent to Dachau, this small town outside of Munich, in order to be retained. They came back, packed all their things and left. I do not understand what they want from the Jews. What harm did we do them? It is just disgusting the way they treat them, like animals sometimes. Obviously a thing like that could never happen here. And in this place, we are not talking about highly cultured people like the people back home. I can understand an outbreak of anti-Semitism from time to time, or even a pogrom, but I think they have carried it too far.

I will end the letter now, as the servant just came to tell me that the carriage is ready to take Judith to her music lesson.

So give my love to my cousin Max and his new wife.

Berta

P.S. Judith my daughter sends her love.

P.P.S. You asked me if I could tell you more about our town. I would say that Siyoma, or even Judith, know much more than I do. However, it is difficult for Judith to write in German and she will not attempt to write a letter in a language she is not fluent in. To get Siyoma to write a friendly letter to one he considers a capitalist is just impossible. So I went the other day to our local library. I got some sort of a pamphlet about our town and I am sending it with the letter. I translated the pamphlet for you in a sort of free style (as the translation from Russian to German is not easy) with some comments here and there.

* * *

Zelig took the brochure out of the envelope and read it, noting Berta's comments sprawled all over.

Ackerman (Cetata Alba): A farming town, population 30,000, which is centered around cultivating wine, wheat and potatoes.

Many people of different nationalities can be found in this town and its surroundings: Rumanians, Jews, Hellenists (Greeks), Russians, French, Germans and Ukrainians.

The harbor, which is the second largest in Rumania, is the main door for Rumanian and Polish products that come via the Dnjenster River, and are sent from here to Istanbul, Alexandria and Marseilles.

[Here Berta inserted one of her comments, in her handwriting, on the side of the brochure:]

The other day when I was taking a walk with Judith and her friend Larissa on the docks, I saw river barges that came from Warschau, Lublin and Piotrkow (as you know, this was the town that Mama and Papa eloped to after I was born) and other cities in Poland and Rumania. They were loaded with wheat and corn. I also saw railway cars on their way to Haifa for the British Army in the Middle East.

Just after the Great War, as part of the Versailles Treaty, the town and its surroundings were given back to Rumania, its lawful owner, from Russia. Until that time, Cetata Alba was the resort town for upper-class people who came from Odessa, wanting to enjoy the beaches along the Black Sea and the atmosphere of a European town. But once the Bolsheviks took over, they cut it off and closed the border. Today, the people of Cetata Alba can only go north as far as the Dnjester estuary. The ferry that used to cross the river, which met the train from Ovideoplice to Odessa, has stopped operating since the end of the war and is rusting away on the banks of the river.

The town still has some visitors who come for summer vacation, but they go mainly to Bugaz, which is on the border with Russia. They only come to Cetata Alba for shopping and recreation.

THE SCHMULEWITSCHES' FIRST YEARS IN ENGLAND

Ackerman, its former Turkish name, is the oldest city on the western shores of the Black Sea.

We still find remains from the Hellenists (Greeks) that settled here in the 7th century and named the town "Tira." After them came the Romans.

[Once more this was written by hand:]

For that matter our street is named after one of the more famous Roman Caesars, Hadrian, who destroyed our Temple in Jerusalem in the 1st century.

Most of what can be seen around here is from the "Turkish" time or what is known here as the "Ottoman Period." These are the same people who conquered Palestine, the Balkans, and held onto it until the British Army at the end of the Great War freed it. They built a big castle [*I sent you a postcard last time*] in order to protect the estuary of the Dnjester River [*called the "Liman"*] against pirates who used to come from the Crimean Peninsula. Most of the Castle is still standing as it was in the 15th century, with its original gates, stables and workshops, as if it were abandoned only yesterday. The Jews still call the city "Ackerman" which means, "The City with the White Castle" in Turkish.

For over 130 years, until the end of the Great War, Ackerman was a Russian city and still today, most people speak Russian. Even the local news paper, *The Ackerman Evening News*, is written in Russian.

[This is what Berta added at the bottom of the page:] *When I first came here in 1928, it was already a Rumanian city, but I learnt Russian long before I knew Rumanian. It was not long after the rise of Antonescu, the man that sees himself as the Füehrer of the Rumanian Fascist party known here as "The Iron Guard" (which is not so different from the Nazi party at home), that King Michael with his new cabinet started the Rumanization of all the former Russian territories.*

Come visit our town and enjoy the hospitality of Rumanians in Rumania.

* * *

Zelig still recalled the arrival of his sister-in-law, Lina, to Leipzig, a few years before the turn of the century with her family from Czestochowa. This coincided with his arrival from the German-speaking town of Koenigsberg in Eastern Prussia, a minor event of historical significance that later helped him and his family get out of Leipzig with all their property some forty years later.

The Oberman and Schmulewitsch families came to Leipzig for the Spring Trade Fair of 1892. The Oberman family came from Czestochowa, 100 KM east of Leipzig, and the Schmulewitsch family came from Koenigsburg, which was part of Germany. He knew the German language, which helped them in their first steps in the new country. That was more or less the time that his wife's family with their three children decided to move their textile factory to Leipzig. It also coincided with the time that Zallel (Adolf and Berta's father) came from Warsaw with his former wife and three children. Zallel and his wife soon divorced, after which he decided to reopen his jewelry shop. Zelig could not remember where Zallel's former family went but he thought it was either to Frankfurt or Bonn. He came to live with his wife's family, the Obermans. Zallel was a lodger at the Obermans. Zelig recalled the scandal when Lina became pregnant, even though they only got married after Berta was born. They left for the town of Petrko in Poland to get married, due to a legal problem that had to do with them being stateless, or maybe the fact that Zallel was Polish.

Max came in later that evening and showed him the headlines of *The Times* that he had picked up in Guisborough on his way home.

THE SCHMULEWITSCHES' FIRST YEARS IN ENGLAND

Friday, October 28, 1938

Late last night the German Secret Police, together with Gestapo agents, started to round up Polish Jews from all parts of the Reich. These poor people were dragged out of their homes, pulled out of bed, and arrested on the streets. They were all loaded onto lorries and trains, and were sent on an all-night voyage to the Polish border town of Zbaszyn. Having arrived at the German border, the soldiers forced them, by shooting, dogs, whips, and other means of violence, to walk across the "no man's land" into Polish territory.

Our correspondent at the border reports that over six thousand Jews were brought to the place by midnight. The majority were men. They were still in pajamas, with no other clothes to protect them from the bitter autumn cold. Our correspondent adds that the whole way from the rail-station to the border is now scattered with the possessions of the few that did manage to take one or two belongings with them as they were forced out of their beds last night. The belongings were dropped or lost in the panic and chaos which was caused by the shooting and the dogs. Our correspondents in major cities and railheads across the Reich report that a curfew was imposed on Jewish neighborhoods, while police, supported by Blackshirt Fascists, went around with lists, arresting Jews and marching them to the rail-stations that had been closed to the public since last night.

Reliable sources in Berlin, tell us that this is the new policy of the Jewish Affairs Department in the Gestapo to get rid of Polish passport holders who still live in the Reich. Due to a declaration, coming from the Polish Home Office on the 6th of October saying: "Any Polish citizen who does not renew his papers by the 29th of October, will lose his citizenship," the Reich does not want to be stuck with over 100,000 Polish Jews in addition to the 150,000 stateless Jews. Jews that live in Germany today will not be able to leave Germany due to fact that they will not have citizenship papers. This problem could hinder the program of ethnic cleansing which Himmler has announced.

The German Jewish community in Great Britain numbers over 55,000, concentrated in cities like Manchester, Leeds, Middlesbrough and London. These people arrived here from Germany since Hitler came to power some five years ago. They are concerned for friends and relatives remaining behind.

From the wires: Reports are coming in of big demonstrations outside the German embassies in London, Cairo, Paris and Washington. The authorities are concerned that they may become violent.

Zelig's face changed color as he turned to Sarah asking her how she thought this would affect her sister and nephew still left behind. Although both of them were stateless, who could know what the Nazis had in store for the remaining Jews in Germany?

Chapter Two

Surviving Krystalnacht

Wednesday, November 9, 1938

THE ENTIRE GERMAN JEWISH COMMUNITY was subjected tonight to a reign of terror without precedent in modern times in the civilized world.

Dr. Josef Goebbels, the Minster of Public Enlightenment and Propaganda, claims the orgy of violence and arson was a spontaneous reaction to the assassination of a German diplomat in Paris by a young Polish Jew, but the events bear all the hallmarks of an officially organized pogrom.

The attacks began simultaneously throughout the country. The violence followed a clear pattern. In marked contrast to former anti-Jewish outbreaks, in which loutish "Storm Troopers" were prominent, this time they were joined by respectable-looking middle class folk. In Berlin, fashionably dressed women clapped and screamed with laughter and some held up their babies to watch Jews being beaten senseless by youths with lead piping.

More than 7,000 Jewish shops were looted. Hundreds of synagogues were burned down. An unknown number of Jews died. To save insurance companies from bankruptcy, the Nazis say they will confiscate any money the Jews may receive and give it back to the insurers.

Broken glass alone accounts for millions of Marks worth of damage. It is said Goering was not pleased when he heard most of the replacement glass will have to be imported from Belgium and paid for in scarce foreign currency. "They should have killed more Jews and broken less glass," he was quoted as saying. "They cost much less."

Leipzig, December 1938

By the beginning of December, the Germans released Adolf Rochman with most of the others. He did not understand why they arrested him, and could not figure out why they let some out and others not. What was clear to him was their warning that if he would not leave Germany within six weeks, they would send him east together with his mother, as they did with the Polish Jews in October. He was determined to do all he could to get out even before the six weeks were up. As he saw it, there were only two options: One would be to go and live with his sister in Cetata Alba. The other option, not any more desirable, was to go to live with his uncle's family in Guisborough. He did not know much about either England or Rumania, but they both seemed to be equally miserable. He liked life in the big city, but at the same time, he understood that the good life in Leipzig was over, and if he and

Mama would not get out soon, that would be the end for both of them.

To get back from what the Nazis called the Sachenhausen Reeducation School for Communists, Socialist, and Jews, they marched them, the whole day, up to Berlin, and from there they put them on cattle wagons like animals, clawing. Adolf did not understand why he had to be reeducated. He was not a Communist or a Socialist, and as a Jew he was forbidden to join the Nazi party. Jews were not allowed to occupy seats in the trains that were allocated for Aryans. To add insult to injury, Adolf was charged the full train fare.

Now once more in Leipzig, he had to somehow, without being seen, get from the train station to Humboldt Strasse, where he and his mother rented an apartment. The Jewish curfew had already started and he could not cover the yellow star on his coat. He only hoped that nothing had happened to Mama while he was in the camp and that she was not sent East or to prison in his absence.

After all, they had no reason to arrest her, but by the same token, they had not had a police decree to detain him either. The Germans had taken him in place of Goldberg, his upstairs neighbor, for whom they had a Gestapo arrest warrant. Since Goldberg was not home, and they had to fill the quota, they took Adolf instead. He hated them with an anger that he never knew was within him. He only wanted out, out, out, and as soon as possible. He decided that he would leave for Rumania, England or Palestine at the first opportunity.

When he got home, his mother Lina welcomed him with open arms and could not stop crying, trying to tell him between one breath and the next what she had gone through since he was arrested. Things were getting worse from day to day, she told him. They had nothing to live on. If not for the food parcels that Berta was sending from Rumania, they would just starve. There was no money to pay for the rent, after bribing the Gestapo for Adolf's release. The hooligans were getting impudent. The police, instead of doing something to stop them, were only encouraging them. Nothing was stopping the Fascists from coming into their house, even when she was in, and raiding the cupboards and icebox, looking for forbidden foodstuffs. Now, they were no longer satisfied in simply confiscating these illicit items; they forced their helpless victims to accompany them to the Gestapo Headquarters to pay a fine.

Adolf noticed that there were letters waiting for him from his sister Berta and from Hans, his mate from the swimming team, who had left for Palestine at the same time that the Schmulewitsch family left for England.

Looking at both letters, he could see that the Gestapo had tampered with them. The letters must have arrived a short time after he was taken to Sachenhausen prison camp. At least Berta had the wisdom to write in Yiddish, so hopefully they did not understand the contents of the letter. He decided to read Berta's letter first.

Translated from Yiddish:
Saturday, November 12, 1938
Trayan St. 50, Cetata Alba, Rumania

Dear Mama and Adolf,

The news about the pogrom [Krystalnacht] reached us today, through someone in town who owns a wireless, a *goy*. The minute he heard, he went to tell the Rabbi, and he came to tell us.

I was shocked in a way that I have never been before. They talked about hundreds of Jewish businesses that were broken into. The hooligans broke the glass from the showcase windows, and it was scattered on the street and looked like crystal. He also said that all the synagogues were burnt down.

Siyoma's family was also in shock; they always considered the Germans to be such cultured people. They cannot accept the reality. In their minds, the Germans, who are civilized folk, a nation that has given the world the best possible musicians, writers, scientists and technology, could not do a thing like that. One would expect this sort of pogrom from the Ukrainians, Poles or Russians, but not from German people. I must tell you that even my German friends in the nearby villages are embarrassed, although I know that behind my back they most probably say, if Hitler had anything to do with it, the Jews most probably deserve it. I wish I would have more details, but we are walking around here in the dark, and all we know are rumors.

Did they burn down the big department store of Bamberger & Hertz, on the corner of Goethe and Grimmaische Strasse? What happened to the Brody Synagogue on Kiel Strasse – was it burnt like all the others? I was told that synagogues that are neighboring Aryan shops or houses were not touched. They say that they arrested all the Jewish men, is that true?

I hope they did not arrest Adolf. They must know that he cannot go long without a proper diet and insulin. They know of his diabetes, or I hope he told them, when they came to get him. Who would have thought a thing like that could happen in Leipzig of all places? But I must say I did see it coming, although maybe not so extreme. Of the Polish Jews that were thrown out in October, one or two families have arrived here in Cetata Alba. They told us terrible stories of the treatment they got from the German soldiers as if they were cattle. I can tell you one thing, something like that could never happen here, because they like and respect us.

I think, Mama, that the best thing is if you pack up the house and come and live with us here. You can live in comfort and safety for the rest of your life (you too, Adolf). What do you need this entire thing for, just in order to go on living with those animals?

Judith has a new friend, Larissa, the one whose mother is my seamstress. It is difficult to keep them apart; they are together all the time, in school and after school, during music lessons and horseback riding. At least two nights a week, Larissa sleeps here, and sometimes Judith goes to sleep there. Do you remember the photo, with Judith dressed up as a Marquise? If you still have the picture, you will see Larissa on the other side by the door. She is also dressed as a Marquise. All that was for a play they did in school four years ago, when Judith was seven years old.

When Larissa stays with us, I always give them a piano lesson. At the same time, I try to teach them some songs from the old country, those that Papa used to sing to us, "A big old fat madam, to catch the train she runs, once she steps onboard, the train can go no more."

Her mother, I told you, comes from Odessa, which is no more than an hour train ride from here. She often tells me about it with lots of nostalgia. She tells me Odessa is like Paris with its big wide streets and boulevards, named after famous French generals and leaders who built the city in the last century, and Dirbasky Avenue, which ends with one of the biggest opera houses in Europe. What I would not give to go visit this town once; it is so near, yet so far. Now that it is in the hands of the Bolsheviks, who knows what they have done to it? They will not let anyone from a civilized country come and visit it.

I will end here as I must go and settle some squabble among the Ukrainian and Rumanian servants.

So do write as soon as you can. Think positively about my suggestion of coming here.

Love to all,
Berta

* * *

Adolf never did get on so well with his older sister Berta; maybe it was the age difference. Four years was not enough for her to behave like his big sister, but then on the other hand, they both had different friends and social lives.

He thought to himself: What would he do in this primitive village on the Black Sea? It would be better than staying here, that was for sure.

Hans was the best-looking youngster in the water polo team, *Hacoach*. Blond, tall and well built, he looked more like an Aryan than a Jew. Together with Margolis and Max Ostrogrsci, they all belonged to the *Bar Kochba* sport movement. They joined only for the Zionist ideology that the movement was engaged in. During the training sessions, the three of them used to always talk about "when they would go to Palestine." Adolf did not like such talk; it always sounded much too fanatical to him.

In the summer of 1935, they all took part in the first Jewish international sporting event in Palestine. They never came back. He knew that some of them were there illegally, and had to go to Beirut and Damascus in order to get visas, but somehow they all managed, and were all still there. They tried very hard to convince him to come with them, but at the time he could not leave Mama. From the letters he got from them in Palestine, he gathered that life over there was no paradise. Nahariya was first built on 2,400 dunam, bought by the Nahariya Society of Small Farms for the price of 34,000 pounds. The former owners of the land were the Tookan family that lived in Beirut at the time. Nahariya was officially established on February 10, 1935. What good would Adolf be in a place like this? After all, he was not cut out to be a farmer, a pioneer or a road builder. He did feel somewhat sorry, though, that he did not join them at the time. In any case, it was too late now to have regrets; he would never get a certificate from the British Consul in Dresden, even if he managed to collect the 500 English pounds that it required. He decided to read Hans' letter next.

None of Them Were Heroes

Translated from German:
Tuesday, November 15, 1938
Nahariya, Palestine

Dear Adolf,

It has been a long time since I last heard from you. I remember that it is you who owes me a letter, but knowing what a bad writer you are, I took the initiative to write. What brought pencil to paper this time was the news coming from home. I heard from my parents about the pogrom. That criminal act has already received the name Krystalnacht. I must say that thank goodness I received a certificate for my brother and parents from the High Commissioner to Palestine in Jerusalem, so they will be leaving Leipzig in a short time. Like most Jews, they had to give up their shares in the well-known department store Kaufhaus Joske. (I recall you working for them for some time, just before I left.)

I think that giving up the business and this pogrom last week were the final straws that broke the camel's back, as far as my father was concerned. You remember what a radical supporter he was of the German people and nation, walking around all the time with his medals from the Great War, as if the whole of the German Army was on his shoulders, always saying, "We, the German people, will not let this hooligan from Austria take over our country." It seems to me that like all the others, he is running away with his tail between his legs. I am only glad that he and my mother have someplace to run to. Just imagine what would have been if I would not have stayed in Palestine after the Maccabi Games in 1935, but relented to his repetitive demands to come back to help in the business which, by that time, was already not his.

As you see by the address, we live in Palestine in this small village called Nahariya. Most of its residents (some 300 families) come from all over Germany, and we all work in chicken farming, something I have never done before but which I quite like. We are by the sea so I can go swimming nearly every day, even in what they call winter here, which is warmer than our summers at home.

Being under British rule is hardly fun, but it's definitely better, more pleasant and comfortable, than being under the boots of those Brownshirt hooligans.

They call us "*Yekkes*" here, which is a derogatory term for German Jews. Although being called that is better than being named "dirty Jew," it does make me think from time to time – who are we? It is ironic, but our relations with the German goyim, known here as "Templers," who live in Haifa, are better than with the Polish and Russian Jews.

We do not have much in the way of comfort, as we were accustomed to back home. Most of us are still living in tents. To go see a film or a concert, we have to go to Beirut or Haifa. But from what I hear about Leipzig, as bad as it is here, it is better than where you are right now.

I know you were never a big Zionist, but why don't you try and come here to live with us in the village? Land is cheap (we only had to pay 1,000 English pounds for four hectares of land plus livestock), the weather is wonderful, and you would still be living in a German environment.

Adolf, you must get out while you still have the opportunity, because in the end the hooligans will throw all the stateless Jews out to the East, like they did to the Polish Jews in October.

I hope to hear from you soon.
Your swimming mate,
Hans

P.S. I have found a hectare of land, by the sea and I am keeping it for you whenever you come.

* * *

Adolf folded the neatly written letter, and handed it over to his mother to read.

It was clear that they must make plans for both of them to get out. Time was short and there was no time to waste. The hooligans meant business. They proved it by their loutish actions. Nothing would stand in their way. He regretted all the time they wasted waiting for matters to improve. Not only did things not improve, but they got worse from day to day. During the last six years, while all their friends and relatives were getting out, they comforted one another by saying that the situation would change for the better. They fervently hoped for better times, believing that each new restriction would be the last one. It never was, there was always a follow-up, which was worse. The only thing that did not change was their disbelief in what "Goebbel's Lip" (the radio station that served as Goebbel's mouthpiece for propaganda) was spouting, "We will kill all the Jews." Now, after his hellish experience in Sachenhausen, it was clear that the Germans were serious about their plans. They were planning to kill all the Jews in the world.

He and Mama must get out of Germany, at all costs, to anywhere and as soon as possible.

Chapter Three

Adolf Plans His Escape

February 1939

ADOLF CAME HOME THAT DAY in a bad mood. He was feeling humiliated and tired after endless visits to the various government departments he had to visit in order to get the permits that would grant him his exit visa. He could not travel on the trolley buses during the hours that were reserved for Aryans, which meant most of the day, and the times he was permitted to use or travel on the trolley buses, the offices of the authorities he had to visit were closed.

Three months ago, just before the occurrence of Krystalnacht, the transport department had confiscated Adolf's driving license and car. When he returned from the prison camp, he found out that his bike was also confiscated for the war effort. He had to walk; there were no other means of transport. It was forbidden for Jews to enter Adolf Hitler Strasse in the belief that they would contaminate the street carrying the Nazis' beloved leader's name. It was also forbidden to go through Rosenthal Park with its Zoological Garden, which was signposted all over *"Fuer Juden verboten"* (Forbidden for Jews).

The yellow star Adolf was forced to wear attached to the top part of his overcoat caused people to spit at him and children to throw stones. But the worst was the humiliation at the hands of the officials he had to confront every day since his return from the prison camp. Some of these officials were old schoolmates or trainees from the Saxony Swim Team, the swim team that, thanks to him, won the golden medal of the "All German Hitler *Junget* (youth) Swimming Championship" last year in Leipzig.

Today, for example, Adolf had spent more than six hours in the municipal sport department, standing in line to get the application forms. He had to wait patiently as Aryans came in and exercised their right to push in front of him. Once he got to the window, he discovered it was Joachim, his deputy on the swim team, who was there to serve him. The same Joachim who could not forgive Adolf when he was defeated three years ago in the Berlin Olympic games, swimming against a black American participant. He blamed Adolf, his trainer, for his humiliating defeat, and the missed once-in-a-lifetime opportunity to shake hands with the Füehrer. He told Adolf that he would not accept a form that was filled out by the hands of a dirty Jew. Luckily for him, his friend, Dina Thorn, happened to be visiting Leipzig and accompanied him that day. She was not Jewish and therefore could fill out the form for him. When he returned to the counter, he had a newly completed form in his hand. Adolf realized that he had not inserted the name "Israel" in front of his real name. This was one of the many formalities that had arisen since Krystalnacht, demanding that when filling out any official document, all Jewish males must write "Israel" in front of their Christian name, and all Jewish females, the name "Sarah." Joachim was not prepared to accept the form with any corrections. After redoing the whole form once more, he was told to pay the sum of 400 Reich Marks, which was supposedly meant to compensate the German People for providing him with training to be a swimmer since the age of ten, 20 Reich Marks per year.

He also had to return all the gold and silver medals he had won. The bronze ones he was allowed to keep.

He was thinking to himself that this time, he was lucky. Last week, when trying to get a similar certificate from the Health Department, he was told to pay 1,500 Reich Marks to Social Security. This was apparently the charge for keeping his late father, Zallel, in the Jewish Chaim Eitigon hospital for five days, some 15 years ago. The assumption was that the German People do not have to pay expenses for sick Jewish people.

To add insult to injury, Adolf returned home to find a note from the Gestapo's office on Koenig Johann Strasse stuck to the door. It warned him, "Israel Adolf," and his mother, "Sarah Lina," that they must vacate their apartment on Humboldt Strasse and move to the Jewish homes on York Strasse by the end of the month, so it could be handed over to real German Aryan people. The note bore its usual signature, *"Deutschland muessen Juden Rein sein"* (Germany must be cleared of Jews).

He tore it off and walked in. Lina came out of the one room of their apartment that they were left with to tell him that their Aryan tenant was threatening that if they did not remove their furniture from the rooms he had received from the Committee for the Aryanization of Haupt Banhnhof Area, he would call the Gestapo to do so.

Since Krystalnacht, when Adolf was arrested with some 330 other men in town and taken to the Sachenhausen retraining camp, the Aryanization committees of Leipzig had been applying constant pressure on the Jews to leave.

Adolf could not understand their logic; on the one hand there was nothing they wanted more than for Adolf and all the other Jews to leave the Fatherland, making it *Juden Rein*, but on the other hand, they were placing every possible obstacle in their way to hinder their departure.

He remembered vividly the night when the Nazi Brownshirt hooligans came and burned down the Brody Synagogue, just opposite their house. They did the same to Jewish Konfektionshaus of Bamberger & Hertz in the Bruel, where Adolf used to work. Luckily, they did not burn down the new Etz Hachaim Synagogue on Schill Strasse as it was too close to Aryan homes.

On the same night, they came to arrest David Ochs, the leader of the stateless Jews. Adolf was forced to come too, just to fill the quota. He begged them to let him take his insulin and other medication that he needed for his diabetes, but they would not let him. Fortunately, Lina managed to stuff it into his pocket without them noticing. That night, they were taken to Berlin and given toothbrushes, and ordered to clean up the shards of glass from the Jewish shop windows that were scattered all over the streets in the Krostberg quarter. These were shops that had been vandalized by the same group of hooligans that came to Leipzig. By the time Adolf and the others arrived in Berlin, it was morning. All the adults on their way to work stopped to look at them, saying, "Let the Jews do an honest day's work." They were not given any food that day. Adolf was to faint three times as a result of his diabetes and the unbalanced diet in the days that followed. He was one of the first to be released from the prison camp of Sachenhausen; at least the diabetes served a purpose.

By the time he got home, he had lost his job, and along with it all, the clients he had worked for in the insurance company. Now that he was out of the camp, his only aim was to leave Germany. His cousin Max was trying to find him a job with Mr. Bellow, Max's brother-in-law. He would work as a sewing machine technician at Bellow Engineering Leeds. Adolf did not know much about sewing machines other than his experience in fixing their old Singer machine, but he was good with his hands and he knew

ADOLF PLANS HIS ESCAPE

he would learn fast. The work and his residence were prearranged in the town of Middlesbrough, which he had never heard of before and could not find on a map. Once this was settled, all that was left was to get his exit visa from the Aryanization Committee, which he had been trying to do for the last month.

Lina handed him a letter that had arrived from Berta.

Translated from Yiddish:
Wednesday, February 15, 1939
Trayan St. 50, Cetata Alba, Rumania

Dear Mama and Adolf,

Today is Esther and Grandfather Moritz's yahrzeit [Remembrance Day]. I decided to write and share with you some of my concerns.

Since my visit last year in Leipzig, much has changed here, mostly after the November Pogrom, although Siyoma did find a new job as an agricultural advisor in one of the training farms of the Baron Hirsch. That compensates us somewhat for the loss of the meat outlets. He thinks it is wrong to send Jewish people from Europe to Argentina to exploit the Indian Tribes, just as what Baron Rothschild is doing with the Zionists in Palestine to the Arabs is wrong. But he likes the work; it always seems to me that he gets on better with animals than with people.

Lately, he comes home and starts big arguments with me or his brothers. He can argue about the rights of the workers for hours. I find it ironic that a person who comes from such a well-to-do family, with servants and peasants, who work for them for close to nothing, goes out of his way to protect the rights of the workers. At home, he and his family exploit their workers to the bitter end. But I do not have any more *koyich* (strength) to argue and fight with him; he always resorts to physical violence when he does not agree with me.

We have lost most of our friends and gained quite a few enemies in the last few years due to his views on Bolshevism; I do not want any part in it. Now, with what is coming out of the Ukraine concerning the starvation policy of Stalin, I can see how right I am in thinking so. Every day, we have refugees who cross the border by swimming across the Dnjestr river. They tell horrible stories about forced Communism in the Ukraine. One of them is working for us in the slaughterhouse. The only thing Siyoma had to say on the subject is that they are capitalists so they deserve it. I sometimes recall how we met through the Leipzig Communist Cell in the University, and how he impressed me with his talk about freedom for the workers, equality to mankind and a better world for our children. But then I was only 19 years old. Today, I can see it was a load of hogwash.

I do understand now that it is only the wealthy, like Siyoma was in Leipzig, who can allow themselves the energy, wealth and time to think and philosophize about these sorts of ideas. Most people, like our family, are too busy fighting for their day-to-day subsistence. What is also clear to me is that they like to implement these wonderful ideas for others, but when it comes to their own comfort and sacrifice, they very quickly forget their wonderful ideologies. He has endless arguments with his brothers about socialism, not so much on the ideological side, but they blame him for the shame he brought on the family by spreading his ideas around the town and in the province area, as he did in Leipzig. Miron, his older brother, the one who is the mayor, says it is very bad for his own position.

Those three German women I was telling you about have stopped sending their children to me for German lessons. It came to my ears that they received threats from local Nazi party activists just after the November Pogrom, warning them not to have any contact with Jews. So, in the eyes of the only people I had any sort of common background with, I am a Jew. To the Rumanians, I am a German. To the Jews, I am a Communist. To Siyoma, I am a capitalist. To the rest of his family, I am a snob and in my own eyes, I do not know who I am.

Time is flying, and Judith is almost twelve years old. She is not only beautiful, but also a very good student. In French, she is not only at the top of her class, but the best in the school. She is very talented in music, and plays the piano as well as I do, if not better.

I do not know if I told you, but I got my Rumanian passport, and for the first time I am not stateless any longer. I do hope it will make it easier for me and Judith to come visit you next year, if things do not get worse back home. Maybe I will wait until you will all be in England, and then come and visit you there.

I am starting to get the "pension rooms" ready for the spring guests who will start coming in April for the swimming season.

Adolf, I do hope this job at this Bellow Engineering company in England will work out, so Mama will be able to follow you there in a short time. I still think that if you and Mama would have come here, it would have been better for all of us. However bad the situation is here, we are not under the threat of war like Czechoslovakia, England or France. But it is your choice; as I always say, "you have made your bed, now lie in it," and I hope you will be happy with your decision. I miss you all, and do not forget to give my love to the Witerlis family before they leave for Palestine, in particular, my dear friend Naumi.

Siyoma and Judith send their love. I miss you and Leipzig so much.

* * *

Inside the envelope, there was another letter that Adolf pulled out and read:

Monday, February 20, 1939

As you can see, I have not sent the letter as something fairly interesting came up the day I went to the post. Do you remember in 1927 when Siyoma was at the final stage of his studies and was thinking of accepting a teaching post at the University? He just got a letter from some well-known chemist scientist from Manchester University by the name of Weizmann. In the letter this Dr. Weizmann was pleading with him to come and be part of a team of scientists, agronomists and teachers that will establish a Hebrew University for Jewish students in Palestine. They were thinking of opening a school for agriculture, and they wanted Siyoma to organize it and be the head of it. Siyoma obviously did not take it seriously. For Siyoma, the idea of this Zionist movement, that all Jews should come and live in Palestine, was preposterous. It would be much better if all Jews would go and live in the land of the workers (the Soviet Union) and help build a new world.

Yesterday, when Siyoma came home from work, he told me that a French Jew from the school of agriculture in Toulouse, a Dr. Wolkovich, came to visit him on the farm. He offered Siyoma a teaching post in the agriculture department of this university, and he told him that although most of the campus is in the town of Jerusalem, the school for farming was outside a small village by the name of Rehovot. Siyoma rejected this proposal outright, saying that it was beneath his dignity to go and live in a place where there was only wilderness and Arabs, besides for which, he is an expert in cattle, not camels. It is interesting, who would have thought, ten years ago, that anything would come of it? Now, in Jerusalem, a place we only mention round the Passover table, and hear about in the synagogue, there exists a university for Jewish people, teaching in Hebrew, a language only our forefathers used to speak.

Maybe this is a sign that the Messiah is on his way and we should all pick up our belongings and go to Palestine, before it is too late. You do not have to be concerned! I have not become religious or a Zionist or any "ist," but somewhere at the back of my mind, I do think from time to time that with this new wave

ADOLF PLANS HIS ESCAPE

of anti-Semitism rising in Germany and flooding the whole of Europe, it will strike at us Jews, in a place, time and with a force we have never known before. Would it not be better if we could all live in a country that is only for Jews? (Do not worry, I am only engaged in wishful thinking.)

Love Berta

* * *

As Adolf finished reading the letter to Lina, he glanced at his mother and saw tears welling in her eyes. She stroked the letters with her rough hands, as if she were stroking Berta and Judith in the flesh.

Adolf still remembered the bitter arguments at home when Berta announced that she was pregnant and was planning to marry the child's father, who was a Rumanian Jew. He came to Leipzig to study animal husbandry in Leipzig University. This was two years after his father passed away (Zallel died in 1924). He also knew that if Papa had still been alive, he would have never allowed this relationship to happen. He thought back to the time, after Papa had died and money was tight, when Siyoma lodged with them. He could not recall if Siyoma had first met his sister somewhere in the music conservatory on the joint campus of the two institutions, and then came to live with them on Humboldt Strasse 23, or if it was the other way around. He did remember his mother saying that history repeats itself. She first met Zallel when he came to lodge with the Oberman family after his divorce in 1904, and she ended up marrying him after falling pregnant with Berta. But she never failed to mention that Zallel was a *mensch* (Yiddish for a decent person) and came from a good Polish family of jewelers that even had relatives in Switzerland, and not some *vilda chaya* (Yiddish for savage) loud-mouthed Bolshevik coming from a butcher's family, living in an unknown *shtetel* in eastern Rumania. How could one compare the two at all?

Adolf was hoping that his mother would prepare the traditional Friday night meal that he was used to, although he knew that this sort of Sabbath meal, with everyone seated around the Schmulewitsch's family table on Manken Strasse overlooking the river that flowed through the Rosenthal Park (the main park in Leipzig; it also had a zoo), was gone forever. By the time he came back from the Sachenhausen camps, it was becoming increasingly difficult to find shops that were still prepared to sell Jews items like candles, *gefilte* fish and other traditional Jewish foods for the Sabbath. At any rate, the Schmulewitsches were no longer in Leipzig and those merry meals were a thing of the past.

He was looking forward to Lotti Katz coming to visit him from Kassel, but since the Jewish curfew began at 5:00 P.M., he gathered that she would not be coming. Any Jew caught walking in the streets could be arrested and sent to Poland.

There was always the poor substitute, Dina Thorn. Dina was prepared to come and see him, any time, any place. Dina had no fear of being arrested. She was a non-Jewish Russian passport holder, and since the improved relations between the two countries, Russians could move around freely at any time of day or night as long as they were not Jewish.

They planned to meet the following day on Humboldt Strasse 3 to talk things over.

Chapter Four

Dina Thorn – A Friend or Foe?

DINA CAME EARLIER THAN EXPECTED. It was Saturday and the Jewish curfew was imposed for the whole day. Adolf tried to sleep late during these long weekends since he could not go out anyway, and had nothing much to do at home. Living in the one room with his mother, and sharing a kitchen, bathroom and toilet with Fritz the Aryan, did nothing to improve the miserable state that he was in. Until the end of last month, he could at least play chess with him, but paragraph D/446 of the Nuremberg race purification law no longer allowed such games. This peculiar law was passed in fear that Aryans might lose a game to one of the *"Unter Mensch,"* an occurrence that would be considered a disgrace to the "True German People."

So most Saturdays and Sundays, he could only stare out of the window and watch the free Aryan people coming and going in and out of the *Bahnhof* (rail-station), as he tried to guess where they were travelling to and from.

The room was cold and damp, there was snow on the ground, but Adolf and his mother did not have any more Jewish rationing cards, which allowed them to buy heating fuel. There was some heat coming from Fritz's room. Aryans had no limit on heating fuel. They could buy endless supplies. Adolf and Lina sat in their one room with their overcoats on, their yellow stars sewn onto them, with *"Jude"* written in the center in big black letters.

Adolf first met Dina in 1933. She came to Leipzig with the Soviet delegation as a translator. They came to Saxony for the Spring Trade Fair that began every year in April. Dina was a native of Koenigsberg, a German-speaking town in East Prussia, and therefore spoke both Russian and German fluently.

He remembered the exact date, April 1, 1933, when the Nazi Party declared a boycott on all Jewish stores in Leipzig for the first time through its official anti-Semitic newspaper *Der Stuermer*. Only 22 years old, he was working at that time as a trainee salesperson for the Konfektionshaus Bamberger and Hertz. He remembered as if it were today the crowds and mobs clamoring outside the store, waving banners that read, "Death to the Jews," "Do not buy from Jewish shopkeepers." Other posters proclaimed, "Go to Palestine to exploit the Arabs." They tried to stop anyone from entering the store. For Adolf, that horrible event marked the first time that he thought of getting out of Leipzig and going anywhere in the world except Palestine.

In the middle of the riot, with all its bedlam and chaos, a small group of five people emerged, led by an outstandingly beautiful woman. This small party walked right into the Konfektionshaus, ignoring all the hooligans trying to stop them. The beautiful woman marched up to Adolf and said in perfect German with a Russian accent, "We understand that the prices are cheaper today. You must have everything on sale." She told him that the five people that were with her were Party members, or as she called them later, "Communist Pigs," who had officially come to Leipzig on business for the *Messe* (Trade Fair). What they really wanted, however, was to buy furs and other commodities for their wives and Party leaders, that were not available in their country.

DINA THORN – A FRIEND OR FOE?

The five of them started to buy everything available in the shop, without any restraint. The woman asked Adolf to take her to Mr. Bamberger, the shop manager.

Once in his office, she made it clear that they should raise prices on anything these pigs would buy and give her a ten percent cut of the profit. The following day, she came back to collect her money and asked Adolf if he would like to come out with her. He said that he would be glad to do so, but as a Jew would have difficulty sitting with her in any public place. She told him to come straightaway to her hotel on Berg Strasse. It was no problem for him to get in as she had the influence and the diplomatic protection of the Soviet delegation.

Dina stayed with the delegation for a month, during which time she met Harold Thorn, a fur trader from London. When the delegation was on its way back to the Soviet Union, Dina could not be found. Adolf discovered this when Gestapo agents came to the store to find out if he had any idea of her whereabouts. Adolf though to himself, "Those were still the times when the authorities spoke to Jews as if they were people, and did not bark at them, and start every sentence with the words 'dirty Jew.'"

Dina was to appear in his life once again last March, just days after the Austrian *Anschluss* began on March 13, 1938. The *Anschluss* was named by the non-German press, "Austria's occupation," while the German press referred to it as "The reunification of the great Aryan people." This time, Dina came as a translator for an English delegation. The British came, among other reasons, to meet Soviet diplomats, and discuss with them the global situation in light of the *Anschluss*. She told Adolf that she managed to jump ship from the Russian delegation with which she came six years ago. She then left for England and got married to Mr. Thorn.

She told him that this was her first time back since then. It took some time for her to get a British passport, and until that matter was settled, she was scared to leave the British Islands, in case she would be abducted by some Communist agent from the "Red Orchestra" spy ring. The Red Orchestra was the Soviet equivalent of the MI6 in Britain. Dina told Adolf that she was unhappily married, and was looking for a way out, but being 36 years old, it was not easy, particularly with a child. She made a point of telling him that he was the only real man she had ever met in her life. She said to Adolf that she would like to marry him once she got the divorce. Dina made it clear that this time she had come to do some private business for herself.

It was known that many Jews in Leipzig were looking for ways to smuggle their money out into England. Dina, holding British citizenship as well as a valid Russian passport, was in a perfect position to help them. She thought that the best way to do this would be to buy gold dust or diamonds on one of the black markets that were flourishing at the time along the Soviet-Polish border, and conceal them in soapboxes. She had no problem traveling in and out of these countries, buying and selling gold, diamonds and dollars. Her assertiveness, self-confidence and British passport stopped short any guard or border official who tried to interrogate her or inspect her belongings. The one time she was stopped by a German border policeman, she offered to sleep with him that night. He accepted her offer, and let her go the next day.

Adolf did not know if she did or did not manage to find clients for her new business. For close to a year afterwards, Adolf did not hear from her, until she had come to see him and his mother two weeks earlier. Dina told them that she was once more in Leipzig for the same business reasons as the last time.

Looking through the window, Adolf saw her coming up the street, hopping over the stones of the burnt-out Brody Synagogue, just outside their apartment. As always, she had the same look in her eyes, as if to say, "the world is at my feet, and God brought me to earth so that people would be able to serve me." He envied her freedom, being able to come and go as she pleased with no curfews or other restrictions affecting her life. She could buy in any store she wanted and talk to anyone she desired; she was even freer than the Aryans who were expected to detest Jews and relate to them in a certain manner, even if they did not want to or understand why they should. He envied her fearlessness. She feared no one: not the Gestapo, the Fascists, the Communists, the anti-Semitic Student Association, the Brownshirts, Blackshirts or State Security Police hooligans.

She was beautiful and attractive and looked much younger than her age, but he knew deep down that she was a real *"Tzazke"* or what his father used to call *"A Polisher Nafke,"* and that he should be careful of her smooth tongue.

Dina was aware of her good looks, and took full advantage of them. As she came into the apartment, she observed the meticulous order with which Lina managed to keep everything. The piano and icebox were in the hallway. Inside their room, which was on the left – where two beds were lined up as if on military parade awaiting inspection – were all the possessions the Rochman family owned in the world: a set of coffee spoons, teaspoons, cake spoons, sugar spoons and soup spoons; to each one of them there was a matching fork and knife. On the table, in the middle of the room, was a cheap art collection made of crystal animals. On the wall were pictures in golden frames of the sort she had seen in the peasants' houses in Russia. Beside them hung framed photos of Adolf with the Bar Kochba Swim Team, Adolf with his father, Adolf with his sister Berta, Adolf with his baby niece Judith, Lina and her father. Resting over the sewing machine were the old silk and lace materials that Lina used in her profession as a hat decorator. The window facing the street was covered with hanging enamel pots, all clean and shining, as if never used. The room was filled with vases, stools, books, and the sort of items that people collect throughout their lives. Dina sat on the leather armchair. Adolf chose the old piano stool to sit on.

They served her water in their beautiful six-piece tea set. Lina apologized for not having coffee, tea, cakes or sugar to serve her; these items were not products readily available to Jews. They could obtain certain items through the black market, but it was dangerous and risky to be seen buying or storing them. The penalty was deportation.

Dina apologized in turn for not bringing these items with her. She could have brought food and other items from her corrupt friends in the Gestapo who would be only too happy to please her for money and sex.

They spoke in low tones. There was always the danger that Fritz from next door would listen and report their conversations to the Gestapo. Adolf presented his plan to her. Adolf was planning to leave Leipzig for England with God's help in a month's time, or as soon as he would get all the permits from the Nazi authorities. Lina would follow a short time after. Both of them would have to have some money to start with in England. The Nazi law would only allow them 5 Reich Marks per person, which would be just enough for a cup of coffee once they got there.

They would have to improvise some way to get some of their valuables out of Germany and into England. Once there, they could try to sell them to cover some of their first month's expenses. There was no point in selling them here, in Leipzig; the money they would get would be significantly less than their real value. Adolf was well aware of the middlemen agents that were hovering like vultures, waiting for the Jews to sell. These men knew that all these sales were done under pressure. The Jews did not have any alternative; they were forced to get out, and would sell at any price. Adolf remembered when he had to sell his DKW automobile for 700 Reich Marks, when its real value was over 4,000 Reich Marks. It was the same story now. Since Jews were no longer allowed to drive or own a car, he had no other alternative but to sell at any price.

On top of that, there were always the informers who were eager to pass on information to the authorities about illegal property owned by Jews. As a reward, the authority would pay the informant a tithe of the confiscated items. At times, they would wait until the item was sold, and then tax them for these items, and at other times, they would just charge you for any sort of paper, visa or form you needed in order to get out or sell any valuables you owned. It was clear that their job was to squeeze whatever they could from the Jews before they left. Adolf also knew that there was nothing they could do with valueless Reich Marks outside Germany, even if they could smuggle some of them out.

Dina suggested that they collect all the jewelry they had in their possession, including jewels that belonged to Lina personally and those they still had from Zallel's jewelers shop in The Bruel. After all, Zallel had owned one of the biggest jewelry shops in town and, because of his expertise as a watchcase maker, he would use lots of gold and silver when making these watchcases for the wealthy class of Leipzig. Zallel did not just service the upper classes; his name was renowned amongst people from Berlin, Warsaw and Frankfurt, who came to him to have their watchcases made. He even had the Herzog of Saxony, a crown prince who lived in Dresden, as one of his clients.

During their conversation, they heard the main door to the apartment open. It was Fritz, who had just come back from morning Mass. Adolf told Dina to put on Lina's coat with the yellow star in case Fritz would enter the room unexpectedly as he often did, just to inspect or harass them. If Fritz saw the coat, he would think that Dina was another Jew who had come to visit them. They switched to Yiddish, a language Dina had picked up from her Jewish neighbors in Koenigsberg when she was a child. Lina was more comfortable speaking Yiddish, the colloquial language spoken among the stateless Jews that came from Galicia at the end of the last century.

Dina took out soap bars that she had brought with her; Adolf dug out their insides. They pushed the jewlery inside the soap. Then Lina brought a broom and took it apart. Inside the hollow handle was all the gold and silver they owned from Zallel's shop. The was no choice but to hide valuables in such clandestine ways since the hooligans, with the help of the police and informers, would break into Jewish apartments from time to time, looking for objects that Jews were keeping illegally. They also knew that Fritz would periodically come into their room and look through their belongings.

Adolf then moved the carpet from under the table. Lifting one of the wooden planks, he moved it quietly so Fritz would not hear and took out all of Lina's jewelry that she had received as an inheritance from her parents and grandparents, as well as jewelry Zallel gave her upon their marriage. There were there also pieces of jewelry from the old shop that had not been sold, some of it belonging to Adolf. It was risky for Jews to walk around Leipzig with ornament like rings, watches or bracelets. They could easily be stopped by the patrol of the Committee for the Aryanization of Stolen German Property, who would grab the rings off their fingers, pull earrings out of their earlobes, and wrench the bracelets off their wrists. Dina stuffed all of the jewelry into her bra, and picked up her skirt, hoarding the rest in her underpants. They decided that she would smuggle the jewelry out of Germany and into England. When Adolf arrived there, he would either sell it all or give it to someone to estimate its value, with the agreement that Dina would receive ten percent of the sales, either in money or in ornaments and gold.

In order to try to confuse Fritz, who they were sure was waiting for her to leave, Dina decided to take her leave by climbing out of the window. Since their apartment was on the first floor, this was not too difficult a task. It was 3:00 P.M., late February, and it was getting dark. The stormy weather kept most people indoors, so there were not too many spectators watching Dina jump out of the window.

The following day, after the curfew was lifted, Adolf went to see Dina in her hotel. Once more, he had to endure humiliation at the hands of the night watchman, who noticed the star, and said to him, "I thought that dirty Jews are not allowed into hotels, and in any case there has been a rumor that you have been all sent to Poland, that is what our beloved Füehrer told us. He said the other day on the wireless that Germany is *Judenrein*, and here you are, coming to defy his words."

Adolf and Lina were among the 3,500 stateless Jews who were unable to get out of Leipzig after the big deportation of Polish Jews the year before on the 10th of October (1938). This was for the simple reason that Poland, and for that matter any other country, was not prepared to take in the stateless Jews. These people had come to Germany in the last century, mainly from Galicia, a country that by 1939 no longer existed. The Weimar Republic was not prepared to grant them or their descendents citizenship. When the Nazi Party decided to get rid of all former Galician and Polish Jews, the Polish Jewish passport holders, the stateless Jews, had nowhere to go and were forced to stay put.

To Adolf, the night watchman appeared to be like one of the thugs who would walk around Leipzig beating up Jews for no reason. For that matter, he was sure he had seen him in a boycott demonstration outside the few shops that were still prepared to sell to Jews. Adolf did not expect him to understand the difference between stateless Jews and those that held German or Polish citizenship. But the night watchman was well aware of the fact that there were still Jews around, since he used to beat Jewish people in the streets, along with all the other Brownshirt thugs. The man grabbed his coat lapel, and was just about to throw him out of the small lobby, when Dina intervened, flashing her British passport at him saying, "I think I will report this incident to the British Consul in Dresden." The watchman promptly let go of Adolf and they left the hotel.

As they were walking along, Adolf was thinking to himself the same thought that recurred in his mind over and over again: Why do I have to go through all this? Would it not just be easier to put an end to it all? The only place they could sit and talk was on the street benches of Notrd Strasse by the river. This was the only street in town where the benches were not yet marked *"Fuer Juden verboten."*

At this hour on a Sunday evening, most of the youngsters were in bars, getting drunk, and there was little danger that Adolf and Dina would be harassed by the Aryan Purification Committee patrols.

Once they sat down, Dina told Adolf of her plan to go to Hungary after she finished her business in Leipzig. There, she hoped to meet a lawyer friend of hers who would arrange her divorce. In a month or two, she would be free as a bird, and by that time, Adolf should be in England, and they would be able to get married. She hoped that afterwards they could go and live in Australia. Once more, Adolf envied her: she could just hop on a train, at any time on any day, and travel on her merry way to Hungary, Poland, England, or any other location in the world she desired. She needed no visa or permit from any committee; neither did she have to report her movements to anyone. No one would stop her from coming and going as she pleased.

She wanted Adolf's promise that the first thing he would do once he had established himself in North England would be to marry her. She hoped that he and her son Herman would get on well so that Adolf would be able to teach him swimming. He tried to explain that he was not decided on the matter, but he knew she would not listen. He knew that she was the type of woman who was used to getting her way.

DINA THORN – A FRIEND OR FOE?

By the time Adolf had formulated a response in his mind to Dina's suggestion of marriage, Aryan youngsters were beginning to leave the bars in Notd-Platz, singing, *"let us go sharpen our knives so we can see Jewish blood dripping off their blades."*

It was time to go. On his way home, Adolf walked through back streets so as not to be seen by any of the patrols. After all, this was the time of night that they were out hunting for their prey. Walking along, he asked himself how this woman constantly managed to manipulate him to do whatever she wanted. He knew well enough that if he would marry her, she would throw him out of the window like an old rag once she squeezed what she wanted out of him, but at this point he was left with no choice; he was a prisoner in her hands. She had all of their money, and might not give it back as agreed; worse, she could inform on them to the Gestapo at any time. It was difficult for him to comprehend why was she interested in him, a humiliated Jew with no rights, money or future.

Once he entered the door to his apartment, he saw the mess that the Anti-Black Market Patrol had made. Lina suspected that someone must have informed the Gestapo that they were holding meat illegally in their apartment, which could only be obtained on the Black Market. Fortunately for Lina and Adolf, they did not have any illegal foods. Even more fortunate was the fact that their valuables had been taken away the day before. Adolf comforted Lina and said, "Better in the hands of this Polish whore than in the hand of the Nazi Pigs."

.

Chapter Five

Uncle Zelig Secures Visa For Adolf

Tuesday, February 27, 1939

FREE AIR RAID SHELTERS ARE to be distributed to London homes. The Home Office announced plans today to provide shelters to thousands of homes in districts most likely to be bombed.

Families earning less than 250 pounds a year will receive their shelters for free.

This announcement came as part of the Home Office's policy to be prepared for war that may break out with Nazi Germany at any time.

* * *

Zelig got home late that day. He was waiting for his son Max and his daughter-in-law Jane. They were supposed to come from the factory in Guisborough.

Although Zelig was glad that Max had decided to marry Jane Gluik, he knew that his son had married more because of her family connections than for her looks. Not only did Jane's looks bother him, but so did the fact that she did not speak German. He found it difficult to converse with her in English. But at least she was pleasant enough, and came from a good family. It was her brother-in-law, Isaac Bellow, who helped so many of their family get out of Germany. Zelig was most grateful to Bellow, not only for guiding them in their first steps in the new country, but also for providing a legal guarantee for Adolf, so he could come over from Leipzig. Zelig himself did as much as he could to see to it that Adolf and Lina could get out.

The Schmulewitsches were starting to receive big contracts to manufacture shirts and uniforms for the armed forces. Even one such contract could benefit them for many years for to come. They were starting to see profits, rewards that he had never seen before either in Leipzig or in England.

On his desk lay the letter that arrived from Adolf after Christmas. It was sent at the end of November, but the mail took a long time to arrive.

Translated from German:
Tuesday, November 29, 1938
Humboldt Strasse 3, Leipzig

Dear Uncle and Aunt,
I hope all is well with you and all my cousins. I am sorry we did not answer your last letter. I have just come home from the most horrid experience that I have ever known. I will tell you something about it if we ever get together. But first, I would like to congratulate for your tremendous success. I was so happy and proud for you that you, together with Max, Herman, Jack and Berta managed to build such a big and prosperous business in such a short time. Your factory business letter heading is impressive with your name at the side "S. and Max Schmulewitsch, directors." I do not understand, though, why it says by your name "stateless,"

UNCLE ZELIG SECURES VISA FOR ADOLF

and who is this Clive Gildon A.C.A.? It sounds like a goyish (non-Jewish) name. Is it like here, that one must take a partner from the people of the land, or is he just an accountant who represents you? I also saw that you have outlets in Glasgow and Manchester. I know about your outlet in London from Herman who told me that he is the representative of the company there.

How does Aunt Sarah manage in the new country? Can she already speak the language? Does she like to go to the theater from time to time; is there a theater in Newcastle? I see from the map that it is not more than ten KM from Guisborough. I assume it is difficult for Aunt Sarah to go and see plays if she does not understand the language.

As I told you, I was arrested on the night of the 9th of November, and after a long and humiliating night, during which we had to clean the streets of Berlin with toothbrushes, we were taken to a reeducation school just east of Berlin. We were woken up every morning at 5:00 A.M. and had to go through endless roll calls till seven or eight in the morning. The temperature was never higher than -3 or -2 degrees. We only were given food at noontime, and that was not much. This whole thing played havoc with my diabetes; I used to faint three or four times a day. This went on for three weeks. One day they called me in with some others. After standing for five hours outside a bureau, an officer from the SS came and announced that we "dirty Jews" could go home. He made it clear that they would give us six weeks to get out of Germany. If we had not left by then, we would be arrested once more. Next time, he said, it would not be a holiday camp like it was this time.

Now, obviously, I am sorry I did not get out before. When you told me to come with you, I thought it was foolish of you to do what you were doing – putting your whole family through such a traumatic experience, uprooting them from home, school and friends and bringing them to a strange country where they did not speak the language. If it would have been London, maybe one could compare it with Leipzig, but to bring them to a place that no one had ever heard of and could not be found on the map? I said to Mama at the time that not only is it foolish, but cruel. Mama said that the situation would blow over in a short time, and we would only remember it as a bad dream. Now Mama and I are standing at the end of the road. We must do whatever we can to get out of this inferno as soon as we can.

I am writing this letter to you in despair, asking you if you can find any way to get us a permit with which to enter England. We have tried to get into Switzerland where, as you know, Aunt Sarah, Mama and Uncle David have a cousin. Although she was prepared to give us a guarantee, the Swiss authorities would not let us enter. Now with the new law that we have to have a "J" stamped into our passport, it is not possible to cross the border into Switzerland.

We have tried France, Italy, Palestine and Rumania, but all in vain. And now we are running around like chickens with no heads. You are our last hope. If you cannot do anything for us, we will be sent to the East, like the Polish Jews were in October. Mama, at her advanced age, and I, with my diabetes, will not survive.

Mama and I have decided that if I can get the necessary papers, I will come to England. We will pack all our stuff and send it on to Middlesbrough. Meanwhile, I will start working and do all I can to send for Mama to follow.

Mama is sending her love and give my love to all,
Adolf

* * *

Zelig had read the letter over five or six times since it arrived a month ago. On the envelope, he noticed the stamp saying "State Security Censorship." This is what most probably delayed the arrival of the letter. Zelig became aware that a new era was approaching. Now, all letters would be opened by the German censorship,

UNCLE ZELIG SECURES VISA FOR ADOLF

something he must take into account when writing letters to friends and relatives back home.

He was proud of himself that within three weeks, he had managed to arrange an entry permit for Adolf. It is true that it was Bellow who gave the guarantee and arranged for the permit, but if not for him, the contact with Bellow would never have come through. Zelig had to admit that he did not get along with Adolf too well. Adolf was the type that did not like to work too hard, preferring that other people do the work for him. It is true that he was a good swimmer, but in England it is hard work that counts, and he, who had worked hard all his life, did not have time for lazy people.

Now that Zelig and Bellow had managed to get all the papers together for Adolf, he was worried that once Adolf came, he would loaf around, which would give the family a bad name. But truthfully, he was more concerned about his sister-in-law Lina. He did not see how they would be able to obtain a permit for her. Lina did not meet any of the requirements that the various categories demanded as a prerequisite. She was too old, and her profession as a hat decorator was not in demand in England due to the economic constraints of war. She also did not have the necessary funds, 500 English pounds, which all refugees wishing to enter England, or any other country for that matter, were required to pay. This was instituted so that refugees would not become a burden on the English welfare system. Additionally, Lina could not speak the language. In one sentence, she had everything working against her.

As these thoughts were whirring through his mind, Zelig heard Max and Jane arriving in their new Morris car, that new toy that Max was so proud to own. When they came in, Max and Zelig moved into the office to talk about the new contract that they might get from the government. Max was very excited. He knew that contracts of this sort would never have come about in Leipzig. Even if they had, by some remote chance, gotten a contract from the German government, it would have only been given to them under the condition that they relinquish the ownership of the business to an Aryan. They talked for some time about the difficulty they may have in recruiting more workers, and whether Berta and the production manageress could handle it. They were both hoping that when Adolf came, they could give him the position of chief sewing machine technician. In general, though, things seemed to be going well and they were hoping for even better times to come.

Berta came over from next door with Jack and Freddy. Max did not like the way his older sister's husband had changed his name from Yacobus to Jack, as if he were ashamed of his German origin. Berta showed them the letter that had come that day from Jack's parents, who were trying to leave Germany.

Chapter Six

Hitler Plans First Stages of War

February 1939

WHILE DINA WAS GOING AROUND Leipzig trying to convince Jews to give her their money so that she could smuggle it into England or Switzerland, and Adolf was doing his best to get out of Germany, Adolf Hitler in Berlin was planning the first stages of the war.

It was now clear to Hitler that Neville Chamberlain, Halifax, his foreign minister, and Daladier, the French prime minister, were unprepared for war. The three of them would do anything in their power to avoid a military confrontation with the Wehrmacht. Hitler was well aware of this fact, and took full advantage of it.

Hitler had taken note of this attitude a few months earlier at the Munich Conference, when Chamberlain and Daladier, together with Mussolini, came to Germany to sign a pact with the Reich, allowing the Wehrmacht's occupation of the Sudetenland. Hitler noted then that the two "worms," (as he called them), were prepared to do anything within their power to appease him, culminating in their giving him a free hand to take over the Sudetenland.

Hitler's basic plan was to create what he called *Leben Raum* ("living space") in Poland, Russia and the Balkans. In other words, any area east of the line marked by Koenigsberg in the North (on the Baltic Sea), Warsaw in the center and Lvov in the South (on the Rumanian border), would be designated for German Aryans. The policy called for complete subservience of the citizens living in these countries to the Germans, who intended to exploit them and their resources. This would not only enrich the Reich, and put it on a par with the leading colonial nations (Britain, France, Holland, Denmark, Sweden, Finland and Switzerland), but would also raise the Germans' standard of living to a height they had never known before. And Hitler would go down in history as the Bismarck of the 20th century. This policy would also nurture a dependency of the German population on Hitler and a dependence of the powerful nations of the world on Germany.

The direction to spread out was eastward, which would not include the nations of the "superior races" (the English, Dutch and Danish people), which lay west of Germany. It was to include the "inferior races" (Russian, Slavs and African people) that lay east of Germany. It was due to their inferiority, maintained Hitler, that Bolshevism and the Jews had taken over. And it was Germany's duty to save them from this misfortune. Hitler was confident that when the time came to occupy the lands in the East, the nations of the superior races would support him.

Hitler always operated with caution and in small steps, each step allowing for retreat, leaving open a window through which he and his armies could turn back if the move was not successful. It was with this attitude that Hitler took over the Rhineland in 1936, giving clear orders to his generals that if there was any sort of French opposition, they should turn back immediately. This policy

HITLER PLANS FIRST STAGES OF WAR

was to repeat itself with the occupation of Austria in March 1938 and Czechoslovakia a year later.

With the Rhineland once more in German hands, Hitler and the Germans had access to its coal and steel industry, which in turn allowed Germany to rebuild its former military industries. Hitler was known to have said, "I am Germany, and what is good for me is good for Germany."

The occupation of Austria and the Sudetenland eliminated an immediate threat from the southeast, and at the same time allowed the Wehrmacht High Command to increase the army by 20 divisions, most of them equipped and armed.

There were three main obstacles that Hitler and the Reich had to overcome:

1. How to finance the first stage of this grandiose idea,

2. From which sources he would find arms to equip another 40 to 50 divisions, which he would need if he planned to occupy the Soviet Union, and

3. The cooperation of Stalin and the Soviet Union might be necessary, until such time as the Wehrmacht would be capable of a full-scale offensive against "the Red menace," as Hitler called it.

Hitler fully understood that Stalin was not Chamberlain, whom Hitler called in private "the King's Clown," and would not be appeased by a phony peace treaty, such as the one signed with Britain and France. Stalin, like Hitler, was a suspicious and cunning person.

Hitler held a clandestine meeting with his generals and cabinet ministers sometime in late February 1939. He laid out his plans, stage by stage, explaining how he intended to confront each obstacle. In this meeting, he outlined the first objective of reaching the Ukraine, which was once considered the "breadbasket" of Europe, before Stalin took it over and tried to force the Ukrainian farmers into collectivism. The second would be the oil fields in the

Ural Mountains. The third was to reach the Pacific Ocean. To Hitler, it was clear that Chamberlain believed that Hitler did not want to go to war. Hitler made a point of not changing Chamberlain's mind on that matter. Neville Chamberlain believed that Hitler did not want to go to war, and it was merely a question of giving Hitler what he asked for.

At the meeting, there were functionaries present from various government departments. Each one of them in turn explained how his ministry or department would handle each aspect of this complicated plan. The president of the Reich's Bank, Walther Funk, displayed with charts and graphs that although there was no more than $120m in the Reich Bank's gold reserves at this time, the funds which were coming in from Jews, or as he called them, "non-Aryans," were replenishing the coffers. These funds were to be collected in two ways: The first one was simple, and was, in part, already being implemented. Walther Funk explained that the Jews had now come to the realization that the German Reich was not the place for them. It was equally clear to the Jews that the longer they delayed their departure from Germany, the more it would cost them. So by now, in the aftermath of November 9, which marked the Krystalnacht pogrom, they were all ready to leave, at any cost.

The plan was, according to Funk, to squeeze from the Jews any money that was left after they had sold their property. Various Aryan committees had been established to execute this plan, beginning with a committee that would estimate the property of those wanting to leave. The committee would recommend what tax to put on the property. This tax would have to be paid to the Reich's Bank before any Jew could leave. Special insurance agents investigated all the insurance policies that had been bought by Jews in the last twenty years. They saw to it that if any Jew would file a claim for the money, they would transfer the money to the Reich Bank. An example of this was after the Krystalnacht pogrom, when

Jewish shop owners and businessmen filed claims to the Allianz Insurance Company for the damages incurred as a result of the pogrom. They were duly informed that they only had to fill in the claim forms and pay the sum to the Reich Bank, and they would be paid back. Of course, they were never reimbursed.

Then there was the *Reichskulturkammergesetz* (The Reich's Education Committee), whose assignment it was to find out how many years the person who wanted to leave was educated. The number of years would be multiplied by 2,000 Reich Marks. The reasoning behind this was that the German people should not have to pay for the education of any Jew leaving the country, who would take his expertise abroad. The fact that Jews were left with no choice but to leave was beside the point.

Then came the long and complicated explanation of the new partnership law. In this new regulation, any non-Aryan (in other words, a Jew) running or owning a business was obliged to take in an Aryan partner, relinquishing control of ninety percent of the value of the business. This transition would be carried out through the Reich's Bank, which would see to it that the new Aryan partner would pay a realistic price for what he bought, while the non-Aryan (the Jew) would only receive a symbolic sum for the shares that he had sold. The difference would go into the Reich's treasury.

Next came the detailed layout of how much they would charge for each form filled out by the person wanting to leave. Any Jew who wished to leave was forced to visit at least seventeen bureaus and authorities. In each of these bureaus, he had to receive a form, pay for it, and fill it in. The form had to be filled in correctly. The person applying for the visa obtains a new one. Any forms that had corrections were not accepted. When the Schmulewitsch family left in 1935, this law had not yet been implemented.

Walther Funk alerted them to the problem they would have with Jews who had invested their money in Switzerland. He explained that the bank account system in Switzerland was based on numerals. Although Funk had a cooperative relationship with Dr. Alfred Schaefer, head of the UBS (The Union Bank of Switzerland), he could not help him much, since a bank account number could not indicate the name of the person who had deposited the money. Dr. Schaefer could divulge, however, that most of the Jews had accounts in National Swiss Bank in Lucerne and the Banque de Paris in Geneva.

Funk did add, however, that they had managed to stop the flow of the money crossing the border, which was the basis of an agreement between Heiruch Riutmun, the Swiss foreign minister and the Reich's department for internal affairs. The agreement stipulated that starting from October 5, 1938, all German Jews would have the letter "J" stamped in their passports and travel documents, so that they would be identifiable. Once a Jew reached the border, the guard would see this stamp, and would stop him from entering Switzerland. In this way, money could not be transferred to Switzerland, unless Jews would give it to Aryans, or non-Jews from other countries, to smuggle in.

This agreement, he told his audience, had stopped most of the money transfers, but he still knew of cases in which Jews had sent money through a third person, a non-Jew who deposited their money into Swiss banks. He made the point that the sum collected until now would only finance the first month of the war. From there on, he told them, the German Reich would have to be dependent on the gold in the coffers and the natural resources of the nations to be occupied. These funds should be sufficient to end the war, which should not last more than a year.

Two of the main speakers in this "secret counsel" were General Reichenau from the Fifth Army and Himmler from the SS. They both gave full details of how the Wehrmacht would get the arms it needed for the upcoming war. In his talk, Himmler briefly summarized the history of Czechoslovakia as he saw it, in light of the Nazi ideology (Czechoslovakia proper which did not

HITLER PLANS FIRST STAGES OF WAR

include the Sudetenland). He proclaimed that the League of Nations had taken it from the German and Austrian peoples after the "Great War," as part of the Versailles Treaty in 1918. By doing so, they created a new nation, Czechoslovakia. Himmler noted that there was some justice in the fact that the Sudetenland and its German-speaking people were returned to its true owner, the German Reich. He emphasized that if these manufacturing facilities with their warehouses were to be under Wehrmacht control, the production would be sufficient to arm 20 or 30 divisions of the army. What Czechoslovakia had in their armories at the time was sufficient to equip 38 infantry divisions and eight mobile divisions. This was more than enough for the first stage of the war which Hitler was planning for the first week of September.

General Reichenau was the C.I.C. of the Fifth German Army. The General presented his point of view at the meeting. He gave a strategic outline of the military forces that were concentrated in Munich, Nuremberg, Leipzig and Vienna, cities that surrounded the Czechoslovakian borders. The crossing of the border into Prague was planned for March 15, 1939; they were only waiting for the order to march. Some months before the planned invasion, Hitler encouraged the Slovakians to demand autonomy from Jan Masaric, the Prime Minister of Czechoslovakia. By doing so, one part of Czechoslovakia was annexed to the Reich and the Wehrmacht only had to deal with the Czech part.

General Reichenau made the point that if things went according to plan, the whole invasion would be nothing more than a drilling march. He said that problems would only arise if the Czechs would put up a fight, which in turn could cause the "soft-bellied nations" (a term used in these secret counsels to describe England and France, who were allies to Czechoslovakia) to come to their aid. He made it clear that if they would do so, the order was to retreat at once. This did not happen. They took over Czechoslovakia as planned, making Germany one of the greatest industrial powers in the world, after the U.S.A. Nations such as Turkey, Russia and Yugoslavia were now dependent on Germany, as the Germans had taken over the entire arms industry in Czechoslovakia. This was a gamble Hitler took and won.

The plan, as Hitler revealed to the "Secret Counsel" at this meeting, was to take over the whole of Russia from the Ukraine to the Japan Sea. Hitler made the point that since supreme races have traditionally had colonies, there was no reason why the "Third Reich" should be denied having colonies. Russia would be Germany's colony and living space, "*Leben Raum.*" For the time being, Germany was still dependent on the cooperation of the Bolsheviks for two main reasons. First and most important was the Reich's dependency on the USSR to supply it with raw materials such as oil, coal and cereals. Second, before launching a fundamental war against the Bolsheviks, Germany still needed the cooperation of the Russians, or, at the very least, did not want any hostility from them. Hitler was referring to a war that could be launched in the future against England and France. The idea was to divert Stalin's attention from the fact that Germany's final goal was to liquidate the USSR and destroy Bolshevism.

Von Ribbentrop, Germany's foreign minister, informed the secret counsel that in his capacity as ambassador in England, he and Maxim Litvinov, the Russian foreign minister, both tried to negotiate a German-Soviet Pact, of which both countries would enjoy the benefits. After Stalin's change in personnel within the Soviet foreign ministry, Von Ribbentrop was given the green light to go and meet Stalin and Molotov. He was welcomed in Moscow with an honor reserved only for kings and heads of state. In his welcome speech, Von Ribbentrop proudly declared, "Until recently the Soviet Union and Germany were enemies. The situation has now changed, and we are partners. The political art in foreign affairs is to reduce the number of enemies of one's country and to turn yesterday's enemies into good neighbors." The result of this meeting was the Ribbentrop-Molotov Non-Aggression Pact,

HITLER PLANS FIRST STAGES OF WAR

which paved the way for Germany's invasion of Poland, which occurred a week later.

The Non-Aggression Pact, which was finally signed on August 23, 1939 (a week before the outbreak of war), outlined the terms of the agreement:

1. To split Eastern Europe into two spheres of influence in which each could do more or less as they liked. The Russian territory would include the Baltic States and Finland. At the same time, Poland was to be split into two between Russia and Germany, with the Wehrmacht occupying Poland, advancing east up the Vistula River, including Warsaw. The Red Army would do the same going west. By doing so, the USSR would annex Poland to the Ukraine. Poland as a political entity would be liquidated.

2. Russia would supply Germany with manganese, cotton, oil, iron-ore and grain.

3. Germany would supply Russia with Czechoslovakian arms and German-made machines.

Russia did not gain much from this pact, except for two or three years' breathing space until an inevitable attack from Germany. The hope was that by then the Red Army would have built a new kedar of officers after Stalin's purges of the officers two years earlier. But the benefits to Germany were endless. They gained the support of all members of Communist parties that were not part of the USSR. The agreement opened the door for Germany to swallow Poland, without the "Lion from the East" roaring, which, in turn, would become a launching pad for the invasion of Russia two years later. It gave them free access to cheap raw materials, and it placed the British and French governments in a dilemma.

There was still one bone of contention, East Rumania (known as Moldavia). Stalin insisted upon having this region within his sphere of influence, which Hitler could not allow. Hitler feared that once that area would be within the Soviet sphere of influence, and the Red Army would enter that zone, the Russians would be too close to Germany's main oil supply in "The Wallachian Plains," which was located in South-East Rumania. This zone in Rumania had one of the richest oil fields in Europe, and the Wehrmacht depended on it for its supply of fuel.

Chapter Seven

Freedom Around the Corner – Adolf Sets Off for England

March 1939

By the first of march, Leipzig was filled with so many scores of soldiers, and such a mass of army equipment, that Adolf feared the Frankfurt and the Alber bridges over the Elsterbecken River flowing through Leipzig would cave in from the pressure of extra weight. Adolf was happy he would not be around to witness such a collapse, or observe the sight of an army advancing towards Czechoslovakia.

By now, Adolf had obtained all the permits, visas, approvals and certificates he needed in order to get to England. There was only one more small obstacle standing in his way: he did not have a visa to go through Holland in order to get to Rotterdam, from where he would board a ferry to Newcastle. Luckily, the Dutch government did not adopt the anti-Semitic policies that were so prevalent in Germany; they did not charge for Jewish visas, nor did they create unnecessary difficulties. Adolf decided to write the Dutch Embassy in Berlin a letter.

Translated from German:
March 1, 1939
Humboldt Strasse 3
Leipzig C-1

To the Dutch Embassy in Berlin;
    I am writing to you in order to inquire about the procedure and cost of obtaining a visa to pass through Holland. I am immigrating to England and have an English visa that is in effect until 1.1.40. I am considered a stateless person and have permission to leave Germany until the 30th of June 1939.
    From the information that I get here in Leipzig, I understand I can get a transit visa at the Dutch border, and will not have to pay. As I do not want any unpleasant surprises, and I do not want to lose either time or money, please inform me as to how I can get through Holland in the quickest way so that I can get to my work in England.
    I am enclosing a return stamp.
    I thank you in advance,
    Sincerely,
    Adolf Rochman

* * *

Thinking that he would have to wait at least a month until he would receive a response, in light of the fact that he was Jewish, Adolf and Lina decided to use this time to start packing the whole household, preparing to send their furniture to Middlesbrough. This was an assignment that required much planning and thinking. What would they need in England? What would Lina need here until she left? This depended on how long she would remain in Leipzig. If it would be longer than a week, she would have to keep more than one dress and some underwear. Would she need any cooking equipment? Eating utensils? Which clothing should Adolf pack? Adolf could not take many belongings with him, as he feared that travelling with a large suitcase would attract the attention of the police, the Gestapo or the Brownshirt hooligans. He could be stopped by any of them at any time, and he could even be arrested on suspicion of attempted escape. Although Adolf had at his disposal all the permits necessary to leave Germany, he knew from other people's experiences that the German authorities could easily take away his permits, leaving him ruined. So, he decided it was wise to be as inconspicuous as possible.

It was eventually decided that all his clothing –nightshirts, summer and winter coats, dinner jackets, house shoes and so on – would be sent along with the rest of the stuff to England. The big question was what they should do with all their furniture, such as the Feurich piano, the Singer sewing machine, stools, armchairs, tables etc. They were not sellable, but if they were left behind, they could be stolen or damaged. Lina insisted on sending all her kitchen utensils: pots, pans, trays, eight sets of mocha coffee and tea sets, and all their silverware. Lina was apprehensive about setting up a new household in England, and felt that she would only be able to manage with the help of familiar items from home. She was too set in her ways to start learning new cooking methods. It was also important for her to keep some small trinkets to remind her of her house on Humboldt Strasse, such items as a beautiful black vase that Zallel gave her for their first wedding anniversary and the Nippfiguren figures that Berta gave them before she left for Rumania. Adolf was against sending all of their personal belongings. He knew they would never arrive in one piece, if at all. He suggested keeping all their things in the house, just as they were. Lina should make use of them until it was time for her to leave. It was not worth the effort of going to the police once more. Sending all their furniture would also require one more visit to the customs or some other authority, not to mention the 23 Reich Marks he would have to pay for registration. He could not see himself standing in endless lines to pay insurance and a fee to the Committee of Restoring Property of Aryan People. He simply did not want to face this ordeal once more, especially not now, when the smell of freedom was starting to hover in the air. Adolf wanted out. He told his mother that when she obtained her visa, which should be in two or three weeks, she should just close the door and let the hooligans, thieves, Fritz and the Gestapo do whatever they pleased. In the meantime, she should carry on using all the clothes and bedding that were in the house. Lina won the argument. It was decided to send most of their goods. She kept one extra dress, and the feather blanket to sleep on, for the short time she would remain in Leipzig.

On March 2, an answer came from the Dutch embassy in Berlin; Adolf opened it with trembling hands.

March 2, 1939
The Dutch Embassy, Berlin

We hereby give you a certificate that will let you enter Holland within the next three weeks through the Krefeld Border Crossing and exit from Rotterdam harbor. You will not be allowed to remain in Holland longer than three weeks.

    Louis de Jong
    Immigration consul

* * *

Adolf was so excited that he was contemplated walking to Berlin just to kiss the hand of this Mr. de Jong. He started to cry. Freedom for him was just around the corner. The train trip to Krefeld would have to be planned in such a way that no one would suspect that he was running away.

Separating from Lina was far more difficult than he had

imagined. He was not sure he would ever see her again, although he could not share this fear with her. But he could see from the expression in her eyes that she was thinking the same thing. He assured her, again and again, that the minute he arrived in England, he would do all he could to get her papers, devoting every second of every day to achieving this goal. Lina turned around as he left the house, but as he was walking down the street, he could see she had gone to the window and was following him with her eyes as he walked down Keil Strasse to the Bahnhof Platz.

Wearing his overcoat that concealed the yellow star, and carrying a small briefcase, Adolf walked the half-kilometer to Haumpt Bahnhof. He had to fight the urge to skip and dance the whole way. It took every ounce of self-restraint not to kiss passersby in the street and yell, "I am free, I am free." A group of Blackshirts passing by quickly quelled his excitement. He trembled with fear as he entered the large hall of Leipzig's main rail-station, recalling that the last time he was here, he was on his way back from the Sachenhausen Concentration Camp, when he had to pass through the goods outlet.

Haumpt Bahnhof was the largest rail-station in Europe, and some said even the largest in the world. With its eighteen platforms, and trains coming and going from all corners of Europe, it appeared to be the busiest place in the world. On the blackboard were announcements of trains arriving from Warsaw, Kiev, Lvov, Bucharest, Frankfurt, Paris, Rome, Moscow and many other places he had never heard of before. The station was zooming with activity; soldiers on their way to the frontline and traders arriving for the Spring Trade Fair. Out of the coaches came farmers from the countryside of different nationalities: Russians, Mongolians, Poles, Gypsies. Some well-dressed members of the aristocracy emerged out of their first-class coaches while laborers in working uniforms were sitting in the bar, sipping their beers. There were even one or two Jews to be seen, conspicuous with yellow stars pinned to their garments. The travellers' conversations were drowned out by the noise of the locomotives releasing steam as they approached the bay. The steam from the engines filled the big vaulted hall with its high ceilings. It was all hustle and bustle. The station looked exactly the same as it always had during the Spring Trade Fair, except that there were less Jews and more soldiers, mostly coming off the trains. Some soldiers leaving Leipzig were being sent off by mothers, girlfriends and wives. As they gave their loved ones final kisses and hugs, and held hands through the train window, it was plain to see that the soldiers were secretly hoping that their train would never depart. Everything appeared to be so normal, as if there were no Nazi Party or Brownshirt hooligans about to wage war.

Arriving at the station, Adolf noticed a guard wearing one of the many uniforms he had seen around. He could not tell if the uniform belonged to the Wehrmacht, Gestapo, SS Abwehr, or if it was simply the uniform of the Deutsches Richsbahn. It made no difference to him. They were all the same. Any man with a uniform, even only a worker's uniform, was a threat to Adolf. For him it meant someone who could take away his freedom with the flick of a finger. He was terrified as he passed by the guards, but luckily they paid no attention to him, looking at him as if he was a regular person coming to the station to catch a train. There was only one more hurdle he had to overcome; he had to buy a train ticket to the border in Krefeld, but feared that he would arouse suspicions if he did so. On the other hand, if he bought the tickets in sections, it would mean going through the hassle of buying a ticket each time. He eventually decided to pay for a ticket only up to Kassel. He reckoned that if he would arrive there before the curfew, he would go and see Lotti Katz. The following day, he would continue on to Dusseldorf, and from there, travel by foot to the border. He was relieved to see that one of the windows was free so he would not have to stand in line, drawing unnecessary attention to his yellow star. The ticket clerk seemed to be at the end of his shift, and gave him his ticket after glancing swiftly at his travel permit. The Gestapo officer sitting beside the clerk was not interested in seeing the documents; they both seemed weary and fed up. Adolf doubted that he would have aroused their suspicions even if he were to shout in their faces that he was a Jew escaping from Germany.

As a Jew, Adolf could only obtain a third-class ticket, which meant he had to walk the entire length of the platform, over a kilometer long, to the dark side of the station. He did not mind the walk. At the other side of the platform, he found a bench that did not sport the sign "Forbidden for dogs, Jews and Gypsies," and sat in such a way that his star was unnoticeable.

Freedom was getting closer. The train came after what seemed to him an eternity. Adolf had to board the train sideways so as not to expose his star. The wooden bench in the third-class compartment was hard; the train wagon was cold, dark and dirty. His fellow passengers were mostly drunken, badly dressed Germans, who in no way presented Hitler's idyllic image of the perfect Aryan. To Adolf, all this did not matter; for him it was the train voyage from hell to paradise. As the train left the western suburb of Leipzig, he looked out through the dirty window at the town in which he was born and bred, the place he knew as home, knowing he would never see it again.

The train stopped in Erfurt and Gestapo inspectors came on, walking through the coach shouting, "Papers, papers, get your papers ready." The inspection was quick, the inspectors did not like to be surrounded by the stench of urine and vomit left by the drunks; they preferred to be sitting in their comfortable first-class carriages or relaxing in the dining car with their fellow officers. Adolf heard them cursing the drunks, "You swine, let's see your papers." By the time they got to him, Adolf was trembling. He was shaking so much that he could not control himself, and it was with great difficulty that he got out his travel document for inspection. The Gestapo officer looked at him and bellowed, "You swine, dirty Jew, stand up when you talk to a Gestapo officer." After showing him his travel papers, the officer looked at them, and said, "You are running away, ha, we are not good enough for you in this country. I will show you exactly where you belong." Saying that, his friend pushed Adolf to the corner of the bench, to the amusement of his fellow passengers. Just then, as if an angel was sent from heaven, one of the drunks vomited on the officer's boot. The SS man took Adolf's papers, cleaned his boot, threw the documents back at Adolf, and left the wagon angry.

Adolf breathed a huge sigh of relief. That was close, he thought to himself. In his anger, the officer could easily have thrown his papers out of the window. Luckily, there were no more incidents of that sort before he reached Kassel. The men that sat beside him moved to other seats in the wagon. From time to time, one of them would pass by and spit at him, saying, "You have milked the Fatherland dry, and now you are taking all we have and running away." Others blamed him for Germany's defeat in the Great War, claiming, "It was the Jews that stuck a knife in the back of the brave German soldiers." By 10:00 P.M., most of them had fallen asleep, leaving him in peace and quiet.

Adolf was too nervous and excited to sleep. Just as his thoughts were beginning to drift to what the future held for him in England, a young man came to sit beside him. "I am embarrassed and ashamed," he said, "of what our people are doing to the Jews."

He added, "There is not much I as an individual can do...." He continued, with his voice lowered to a whisper, "All this will not end well. Today they are discriminating against Jews and communists, tomorrow it will be against anyone who stands in their way."

The young soft-spoken gentleman offered to help Adolf once they pulled into the Kassel rail-station, and so he did. The stranger told Adolf to wait at the dark side of the station while he went and bought his ticket. When he finally returned with the tickets, he would not hear of taking money from Adolf. He confessed that it was the very least he could do to compensate in some small way for the atrocities that his people had performed. His generosity did not end there. He pulled out of his rucksack a clean SS uniform. After putting it on, he saluted anyone coming or going who was wearing a uniform. He remained with Adolf as his protector until they arrived at the border. He bought Adolf his ticket at every station where they had to switch trains, sitting and standing beside him each time there were people around, in order to cover his yellow star.

There was one more inspection left in Dusseldorf. After acknowledging the inspecting Gestapo officer with the customary "Heil Hitler" salute, the stranger took the officer aside and told him that the person sitting beside him was his cousin who was deaf and dumb. He explained that he was responsible for bringing his cousin to his family in Duisberg, a city on the Dutch-German border, which Adolf was planning to cross to get into Holland. The SS officer suggested they move to the dining car with all the other SS officials, but the stranger preferred not to shame the pureness of the SS with people such as his cousin. They traveled together on the train throughout the night. The last leg of the voyage was by taxi, which the stranger insisted on paying for. At the border, he told Adolf to wait for him to arrange the papers. It did not take long. Once Adolf got to the border officials, there were no questions asked or papers or baggage checked; the stranger had seen to that. The stranger waved goodbye through the fence and thanked Adolf for giving him the opportunity to prove that not all Germans were Hitler supporters. "This is the only way I can express my resistance to this regime," explained his guardian angel.

By daybreak, Adolf was already in Holland. He was free once

again. The first thing he did, as he left the border guardhouse, was to rip off the oppressive yellow star, and with a sigh of relief, toss it to the ground, where countless other rejected stars lay.

On the Dutch side of the border, the officials were polite and courteous. They looked at his papers and within minutes, he received a visa for three weeks. After exchanging his Reich Marks for Dutch Guilden, he bought a ferry ticket that would take him from Rotterdam to Newcastle. With his few remaining coins, he sat down in the rail-station café. For the first time in what felt like years, he was free to order whatever his heart desired. No one asked him for his ration card or if he was a Jew. For that matter, it seemed to him no one really cared who he was. There were no signs saying, "Not for Jews," "Jews are not welcome here," "No entry for Jews, dogs and Gypsies." There were no sounds of barking dogs accompanied by SS officers, no hollering, and no signs of any Brownshirts, Blackshirts or Gestapo officers in uniform. People were simply going about their business, as they would in Leipzig before the rise to power of the mindless thugs and hooligans.

Adolf felt an exhilarating rush at the thought of being able to travel to Rotterdam without any restrictions, with a second-class ticket, no inspections, no fear, no yellow star, no papers to show or travel documents to present. He was once again a free man.

Adolf savored the dawn breeze on the overnight ferry from Rotterdam to Newcastle; it was the sweetest wine he had ever tasted. It was the feeling of freedom brushing against his face. He had never felt so good or so happy. It seemed as if all the passengers on the boat were rejoicing with him. The thought of Mama, though, who had remained behind in the "inferno," dampened his feeling of being born again. Adolf was sure, though, that Aunt Sarah and the entire Schmulewitsch family would do everything within their power to ensure that Mama would join them in a week or two. Adolf was convinced that once they heard first-hand of all the atrocities taking place in Leipzig, the place they once called home, they would immediately make plans for Lina's move to England.

It was Max, with his English wife Jane, who was waiting for him on the quayside in Newcastle. Adolf could barely recognize Max; he had changed so much since he'd last seen him some five years ago. It seemed that life in England was treating him well.

Adolf was overwhelmed by the sights before him; everything was new, fascinating and impressive. Seeing Max in his Morris motorcar was a sight for sore eyes. In the last three years, Adolf had not seen a Jew driving a car, or for that matter traveling in one. Driving on the wrong side of the road scared him. Through the rain and fog, he could see road signs saying, Middlesbrough, Guisborough, Newcastle, Hartlepool. Suddenly, these places that he had only seen written as addresses on envelopes became real before his eyes. Within an hour, they arrived at the Gray House, the Schmulewitsch family home, on Cambridge Road.

They were all there waiting for him, Aunt Sarah, Uncle Zelig, and all his cousins: Herman with his new English wife Ray, Dora, Yette, and Berta with Freddy, who was by now a big boy. They stayed up the whole night talking, drilling Adolf for the lowdown on what was really happening in Leipzig. Their German neighbors also came round, thirsty for more information about their friends, family, neighbors and acquaintances. Had they been deported, did they manage to get out? If so, where to? What happened to the synagogues, to the businesses? Were Jews still allowed to pray in the ruins? Was it as bad as they said? Were the stories they were hearing exaggerated? There were quite a number of German Jews who had arrived in Middlesborough between the years 1939–41, most of them thanks to the Schmulewitsch family.

Adolf was amazed at the quantity and quality of the food that was being served. It appeared they had never heard of rationing, Jewish food curfews, or any other food restriction. That night, he saw, smelled and tasted foods that even the Aryans, with the best rationing cards available, were prohibited from buying. Rationing cards for Aryans were divided according to social status, military rank and membership in the Nazi party. The closer one was to any of these categories, the better the ration card he received. There was a lot of laughter and crying that night from everyone who came to see Adolf.

Adolf wanted to meet Ike Bellow, Max's brother-in-law, to thank him for all he had done to help get him there. Adolf hoped to meet with him once he had settled in; after all, he would have to go and work for him soon. Bellow lived in Leeds. After all the guests left, the family discussed Lina's situation. The question was, how could they possibly get her out of Leipzig? Uncle Zelig hoped that with all their efforts combined, they would manage. That night, they promised each other that they would not give up until Lina was on her way to Middlesbrough.

Adolf went to bed that night content, his heart filled with hope and excitement about his new life in England.

Adolf was to awaken the next day to the news of *The Middlesbrough Chronicle*:

Wednesday, March 15, 1939

Jeers greet Hitler's entry into Prague:
Herr Hitler entered Prague as a conqueror last night and raised his standard on the Hradzin Castle, ancient palace of the Bohemian Kings.
Czechoslovakia came under the Nazi boot just as Austria had the year before.

Chapter Eight

Adjusting to Life in England – Adolf Becomes Peter

April 1939

Jews around the world will be sitting down tomorrow for the First Seder night of Pesach.

Round the Seder table this year in the British Isles, each family will be asked to host at least one Jewish refugee that has arrived recently from Germany, Czechoslovakia or Austria.

The Chief Rabbi of England has asked that in each and every Jewish home there should be a prayer recited for the safety of Jews in Germany and Czechoslovakia.

Monday, April 10, 1939
From our correspondent in Rome

On Friday (Good Friday), the Italian Army, led by Marshal Rodolfo Graziani, invaded Albania.

This was less than a week after Neville Chamberlain's momentous statement that Britain and France would come to the aid of Poland if Germany or any of the other Fascist countries would attack it. The statement came following the unresolved dispute over the Danzig Corridor, which was reported in the Evening Standard of the 3rd of April.

Our Roman correspondent reports that Italian units headed by Marshal Rodolfo Graziani invaded a small Islamic country on the Adriatic Sea. The Italian forces met with little resistance and managed to arrive at the capital, Tirana, by the end of the day. Early Saturday morning, Mussolini, in his victory speech, said, "The conquering of Albania by the heroic Brigade of the Blackshirts, which fought courageously against forces and equipment far suprior than its own, was part of my Fascist policy to extend Italian rule over the whole former territory of the glorious Roman Empire." Mussolini added, "As the heir of Julius Caesar, it is my duty to history to rebuild Italy as it was in the first century, the Empire that ruled over Asia, Africa, and Europe."

Mussolini continued, "'Believe, Obey and Fight,' these are the three principles that guided our troops in Albania, and brought them to glorious victory."

Our correspondent in Whitehall reports of an urgent meeting that took place last night. Prime Minister Neville Chamberlain, the Foreign Secretary Lord Edward Halifax, and the Prime Minister of France, Daladier, attended the meeting. All three came out with joint proclamations that "denounce the invasion of Albania as a dangerous move and an act of aggression. The leaders see it as a continuing policy of Hitler in Europe."

Our political correspondent adds that the invasion of Albania is a direct result of the agreement that was signed in Munich last September by Hitler, Mussolini and Neville Chamberlain, known as "peace in our generation." This agreement gave legitimacy to Hitler to invade Czechoslovakia in the name of German unity. Mussolini in Albania used the same argument. Our correspondent also adds that the Duce is worried that his ally, Hitler, will conquer the whole of Europe in a short time, while Italy will only be left with the crumbs. In light of that, Mussolini has decided on the policy that each time Germany takes over one country, the Italian army will follow suit in another place. In this way, the Duce thinks, he will at all times be able to sit alongside the Führer and talk with him on equal terms when the time will come to divide up the conquered territories. It was also noted that Albania, being a protectorate of Italy, and in some ways an ally, did not offer much resistance to the occupation. It is clear that Mussolini took advantage of the long weekend holiday of Good Friday in order not to arouse the suspicion and condemnation of the press and politicians around the word. The Duce estimated that by the time they would be back in their offices on Monday, any denouncements would be too late.

* * *

Coupled with the new regime in Tirana came the news that Franco with his Fascist army had overrun the final resistance of the International Brigade, and entered Madrid on Friday. He also took advantage of the Good Friday prayers – Franco knew that most Spaniards from either side of the barricade (Communist and Nationalists) would be in church then. Therefore, there was almost no street fighting. The enactment of the takeover was by now a fait accompli.

10 Downing St., the White House, the Quai d'Orsai in Paris, and other democratic powers, have voiced concern over the growing influence of Fascistic regimes all over the world.

Translated from German:
Saturday, March 25, 1939
Middlesbrough

Dear Mama,

I am sorry I did not have the opportunity to write before. I have been so busy trying to get things sorted out. I had a long talk with Bellow to see what can be done in order to get a visa and permit for you. The conversation in itself was not easy, as he could not speak one word of German. Cousin Berta had to come along and translate for me. It is funny how people here can only speak English. At home, most people can speak Yiddish and Polish. (Not goyim of course, but he is a Jew.)

Bellow suggested that the best thing is to put the case in the hands of a lawyer. He himself does not have the time to deal with it. It seems that he is saying, in not so many words, "I have other responsibilities and I cannot be bothered with this." I guess he thinks he has done his duty by getting me the papers and the visa. He also suggested that the first thing I should do is change my name. He is right; to go around in this country at times like these with a name like Adolf is not a good idea. I decided to adopt the name of Peter. Do you remember it was the name we gave the dinghy that we used when we would go to the Water Polo competitions? It is a funny feeling. At first, I did not react when people called me Peter, thinking that they were talking to someone else, but with time, I got used to it. It feels as if I am a different person, as if I were reborn. I just think, react and talk differently when someone calls me Peter. For one thing, I expect him to speak to me in English, and that I should answer in English.

Auntie and Uncle are very busy trying to find their way in the new country. They think they cannot do anything that is unorthodox, as it may anger their English neighbors. They are more preoccupied with preparations for the Passover than with anything else. Uncle and Max go every morning to the factory in the nearby town, Guisborough, 15 kilometers down the road.

Herman is in London working as the firm's representative for the south of England. Berta is the main work manager on the factory floor. At the same time, she is taking care of her family, and does all she can to get Jack's parents out of Germany. What I am trying to say is that they have left me alone to deal with the permits and papers we need in order to get the visa for you to come here. The first problem is that I do not know my way about, I do not know where to go and who to approach. Worst of all, my English is not good enough. I hope I will learn more before I start working. Second, I do not have enough money to pay a lawyer, so as to put the case in his hands.

I hope that sometime soon, I will go down to London to get the jewelry from Dina and pawn it. With some of the money, I will get myself a place to live; the rest of it I can use to pay for a lawyer.

The news from Czechoslovakia is very worrying. Here people are saying that they could have told Neville Chamberlain that Hitler would not keep his promise. For anyone that comes from the old country, it does not seem astonishing that the Wehrmacht has occupied Prague. For the English people, they can only think of it as, "Hitler did not play fair." They somehow think that the whole thing in Europe is no more than some sort of cricket game.

I feel well, and it is a wonderful feeling to be free. It is a feeling I cannot describe. But I have some problems with my health. I think it is from the food that I am not used to.

I do hope that within two or three weeks we will be together once more. I just know you will love England, although you will think that people here are somewhat strange, and you may have some problem learning English, but if Aunt Sarah learned, you will also pick it up.

I am longing to hug you and hold your hand once more.
Adolf

* * *

Lina was ordered to come to the offices of the Jewish community on Keil Strasse 5. Since the night of the big pogrom in November, she, and all the other stateless Jews, had to report once a week to the headquarters of the community to renew their residents' permit in Leipzig. After October 1938, any Jew (non-Aryan) still remaining in Germany resided there on a temporary basis, and had to renew their residence papers weekly. At the same time, they received food coupons, nourishment and fuel. These allocations were enough to stay alive, but they were not sufficient, even if certain foodstuffs could be found in the Jewish shops. There were only a small number of shops that were allowed to sell to the Jews. Often, these shops did not stock the food that was specified on their ration cards.

Lina had just been to the offices on Keil Strasse two days ago. She could not understand why she was being summoned there once more. Maybe, she thought hopefully, her exit visa and papers had arrived. As she entered the building, she was shown to the room of the Chief Rabbi where a Gestapo officer dressed in black was waiting for her. He ordered her to come close to the table where he was sitting.

He looked at her with angry eyes, and sputtered, "Who does your dirty Jewish son think he is, talking about our beloved Führer in such a way, and humiliating our Fatherland in front of enlightened nations?" He slapped her face so hard that she fell on the floor. Then he threw at her the letter that had arrived from Peter. The censors had obviously read the letter. The officer came over to her side of the table and kicked her out of the room. He warned her that if her son would ever write or say one more thing against the Third Reich, they would get him even if he was in England, and she would be sent to the East. Lina took the letter and crawled out of the room.

She had to stay in the building until the end of the Jewish curfew. When she got home, she opened the red seal of the censors. With shaking hands, she pulled out the letter. By the time she had finished reading it, she had totally forgotten that she had not eaten anything for the last two days. The humiliation she had suffered this afternoon was erased as she read her son's letter. She was happy and relieved that Peter was alive and well, and she was sure that within two to three weeks she would be with him safe and sound in England.

Lina wanted to respond to Peter's letter immediately, but she could not find any paper or pen to write with. She recalled that all the pens were sent with the shipment to England. After a long search through her empty house, she found a pencil between two floorboards. She was sorry she did not have a knife to sharpen it with, knowing that her writing would look sloppy and unreadable, but it was better than not writing at all. Knives and writing paper were among the long list of items that Jews were prohibited to own. She also found some of Peter's old writing paper, with his letterhead:

Adolf Rochman
Insurance Agent
Humboldt Strasse 3
Leipzig C1

She knew she would have to cherish these few pages she had found, and use them sparingly. Even if Jews were allowed to buy paper, she did not have the money to do so.

Translated from Yiddish:
Saturday, April 15, 1939

Dear Adolf,

Why are you complaining about your health? Are you not healthy because you do not eat enough? Or is it because you are eating things that you should not? Why do you not go to the doctor? Do you do your injections regularly? You definitely eat things you should not; you should take more care. You could eat cucumbers with sour cream; this sort of thing you can prepare for yourself without cooking. Obviously, you can buy butter, as there is no Jewish rationing in England. I got the rent for the two rooms from Fritz, and there are still 100 Reich Marks due. Is that his debt? Ask Aunt Sarah what a common family he comes from, and she will tell you some stories about him. I would not lie to you about these things. I asked him to give me the money that he is holding back, but he was not prepared to do so.

When the things arrive, you should not give away anything until I get there, so I can see for myself what we need and what we can sell or give away. Now I am sorry that we sent my entire wardrobe. It is still quite cold here and I have only the one dress to wear. My shoes are getting worn out. I try to do as much walking as I can so I will look good when I will have to go to the consul to get my visa, but I am sure that that will only last a week or two until I get to England. You must remember, when you come and meet me at the quayside, to bring my red dress and black shoes with you. I will need to change before seeing the rest of the family. I do not want anyone to see me in the old rag I am wearing now. I especially do not want Aunt Sarah to see me looking like this; she may think we do not have any money for clothes.

On Thursday the 13th, Herman Uko and his young wife Ayala left for Palestine. Somehow, they got a certificate. You know that Herman's father was well off before the bad times, and I think he bought land in Palestine some 10 years ago. Herman told me it is someplace in the north, not far from a big city in Lebanon; I think he said it began with a "B," Babylon, Beirut, or something like that, but I never know with these Biblical Arab names, what they mean and how one is supposed to pronounce them, let alone remember their names. To me, they all sound the same. He did say it was not far from another port on a big mountain, about which the only thing I could remember is that it has something to do with the prophet Elijah, the one we open the door for, and give a cup of wine to, on *Pesach*. Ayala said that in this city, "Hif" or "Hifel," or something like that, there are a lot of former Leipzigers that have come to live there in the last five years. I met him in the community office when I came to collect your letter. As you must have known, all letters that are sent to Jews come to the community headquarters where they are looked over by the Gestapo before we receive them. You must be more careful what you write, or write in Yiddish. Herman told me that they plan to go by train to Budapest. From there, they will travel with many more Hungarian and Czechoslovakian "pioneers," as he called them (the word "pioneers" always makes me think of the Europeans that went to fight the Indians in the Wild West of America), then on the Danube to Constantsa in Rumania by the Black Sea; and from there, they will take a boat to their final destination, Palestine. In Palestine, they are going to someplace or another (he told me the name of the place, but I cannot remember) to drain swamps. As he told me that, his eyes glittered, as if they were going to America to find gold. I am glad I do not have to go with them. It seems to me that as bad as it is here, it is evidently worse there, with all the Arabs, deserts, swamps, malaria, camels, and God knows what other calamity one can find over there. They expect to arrive in about three months. He gave you his regards. He said to tell you he is very upset that you did not answer his letter.

Dear Adolf, Aunt Sarah could drag me out of here as a housemaid. She needs no money for that. You think I have nothing to do all day? So, I will tell you: we have to go and work every day in some sort of an ammunition factory from morning until night. We do not get paid and we have to walk to the factory. Sometimes they give us some food, but usually the strong and young get to it first so I go hungry. I have so many troubles that I do not know where to start.

By the 1st of May, the stateless have to move out of homes that are in Aryan areas, and move to "Jewish Homes." I do not know what to do with the rest of the furniture. No one will buy it, and I cannot lift it or take it with me. Most of the people who rent rooms in the "Jewish Homes" zone are very primitive; they do not let us (the stateless who come from the other parts of town) into their kitchens, even if it is only to prepare food to eat. Gaunter Witerlis is already out. He gave his house back to the landlady.

I just do not know where to get money from to pay for the rent and for moving. I have no money for food, let alone for heat, rent and stamps. I am just totally lost. Luckily, I met Mr. Paul Niederland, a teacher in the Jewish school. He and his family will be leaving for France next week; he will take my letter and post it from France.

From the Jewish community, I receive nothing. I have already told you how they humiliate me each time I go there. They are very simple people that cannot do anything without the approval of the Gestapo who prowl around like lions waiting for a kill.

You must ask Aunt Sarah if she could send me some butter. The only thing I can eat is dry bread. The only thing I get from the community is five Marks a week and one ration of oil, which I cannot cook with, so I use it to put on the bread. The only bread we get is usually five or six days old.

* * *

ADJUSTING TO LIFE IN ENGLAND

At this point, Lina had filled the paper with her handwriting, so she started to write on the edges and around the sides of the paper, so as to get the most use out of it.

* * *

Dear Adolf,

I think the best thing to do at this point is to put an announcement in the Middlesbrough local newspaper to get work for me. Maybe you can ask around in the Jewish Committee if they need someone to work for them. I do not want to come and live under the wing of Uncle Zelig. We did that once. Do you remember the time after father died on Humboldt Strasse 23? From then on, they always mention it each time we meet. What do I need all this for? I would like to get off the boat in Newcastle, and start working the next day.

Dear Adolf, I do not understand. Are you so busy that you cannot find any time to do these things for me? You did not tell me anything about the furniture – did it arrive safely? What have you done with it? You must do something so the moths do not eat everything up. Go buy some mothballs, give them to the movers, and tell them to roll the carpet open, put them in and then roll the whole thing back up again. Do not open the boxes before I come. Did you get the money and jewelry for this *Tzazke* (Yiddish: a derogatory name for a woman) of yours, Mrs. Dina Thorn? Did she run away with our property? Why didn't you write to me about that?

You must give me an answer when I ask you something. This business of you changing your name is of no interest to me. I do not care that you changed it. It is your business. To me, you will always be Adolf. Better spend your time and effort on writing things that are important.

Adolf, do not forget me here, do not leave me in Leipzig. You must get me out any way you can. Whatever you do, don't let them sent me to the East.

I have no more room on the paper to write, so I will stop here.
Love from your sad Mama

Chapter Nine

Blood is Thicker than Water – a Testing Time for Family Loyalties

WHEN DAVID OBERMAN GOT UP that day, he was nervous and annoyed. He did not like life in London – it was too cold, damp and noisy. Neither did he enjoy his work at the accountant's office of Goldberg and Jackson, where he spent most of his day having to deal with small accounts of grocery shops on street corners in Hendon and other slums of London, or of third rate hairdressers in the back streets of Golders Green. David found it difficult to comprehend the idea that he must cover up for the tax evasions of slumlords who took advantage of refugees like him. Life in England was not what he had imagined when he left Leipzig, less than a year ago.

Back home, he worked as the chief accountant for the Jewish Kroch Bank in Augustusplatz, which dealt with international clients, big fur traders in Leipzig, and had contacts with banks and financial institutions in London, New York, Alexandria and Bolshevik countries. David was fortunate enough to have a boss, Mr. Kroch, who advised him to transfer some of his money to Barclay's Bank in London. This meant that he had some money to live on once he arrived in England, and did not have to ask for charity from the Jewish Committee, like so many of his friends from back home did.

He walked to work through the dark morning streets of Hackney Borough, with the wind blowing in all directions. His office, located on the corner of Curtain Street and Old Street, was nothing more than an old warehouse that had been converted into an office. Every time he would use the outside toilet, David remembered with nostalgia his beautiful office on the top floor of the Kroch Hochhauses, where he had the most magnificent view of Elsterbecken River and Rosenthal Park.

That day, David still had to turn in his final summing up of Hirshberg's notions shop, whose owner was constantly trying to fiddle with the books and evade taxes. In Leipzig, he thought to himself, this would never happen. In all the years he worked for the bank in Leipzig, he never once was expected to cover up the correct figures. Of course, there was the money from the Jewish businesses in the Leipzig Brüle, a world trade center for furs, that had to be sent overseas so the Nazis would not lay their hands on it, but that was something else entirely. As David walked into his office building, nodding at the cleaning staff that were just walking out, he thought of the workers in Leipzig, who would always greet him with a pleasant *"Gutte Morgen*, Herr Oberman;" a cup of coffee would be waiting for him at his desk. In his mind, the army of secretaries and accountants were there to carry out his instructions.

David could not rid from his mind the image of boardroom meetings at the Kroch Bank, at which he was expected to give his opinion on world financial evaluations. Here in London, in contrast, he had to contend with scraps of papers with illegible writing scribbled in a language he could barely understand, which they called "receipts," trying to work out the profit of some shop which was worth no more than a hole in the wall.

David constantly tried to remind himself that a lousy job is better than no job, and at least he had a roof over his head, and, most importantly, he was safe in England. Thank goodness he did not have to endure what his sister Lina was suffering at this moment in Leipzig. It had taken David a long time to finally make up his mind to leave. Like most Jews in Leipzig, he thought things would get better. From 1933 onwards, he knew of people who had lost their jobs, but he thought that this would never happen to him. The bank could never manage without him, and the state of Saxony could never manage without the bank. The Kroch Bank not only ran the lottery for the State, but was also its only window to the outside world. So at least he was safe, or so he thought. They would never hurt him because if they did, they would only be hurting themselves.

Two significant events occurred that were to prove him horribly wrong. First came the nationalization of the lottery and the transfer of the money and profits to the state bank. A short time after that, the Reich came out with the Nuremberg Laws, which forced every Jewish business to take on an Aryan partner who had the right to take over at least ninety percent of the business. The day the "new owners" came into the bank was the 9th of November the previous year. David remembered it as if it were yesterday. The two "new partners" came into Mr. Kroch's office and ordered him to get out of his seat behind the desk. Mr. Kroch said, "Here is my Argentinian passport, you can take the whole bank and do with it as you like," and left the building. He had obtained Argentinian citizenship through his connection with the consul in Dresden and, knowing the new partners would come, he organized for himself and his family a train and boat trip out of the port of Danzig. He was determined not to sign the bank over to the hooligans, come what may, so he said to David, "They can control it, but they will never own it. The day will come when my inheritor will get it back." David had not seen him since that day.

A letter came from him a short time after his departure, saying that he had reopened a branch of the bank in Buenos Aires, and at the same time bought land in Palestine, somewhere on a hill west of Jerusalem. He was also thinking of building a hotel over there. It was on that day that David decided that it was time to leave. David was lucky that he took Kroch's advice and had savings of more than 500 English pounds, which gave him the right to migrate to England.

After talking to Peter last week, he realized that not only had he made the right decision, but he had also left at the right time. He did not have to experience the humiliation and the run-around that Peter had to endure in order to get a permit to leave Leipzig.

There was a letter waiting for him on his desk from his sister, Lina. Since the pogrom, he had started to receive letters from her on a weekly basis. He also got letters from friends and relatives in Leipzig whom he had not heard from in years, acquaintances that he did not know existed; they all asked for the same thing – a visa, or any other arrangement so they could come to England. Sometimes he wondered from where they had gotten his address.

Translated from Yiddish:
Thursday, April 13, 1939
Humbold Strasse 3
Leipzig

Dear David,

This is the third letter that I am writing, and you have still not taken the time or the effort to answer me. I also gave Adolf a letter to hand over to you, which I thought you would have received by now. Yet there is nothing from your side except complete silence. Am I not your sister? Am I not blood of your blood? Am I not the closest relative you have? David, we are all Obermans, and we have to help each other. If we will not give a hand to each other, who will give a hand to us? Don't you know that I must get out of Leipzig? I only have a permit to stay here for another month. If I do not get out by then, they will send me to the East, like they did to the Polish Jews.

I know that Adolf is trying his best to get a visa for me, and that Sarah and Zelig are helping too, but as yet nothing has come from all their efforts. Time is running out. Since Reinhard Heydrich took over the Bureau of Jewish Affairs at the end of last month, things are getting worse from day to day, from hour to hour. It is something I cannot even describe to you. Every day, every hour, there are new decrees, injunctions and regulations about what Jews are allowed, or rather not allowed, to do, eat, talk about, read, buy, sell, listen to, travel in, or places we can travel to. There are so many rules, and they come so often that I spend most of my time going around trying to find out what new restrictions have been issued during the course of the day. This, of course, is not announced on the radio, as Jews are not allowed to listen to, or for that matter own, a wireless, but they paste them on the walls of the Jewish homes. If you happen to pass there and see, then you know, otherwise, they will punish you, mostly by beating, for violation of the laws of the Fatherland.

The other day, I found out that starting from the 15th of April, Jews are not allowed to buy chocolate. Not that I was thinking of buying any, it is too expensive for me, but I ask you, why? Why only starting from the 15th? Why not a day before or a day after? Do Jews eat more chocolate than goyim? I do not know the answers to these questions, but what I do know is the result. I can promise you that on the 16th or 17th, we are due for a raid on the Jewish homes, by the Brown or the Black or some other color shirts, looking for chocolate that Jews are hiding in their kitchens. At the same time, they will confiscate, thieve, rob and pilfer other things that they fancy in the house, whatever is left from the last time they came.

I am not talking about the beating, slapping or rape that they perform if they find a woman that they like. Complain? If you dare complain to the police or the Gestapo, the first thing they will do is arrest you for defying the honor of an Aryan. How could a woman defy the honor of the Reich by claiming that an Aryan would sleep with a dirty Jewish woman, or what they call "Unter Mensch?" They would send you to the East if you dare make those accusations.

I ask myself which is worse: to be humiliated every time I go out, or to receive charity from Zelig or Berta, with the knowledge that twenty percent is taken by the Germans? That is before they even give it to me. They say it is in order to repay the damage that the Jews caused on the night of the big pogrom in November.

David, I am an old woman, and do not have many years to live. You must do something to get me out of this hell. I could be sent to the East for the slightest offence. You know, David, they send Jews to the East for "crimes" such as not moving off the pavement when an Aryan comes along. If that happens to me, it will be the end. I will never see Adolf again, and I will perish in one of those small villages beyond the mountains of darkness.

David, save me. It is within your power to do so, and to forget once and for all the misunderstanding that we had.

Your loving sister,
Lina

* * *

David put down the letter. Yiddish was difficult for him to read, and he was not sure he understood it all, but what he did understand was bad enough. He tried to get hold of Peter in Middlesbrough, but it was hopeless; with only a few telephones in the town, he knew it would be impossible. Lina's letter continued to bother him throughout the day. If only there was someone he could consult with. David did not know anyone in London, and the few people he was acquainted with were English. They would not understand the urgency of getting some old woman out of Germany, even if it meant she would otherwise be sent to the East. The English perception of East extended as far as Kent on the southeast coast of England.

As for the few German refugees that David happened to know, they were all preoccupied trying to get their own relatives out, and could not help him. He decided he would go and see Lily, an English Jewish woman who worked in a lawyer's office. He met her some time ago at a dance that was given by the local Jewish committee in Hendon. Although she was more than 15 years his junior, he quite liked her, and thought that discussing his sister's plight would be a good pretext to ask her out with him to the next dance.

David left his office early that day so he could get to Lily's office before she left. While sitting in the waiting room, he picked up a newspaper, and was amused to see the headlines.

Friday, April 21, 1939

> Commons cheer Neville Chamberlain as he pledges to defend Poland:
> > Britain and France pledged wholeheartedly to defend Poland against attack. MPs on all sides cheered Mr. Neville Chamberlain when he gave his solemn undertaking today. An Anglo-French-Polish military alliance will be sealed next week.

* * *

David had to smile; these were the same words that were uttered by the same people only three months ago with regards to Czechoslovakia, and look what happened there. Besides making a feeble gesture to Hitler that England did not look favorably on invasion, nothing had been achieved. Why on earth should the Polish government or people be reassured that anything was being done on their behalf?

After waiting a while for Lily, she finally emerged from her office. It was good to see her. Every time they met, she seemed to grow more and more beautiful. David explained his sister's predicament in as much detail as he could. Lily did not seem overly interested, and was more eager to tell David about the new dress she had bought for the big dance that was planned for the Jewish festival of Pentecost, which would take place in the big synagogue. As for Lina's problem, she told him she would look into it when she had time and would discuss it with her boss, Mr. Liayd.

They left the office together, walking hand-in-hand along the dimly lit streets of London. They decided to go to her parents' house for the Friday evening service.

On Monday morning, he walked into his office to find another letter, this time from Peter in Middlesbrough:

Translated from German:
Saturday, April 15, 1939
Middlesbrough

Dear Uncle David,

I hope this letter finds you in good health, and that things are going well for you. I heard from Aunt Sarah that you have found an English woman and that you are thinking of getting married. Is it true? If so, *mazel tov*, and as Mama says, "Better late than never." I am sorry I did not write before, but as you know, I have not been over here a long time, and it has taken me some time to find my way around. Herman told me that he met you some time ago and informed you that I would be coming.

Aunt Sarah and Uncle Zelig, and the whole Schmulewitsch family, for that matter, are taking good care of me. I am still living in the Gray House; it is somewhat crowded here with the entire Schmulewitsch family, including children and grandchildren, but Aunt Sarah is doing well in navigating this ship. She even manages to keep the house Kosher.

I hope that by the end of the month I will get all my papers in order, so I will be able to start working for Mr. Bellow (Max's brother-in-law). He is, by the way, the one that vouched for me and arranged my exit visa. Once all this is done, I will move to Leeds. Then I will be able to get out of the madhouse and find a place for myself. Not that I do not like it here; it reminds me of the good old days back home, when we used to all gather at Aunt's Sarah's house on Humboldt Strasse 23, before father died and we still lived in the same building. But I think now that I am older, I would like a place for myself.

I am sending you a letter I received from Mama a few days ago. As you will see, she expresses hope that I will have a visa for her in a day or two. As yet, nothing has been done. My feeling is that Aunt Sarah and Uncle Zelig are more concerned with the factory and helping Jack's parents get out than with their own sister's problem.

They have hinted to me that they have seen to it that I got out, and now it is my duty to see to it that Mama gets a visa. But as you know, this is no easy accomplishment: it requires money, contacts and a minimum command of English, all of which I do not have.

I am sure that you, who have been here longer than I, and live in London, can do more for her than I can. If you read the letter, you will see how desperate the situation is. We must do something to get her over here before it is too late.

I hope all is well with you,
Peter

David took Lina's letter out of the envelope. The truth was that he really did not want to read the same thing over and over again. Besides that, he felt he had done all he could from his side, and he was annoyed at his nephew and sister for throwing this hot potato into his hands. His conscience pricking him, David decided to read her letter, as, after all, she was his sister, and the very least he could do was to read what she had written.

Copy of letter to Peter, translated from Yiddish:

Dear Adolf,

I told you to ask David about what I asked you. If you don't ask him, I just do not know what I will do. You should take back what you gave to Uncle Zelig and give it to David. When God helps me and gets me out of here, I will take all my possessions, sell them and pay him back. If this doesn't work out, I do not have any other way to get out of here.

How are things with you and your health? Do you belong to a health insurance group? You must see to it that you do not eat things that you should not. You should not drink much; you should buy yourself some Cognac and drink it if you feel thirsty. I do not see any problem with you eating cucumber with sour cream; this is after all something that you can prepare with no help. You should not go swimming. Know that I just do not sleep at night. I am too worried about all of these things. How do you eat? Do you have all your things with you? I sent my best underwear with you, and the best suit also. These things should not be used for every day, you should only use them for special occasions. But you can use your training suit for day-to-day use.

Do you think you need an overall? I can send one from here; all you need to do is ask.

I will need a suitcase to pack all the things I plan to bring to England. I only have a basket, which would not be suitable for the journey. I do not want Aunt Sarah and Uncle Zelig to see my poverty, but I do not have any money for this. What do you think I should do? What is with the mover? He said that he did not receive any money as yet and also did not get the money for the insurance, which he said he paid from his pocket, and now I will have to pay with something from our possessions. If I cannot pay, I will have to get new documents. My permit to stay in Leipzig is expiring, and I must get a new one that costs 10 Marks. I do not know where I will get the money for this.

Dear Adolf, do you think I should bring a paraffin cooker with me, since I do not know how to cook on a gas cooker?

I told you that I must go to Berlin. I must visit the tombs of Grandfather Moritz and my Uncle Simon for the last time before I leave. I must see that all is in order with their graves, and that the hooligans have not damaged them as they did to the graves here in the New Jewish Cemetery in Leipzig on the day of the big Pogrom. I do hope you remember that the *yahrzeit* (Remembrance Day) is coming up. You can tell that to David too. After all, it was his brother and father also. Sometimes I think he would like to forget that he belongs to the Oberman family.

I am sending you a letter with all the documents from the passport bureau, so you will have all the papers in hand when you go to collect the visa for me. I must have them back soon.

Dear Adolf, you must send me an answer to all my questions. I beg of you once more to go to Uncle David, because if not, I do not see any way I can get out of this furnace.

I love you as always. Do not forget me,
Mama

* * *

David sat down to write a letter to Peter in German.

Translated from German:
Monday, April 24, 1939
London

Dear Peter,

Thank you for your letter that I received this morning. I am glad to hear that things are going well for you, and I am sure you will learn the language in a short time.

I also stayed in the Gray House for a short time when I came, it seems as if it is a station for all Leipzigers that arrive here. As for your mother, I have spoken to a lawyer here in London, and he said he would try and do his best, but of course, he expects payment. In addition, he said that your mother's case is difficult, as she does not fulfill any of the categories that are required by the Home Office to grant her an entry visa. She is old, has no profession (a hat decorator is definitely not a required trade), is a sick person, comes from an enemy country, and has no money to cover her expenses. I cannot find an English person who will vouch for her. When you try and talk to them about this, they say, "The Germans that have come over have caused us enough anti-Semitism as is, why do we have to help import more of this feeling among the goyim?" What is more, they cannot see what is so desperate about the situation. So it is clear that help will not come from those quarters.

What I think we should do is somehow pool together all the money we have – maybe Max or Herman will also contribute – and get a good lawyer with contacts in the Home Office, and see what he can do.

By the way, the girl I am going out with now works for the lawyer that I told you about. It is important, though, that you send me the papers that Lina sent to you.

I am waiting to hear back from you so we can proceed in this matter.

Love Uncle David

* * *

He sent the letter to Peter immediately, as if by sending it he was washing his hands of Lina's predicament. He had done his bit. Let the others also do something.

Chapter Ten

Trapped in Leipzig – Lina Cries for Help

After two months in Middlesbrough, Peter became confident enough to speak English, and meet with people other than his family. He was still at a loose end about Lina. It was clear by now that salvation would not come from the Schmulewitsches. Herman was in London and thus removed from the problem, busy with running the factory and firm. Max, Uncle Zelig and Berta were devoting all their time to the new contract from the War Office. Berta, besides being a sick woman, was occupied with her family, and any strength she did have, she devoted to getting Jack's parents out. Shnoki spent most of her time with her boyfriend Carol Katz, whom she planned to marry in the near future.

Aunt Sarah's attitude to her sister's predicament in Leipzig was, "This is a matter for the men to deal with, we will do as they tell us." In the meantime, the heartbreaking, demanding, and desperate letters did not stop coming from his mother Lina, still trapped in Leipzig.

Then there was the other problem: the furniture. Peter just did not know where it was. He remembered clearly that the movers from Möbelpaker and Hoffman in Leipzig told him that they would come to take the boxes the following day. It must be on its way, he thought, from there to here. But did the movers steal it? Perhaps it only reached the Gestapo warehouses, where they were now distributing the loot. Or was it just stuck in some transit station along with furniture belonging to petty Jews like themselves who believed that saving some of their property was more important than their lives?

He was faced with yet another dilemma: he had not heard anything from Dina regarding the jewelry. Although he had written to her twice since his arrival, he had not as yet received a response. He was not sure how she was planning on transferring the jewelry to him.

As these thoughts were racing through his mind, Sarah came into the dining room with a letter that had just arrived from Dina. Peter sincerely hoped that he could at least resolve the problem of the jewelry.

Translated from German:
April 15, 1939
The International Language Club
(Dina taught English to Russian students in this school)
202 Lewisham s.e.4 East London

Dear Adolf,

I am sorry that I did not have time to answer your letters, but what with my work (I told you I teach Russian) and having to take care of my son and husband, I am not left with time for much more.

I am glad that you managed to get out of Leipzig. You may find it somewhat difficult for the first two or three months until you learn the language, but once you have mastered the English language, you will find the common folk here quite pleasant, if at times somewhat phlegmatic.

After I came back from Germany and Hungary two months ago, Harold and I have discussed divorce. He thinks it is better to wait till Herbert is a bit older, but I am fed up with living with him. When we are in bed together, I think only of you. You must let me come and visit you in Middlesbrough, although I cannot come as long as you are living with your aunt's family. So maybe we should wait till you move to Leeds and start working for Bellow. By then, you will have a place to yourself.

I am saving as much money as I can (but as you know, things are getting more and more expensive) so we will have something to start with once I get the divorce, and we will get married.

Longing to hear from you,
Your love as always,
Dina

* * *

Peter read the letter once more. He could not believe his eyes. There was absolutely no mention of the jewelry. Why did she not mention it? He did, after all, specifically ask about it in his letter; did she steal the jewels? Or maybe she just didn't want to give them back? May be she was using the jewelry as leverage against him, so that he would be forced to marry her? Whatever the reason, Peter could not think of a way to legally retrieve the jewelry. The jewelry constituted their entire savings, which was meant to pay for legal expenses incurred in getting Lina an entry visa.

Later that day, Max came home and showed him the newspaper:

Monday, May 1, 1939

Territorial Army is to Double:
    Preparation for a war with Germany is going ahead.
    The announcement came today that the Territorial Army is being doubled in strength to a total of 340,000

men. The government has ordered the building of more weapons factories and camps, and vast supplies of boots and uniforms have been ordered from privately owned factories all around Britain and the colonies.

The following day, a letter arrived from Lina:

Translated from Yiddish:
Monday, April 24, 1939
Humbold Strasse 3, Leipzig

Dear Adolf,

I received your letter in which you told me that you do not know where the furniture is. It was your idea in the first place, so why do you reproach me? This is what you wanted. You know I have nothing to wear, nothing to eat, nothing to cook in, and no place to live. I do not even know how I will pay for the moving. I must move by the end of the month to the Jewish Homes on Humboldt Strasse 6. Over there, the only water I will be able to get is from the lavatory; they will not let newcomers into the kitchen. If you do not believe me, you can ask them yourself. They are very primitive, but they will tell you the truth.

All the Jewish shops have to be closed, and there is simply no place Jews can buy food. I have placed an announcement in the newspaper to try and sell, but no one is interested. I cannot even sell the wireless. Now that the Polish Jews are allowed to come back for two weeks and sell all their things, nothing has any value any longer; people are just throwing things away.

Dear Adolf, you tell me that I should write to Mrs. Thorn. I cannot write to her, I do not have money for stamps, they cost more than 15 pfenigs. I had to borrow money from Witerlis to send you this letter, but even if I had the money, what could I tell her? If she will not give the "furniture" [code word used between

Lina and Adolf for the shipment of jewelry that was sent from Leipzig to London] to you, why would she give them to me?

I was talking to Sukerman's mother-in-law the other day, and even she was very upset about the whole story.

Wednesday, April 26

Dear Adolf,

I had to stop writing the letter yesterday as they came from the Jewish committee and told me that I must pay 50 Marks for them to dispose of the rest of the things. Where am I to get 50 Marks from?

Have you already received the things? Write immediately as I am worried. Have you checked that everything is in the boxes? Take out whatever you need and seal the boxes up.

Dear Adolf, do you think that I am complaining? There is no need to reproach me as if I am. As yet, I have not done so, and you can believe I have as many *zurise* [Yiddish for troubles] in one day as a person has in a lifetime.

Send my regards to all the family and tell them not to forget me.
Your love,
Mama

* * *

As time passed, there were more and more headlines in the newspapers and broadcasts on the wireless that once more Germany and England were on the brink of war.

Tuesday, May 2, 1939

Britain plans to introduce conscription:
A grave and subdued House of Commons endorsed the government's decision to conscript men over 20 for military service.

Wednesday, May 3, 1939

Moscow's "Pro-Western" foreign minister Litvinov is dismissed and replaced by Vyacheslav Molotov:

From our political correspondent: Following the German invasion of Czechoslovakia, there has been a constant rapprochement between the two countries. Litvinov was dismissed from the post of foreign minister because he is Jewish. He was also known for his pro-Western political outlook. The attack on Britain as a war-seeking nation comes as part of the Bolsheviks' pro-German policy, and a diplomatic signal that Stalin's government is prepared to sign a non-aggression pact with the Nazi regime in Germany.

Tuesday, May 11, 1939

Chamberlain warns Hitler that the use of force in Danzig means war with Britain

* * *

Translated from German:
April 12
Ipamena 2
Rio De Janeiro

Dear Papa & Mama,

I am sure you will be astonished to receive this letter from me in Brazil. I must say that I myself am wondering what I am doing here instead of in London. So I will just tell you in short how it all happened that I am over here and not there.

I will start with the 15th of March, the day you all came with me to see me off at the rail-station at home. It was also the day of the invasion into Czechoslovakia; that is how I remember it so well. Do you remember, Papa, we were both wondering what all those soldiers were doing at the rail-station? We had planned that I would catch the 8:20 A.M. train to Bremen, so that I could be there at night in order to catch the S.S. *Hindenburg* the following morning. The train journey was itself another story. Five or six times the Gestapo came through, checking papers and looking for Jews and army deserters. They found a deserter in my compartment. The way they treated him, I said to myself, "it's better to be a Jew with a travel permit that does not or can not serve in the Wehrmacht, than to be a deserter from that army." Short of killing him then and there they did all kinds of things to that poor youngster, including hanging him from the window as the train was on its way. I would say that the only good thing that came out of that was that they ignored me entirely. At another checkpoint they did not like the "J" in my passport, and I had to do some explaining as to why I don't have a yellow star on my clothes, but other than that it was okay.

The problem started once we got to Bremen. It was around noon and I walked the streets until the curfew, but I could not find a hotel, hostel, or private room that would take me in once they saw the "J" in the passport. Some just called me the "ordinary" things like filthy Jew, Christ killer, blood sucker, Jewish whore and so on. One man said he would call the Gestapo if I didn't get out of his place, which looked to me to be nothing more than a brothel. One hotel owner apologized, saying he feared trouble with the Gestapo if they found someone with a "J" passport on the premises. In the end I slept in the central park; that is where the trouble started and that is why I am here. Being so exhausted from walking and carrying a suitcase the whole day, I didn't notice the sign at the gate which said *Für Juden verboten,*" (No Jews allowed). I had just fallen asleep when I was awakened by a big man in a Gestapo uniform dragging me to the police station. Nothing – not a permit, nor an explanation that I must catch a boat the following day, nor a bribe, not even an offer of sex – nothing stopped them from putting me behind bars. I was there for five days when for no apparent reason they told me to take what was left of my belongings (after they had taken all they thought would be of use to them or to their wives) and told me to get down to the harbor and out of their sight.

I thought it was the intervention of God. But when I got down there, I found out that the S.S. *Hindenburg* had not waited five days for some Jewish woman, even if her father was a hero of the Great War. I was at a dead end. No money, no belongings, a worthless passport, and an outdated ticket were all I had to my name. I did not even have money for a stamp to send you all a letter to ask you what to do.

As I was walking along the docks I saw the offices for the Deutsch Südamerika Schiff Leine (The German South America Ship Lines), the same company which owns the S.S. *Hindenburg*. So I went in, if only to sit down and rest for a short time. Luckily for me, I was the only one in the office. The young clerk behind the desk, ignoring the way I looked, asked with a big smile if he could help. I told myself that I had nothing more to lose, and decided to tell him my story. He listened carefully, occasionally exclaiming, "How terrible!" After waiting patiently until I finished, he said, "I think I can partially solve your problem. We have a boat leaving tomorrow for Brazil. I can see to it that they honor your ticket, but that will only pay for part of the journey; for the rest, I suggest that you work as a chambermaid." He told me that due to the mobilization, most of the ship's younger staff had been taken away.

It is true that I had no desire or intention of ever going there. "Brazil!" I said to myself; the only things I knew about Brazil were that it was somewhere in South American, that they have a carnival over there every year with naked women walking the streets, and that they speak Spanish. I soon found out that I was quite wrong. At any rate anywhere – be it Brazil, the North Pole, or even Palestine – had to be better than staying on the docks in Bremen.

The voyage took over two months, including stopping at Miami and Havana on the way. I tried to get a visa at both places to go ashore, but the "J" in my passport made the option a clear "no." We arrived in Rio de Janeiro ("Rio," as they call it here) three days after Franco took over Madrid. That made very big headlines here; there are many former veterans of the civil war in Rio. It took only a short time for the Jewish community to obtain a temporary visa for me, and as you see, I am still here. I live in a hostel by the sea, which the community has provided for refugees like me. There are many German and Austrian Jewish refugees in the hostel, each one with a story like mine. Work is plentiful for anyone who can speak German and there will be even more opportunities once I've learned Portuguese. The Jewish community embraces us as much as they can, and are prepared to do anything for us – from finding us work, arranging for visas and housing, finding lost relatives, teaching us Portuguese, even helping people my age find a husband or wife. This is in addition to the constant stream of invitation to weddings, community functions, Friday night meals, and family happenings and all kinds of other things that we receive. The Jewish community here tells me that since their parents were treated this way when they came, they, too, want to give back to the community, as will we, once we are established. They are very well organized and they have arranged it so that each refugee is adopted or fostered by a family who are like temporary parents for them. I must say, I never had it this good at home – even before the hooligans came to power.

I will write once more in a day or two.
Love, Kate

* * *

On the same day that Peter received a letter from his mother, a letter also came from his friend, Lotti Katz.

Translated from German:
Sunday, April 23, 1939
W. Hartlepool

Dear Adolf,

Shnoki came to see my brother on *Shabbos* (Saturday), and I was overjoyed to hear that you had arrived, and are staying with them in Middlesbrough. Why did you not tell me that you were coming? The last I heard from you was your plans to leave Leipzig sometime in March, and that on your way to Holland, you would stop in Kassel while waiting for the train. But I presume something happened with the Gestapo, or God knows what, and you could not make it. In any case, I was so relieved to hear that you got out.

I myself had a very big ordeal since the last time we met in Leipzig. Do you remember that my father was honored with an Iron Cross from the war? So we all hoped, or should I say wanted to believe, that we were safe. Even when they threw out the Polish Jews, we did not feel any threat. Father would say, "We do not have to worry, we are German and they will not touch us." For that matter, if you remember, he was very furious with my brother Carol, who left two years ago. Of course, he liked to ignore the fact that Jewish lawyers were not allowed to practice law any longer. (You may remember that he is, or was, a lawyer.) For him nothing had changed, and no matter what Kate and I tried to point out to him, he was firm in his opinion that it was only a passing phenomenon. Things changed very radically after the Pogrom. Not only did he lose his position in the town council, but he was also arrested. When he came home from prison, which was more or less the same time that you came home, he decided we must leave.

Fortunately for us, he had some contacts, so he could get permits for all of us to leave, and even luckier was that Carol was in England and could arrange work permits for us on this side. My father arranged seats for all three of us in a Portuguese train carrying other refugees. We stayed in Lisbon for some time until Carol finalized our papers, and two weeks ago, we landed in W. Hartlepool. In the meantime, things are not easy. Father has no work and is feeling very humiliated because of what happened, and not knowing or understanding one word of English does not help things. You can imagine how he feels after having his own law firm, where language is the most important tool you work with.

I presume you know how they squeezed every pfening out of us. So in the meantime, we live with Carol in one room at the back of the store. After living in a big house, it brings a lot of tension, particularly between Carol and Father, who still treats him as if he were the youngest child. Mama and I started to work last week for some English people, cleaning houses. Father finds this difficult to digest.

My sister, Kate by the way, who planned to leave a day before us, somehow got on the wrong boat and ended up in Brazil. When we arrived here, we were astonished to find she was not in Hartlepool, and Carol had not heard from her either. But just yesterday, we received a letter from her telling us about the whole ordeal.

It is just terrible what Hitler and his army of hooligans have done to us. But in any case, we must stop complaining. After all, we are safe and sound now, and there are people who are in a worse situation than us. By the way, what is happening with your mother? Is she already here or is she still on the way?

Adolf, what can I tell you? It was just wonderful to hear that you are not far away and I do hope we can meet as soon as possible.

Love as always,
Lotti

Peter sat down immediately to reply. Although W. Hartlepool was only a few kilometers from Middlesbrough, it was more common to write letters than to phone people, as there were very few phones in either town.

Translated from German:
May 2, 1939
Middlesbrough

Dear Lotti,

I cannot tell you how glad I was to hear from you. I must tell you that your ordeal pales in comparison to what I had to go through. I will tell you about it when we meet. As for Mama, she is still stuck in Leipzig and I am at a loose end trying to get a visa for her.

In any case, it is a funny coincidence that I received your letter now, as I am leaving Middlesbrough in a few days for Leeds to start working for Bellow Engineering. Maybe you can come by train to visit me. My address in Leeds will be: c/o Alexander Boarding House, 15 Reginald Terrace, Chapeltown, Leeds.

I do hope to hear from you soon.
Adolf

P.S. By the way, I have changed my name now to Peter.

* * *

By the end of the first week of May, Peter had received most of his papers. It had only taken a week for him to get a work permit that would allow him to start working for Bellow in Leeds. Max and Aunt Sarah insisted on coming with him this first time to his new residence in Leeds. It was simpler than he thought to find a place to live.

He moved into a bedsit on Reginald Terrace, better known as Alexander's Place, where mostly German Jewish refugees lived. He found some comfort among these people who were in the same boat as him, all looking for work and accommodation, and had family, mostly parents, still in Germany, who they were desperately trying to get out, one way or another. Like Peter, they had relatives in Britain who were trying to keep themselves aloof from the rest of the family. They all understood what was going on in Germany and could help each another with useful pieces of advice and a listening ear. They could exchange information about lawyers who were experts in immigration, or information about work, places to live and how to deal with the English.

The same week, another letter arrived from Lina.

Translated from Yiddish:
Saturday, April 29, 1939
Leipzig

Dear Adolf,

On Thursday, thank goodness, I got a message that they will come to pick up the furniture with a lorry that is on its way to Chemnitz. In Chemnitz, they will pick up the stuff from other people. In the middle of the lorry are the belongings of other people, and on either side are our things. When it arrives, with the help of God, you must find a room immediately and store all the things. Remember the mattresses on the floor and the furniture above. You must check personally that everything is there. Take someone with you to check it and then close it immediately. Do not pack the wash kit in the big suitcase. Wait until I, with God's help, arrive.

I absolutely cannot cook in the room. They do not let me. When I need water, I must take it from the toilet bowl. Adolf, I cannot live through this. I cannot go all the time to the Witerlis family when I need some hot water. They are not the best of people. I am withering away from the stress of it all. As far as I am concerned, they can go to hell. I curse the Kaufmanns and the Arens. They should not have a better life than I have. They should leave me alone. Write to the Kaufmanns that they should give me the 50 Marks they promised to pay for the room. You do not have to be ashamed to write to these people. But do not write your address so they will not know where you are.

Now we, I mean those over 50, have to go and work in the garbage site for hours on end every day. All this labor for a measly six Reich Marks from the committee, so we can survive. We work there from morning till night, sorting out garbage. I would say the only thing that is good about it is that I can find food in the garbage from time to time; that is the only thing that is keeping me alive. But the work is very hard and the weather cold, and my shoes are ruined. Maybe I will find something to put on my feet. It's forbidden to take, but the German in charge is a kind person and allows us to take things from time to time, and even to work sitting down, if there is no Gestapo inspector around. He is also very afraid of the *bal-la-goles* (horsemen) who bring the garbage from town in case they might inform on him or on us, so we must be careful when they come in.

You must not tell Uncle and Aunt what I told you; no one must ever know that I work in a garbage dump. I do not want to imagine what they would think when I come over. Please write to Uncle David and tell him that I am starving, if it is not already understood. If I do not get rent money for the room, you will not have to trouble yourself about me anymore.

Your loving Mama

* * *

The constant stream of letters coming from Lina placed enormous pressure on Peter. As much as he tried to discuss them over with the family, they were just not interested.

Chapter Eleven

Britain Prepares for War

B<small>Y THE END OF MAY</small>, the first letters from Lotti started to arrive to Peter's new address.

Translated from German:
Thursday, May 18, 1939
British Dolls & Toys LTD
Therpe St., W. Hartlepool, Tel 6277
Manager Carol Katz (German)

My beloved dear Adolfi,
    Only once more, I would like to be honest with you and call you this name.
    My visit to Leeds has not changed my feelings for you. I am still under the influence of our last day together in Leipzig, just before the November Pogrom. The wonderful friendship that developed between you and me was a bond free of any egotistical feelings. I would like you to know that already in Leipzig, my feelings for you were growing stronger by the day, but I was reserved, and no one knew this. Even you did not know; I was too proud

to show it. Now I must live with what you said to me, "When someone loves, one does not look at one's honor." So for the first time, I am writing to tell you what I feel inside. Never in my life have I experienced such pain since the last few hours we spent together in Leipzig. I thought that would be the last time that I would ever see you. I must tell you that never in all my thirty years have I felt so strongly as I do for you right now. I suffered with you when you were ill and your pain was my pain. Likewise, your joy was my joy. Maybe now you can understand the depth of my feelings. I could never tell them to you as that is my character. On the other hand, I felt compelled to share my emotions with you, as there are many women who turn your head – that is the weak side of your character. But the sort of women who catch your eye only like the manly side of a man, and do not look inside the heart, and when a man is not a man anymore, they will leave him and find someone else. As you know, there are many men! Not only do I say so, everyone knows it.

I mean one woman in particular, this Russian woman. She has some sort of grip on you. The truth is that you do not deserve to be miserable; you have a heart of gold.

On the 9th of December, I must go to Harrogate. I was told that the journey is no more than a twenty minute bus ride from Leeds. I would love to come and see you once I get there. I want to feel you and I want to be close to you.

I was so happy you wrote me a letter.

From your sad Lotti

* * *

The morning newspapers carried the story about the fate of the Jewish refugees coming from Central Europe to Palestine.

Thursday, May 20, 1939

Illegal Palestine immigrants face curbs:

Malcolm MacDonald, the Colonial Secretary, warned last night that the illegal entry of thousands of Jews into Palestine was fanning the flames of Arab revolt. Suspicious Arabs thought that Britain was condoning it so as to get around declared policy, and this was perpetuating dangerous bitterness.

He told the Commons of an organized attempt to smash the government's policy by breaking the Palestine law. The immigration quota for October to March next year has been suspended because of large numbers of illegal Jewish arrivals; that total will now be deducted from future quotas. Steps are being taken in countries of embarkation to check illegal immigration and detain the ships being used.

Denying that the government was indifferent to the plight of the refugees, he said that 75,000 were allowed to enter over the next five-year period. But Palestine could not solve the whole refugee problem, although special provision was made for people from Central Europe.

What the Colonial Secretary condemned was the organized traffic in immigrants. In two months 8,000 had tried to smuggle themselves in. Of those entering now, forty percent were Polish and Rumanian, not from Germany and its new territory. Most of those coming are either from the Germans' newly acquired territories (Czechoslovakia, Austria, Germany) or Jewish citizens of Galicia that migrated to Germany at the end of the last century, and therefore do not have German citizenship or hold German passports. Within Germany, they are considered "stateless." Palestine and the Dominican Republic are the only two places open to them at this late stage.

> As for those holding German statehood and passports, it is easier to migrate to any other country.

* * *

What Peter understood from this article was that yet another gate to freedom was being closed to his mother. Once more he felt pangs of regret that they had not grabbed the opportunity in 1936 to emigrate to Palestine, but at the time, such drastic measures seemed ridiculous and unnecessary. Mama, of course, would not hear of it, saying, "What, are you crazy? What do you think we would live off, scraps from the garbage that the Arabs have left behind?"

A letter from his sister, Berta, was waiting in the mailbox the following day.

Translated from German:
Monday, May 15, 1939
Trayan St. 50, Cetata Alba, Rumania

Dear Adolf,

Today I received a letter from Mama, claiming that I spoke about you in a very bad way. In spite of the fact that you did not see any reason to write even a postcard, and that I am older than you, I will make the first step and explain to you what I wrote, as you do not know what was actually written in my letter to cousin Berta. First, I must say that when I wrote to Berta in Middlesbrough, having received a letter from Mama, telling me that she did not know where to find you. You, Adolf, did not see any reason to write to us or to Mama for that matter. This is on top of the fact that Mama lost her house because of you, and now she must go from one family to the next, living in servants' quarters with five or six men and women in the same room, with no money to live off.

All that I say here is the pure truth. If Mama had stayed in the Humboldt Strasse 3 house, she would not have needed help.

How terrible it is that Mama must live with the Witerlises in this awful room that was once servants' quarters. To my regret, I know that room too well, as I spent many hours in it with Siyoma before we got married, but at least then it had a bed inside. The thought of Mama living in it breaks my heart. I think often of what has happened to all of us, and tears come to my eyes. Mostly, I think of Mama. If Father could see what is happening to her, he would have turned in his grave. I am not writing with the intention of hurting! It is so dreadful that because of some cheap woman, Dina, all this happened to us.

I can understand that to live with an old mother and take care of her is not easy. I have already written to you about this. Do you think that I write all this with a light heart? Do you not think that the whole thing troubles me? I think the impudence of this Thorn woman is terrible.

I would be the happiest woman in the world if Mama lived in safety. I ask you once more, from the bottom of my heart, to do something to get Mama out of this inferno. From here in Rumania, I cannot do a thing. Maybe it would be a good thing if Mama would marry in a fictitious way? If this is possible, she can come and live with us. We do not have much either, but where there is food for three, there is food for four also. If Mama stays much longer in Leipzig, she will not survive. I cannot go there because I do not have the money and I cannot get the travel papers to enter Germany as a Jew.

Where is all the furniture? Where is all the silver? Where is the piano? How terrible it is that it is all going down the drain. When I left the house in 1928, I did not take anything. I did not want to take anything away from the home of my parents. I only took my garments, and now look what is happening. I am raising a daughter and have nothing to give her. Tomorrow, Judith will be an adult, and she has nothing and no future in front of her.

How is your health? What are you studying? What are your

plans? Would it not be better to marry into a respectable family? By doing so, you will be able to get on in life. This is what many young people do today.

How is Dora? How is Herman? I do not hear from them anymore. I think that to them I do not exist any longer. Has everyone forgotten me?

I do not feel well, my heart is bad and my nerves are gone. I have bad rheumatism and life is over for me. I do not have any more happiness in my life. Judith is a big girl now; she will be 12 years of age. She will be going to high school; she is a good student. Judith already looks like a young woman, slim and beautiful.

That is all the news from our side. I ask you once more not to let things go on as they are. Do something so Mama can get a visa before it is too late.

I hope all is well for you, and that God grants you health and prosperity.

From your loving sister,
Berta

* * *

It was late May by the time the letter arrived. Peter had already been working for Bellow for over a month. He did not like the discipline that working for Bellow Engineering entailed. It was not easy getting up every morning at 6:00 A.M. and being at work by seven, working all day with someone standing over you, telling you what to do.

Day-to-day life was becoming increasingly tense in Leeds as Britain prepared for war. There were an increasing number of young men in uniforms on the streets, most of them from the newly established flying corps. At Bellow Engineering, there were hardly any men left; women had taken over the machines. There was an increased demand for sewing machines, mainly for the colonies. Peter suspected that the sewing machines were needed by factories to sew uniforms.

Peter was amazed to see so many flying machines in the air; he was told that they were from the R.A.F. base just outside the town. Among the workers in the factory, there was much anti-Semitic talk. Most of it centered around the fact that the English boys must go to war once more, this time to save the Jews. The newspapers were filled with articles about the Polish-German border conflict, making the point that most people in Britain do not know where Poland is, let alone want to go and fight over there. They could not comprehend the dispute between Poland and Germany. Their criticism had been directed at the politicians who signed a treaty with a Catholic country, which had no cultural, economic or religious relations with Britain. They could not see any reason why their boys should fly over the continent, just to lose their lives in a country they had never heard of before. "Let Poland solve her own problems. Why do we need to take the chestnuts out of the fire for her?" This was a classic example of a newspaper headline during the months of June and July of 1939.

By mid-July, the first children from the Kindertransport began to arrive in Leeds. Some "Kinder-children," as they were called, rented rooms in Alexander's Place. The stories they told were ghastly. Peter had forgotten his personal experiences, and the appalling experiences that these children had endured only served to reinforce his own horrible memories.

The Kindertransport
(taken from the Encyclopedia of the Holocaust)

On November 21, 1938, only two weeks after the Pogrom, the House of Commons debated the Jewish refugee issue. On the same day the government announced its decision to permit an unspecified number of children up to the age of 17 from German-occupied lands to enter the U.K. as "transmigrants" (A 50 pound bond had to be posted for every child).

On December 8th, the former Prime Minister Stanley Earl Baldwin issued a radio appeal. In this appeal, he said, "I ask you to come to the aid of victims not of any catastrophe in the natural world, not of an earthquake, nor flood, nor famine, but of an explosion of man's inhumanity to man."

The Jewish Agency wanted to bring 10,000 Jewish children from Europe to Palestine, but the British Government was certainly not keen on that. Following Krystalnacht, Neville Chamberlain and the Home Office Secretary, Sir Samuel Hoare, were strongly urged to make a tangible gesture to assuage public opinion in the U.K. Neville Chamberlain had a very low PR rating following his appeasement of Hitler in Munich. "Allowing the refugee children into Britain was an easy way to improve his and the government's image," said Tydor Baumel (an opposition MP).

The first to arrive were 502 children who arrived in Horwich on December 10th, 1938, in the first Kindertransport from Vienna. Among them there were some 100 who were not Jewish, but were labeled by Nazis as "non-Aryan, having had grandparents who were Jewish."

The size of further groups ranged from 30 to 500. They came via Riga, Holland, Danzig and Warsaw, most of them by train and boat, some by air. In England, they were divided into two categories: "Guaranteed" children, who already had sponsors in England through prior direct contacts, and "un-guaranteed" children, who were chosen by the Reichsvertretung der Juden in Germany and the Kultusgemeinde in Austria.

The last to arrive in Britain was a group of 40 children that came from Leipzig through Holland in May 1940.

As none of the child refugees were allowed to be accompanied by their parents, the children were "adopted" by foster families, and those new parents become their closest relatives. In years to come, most of these children never saw their biological fathers and mothers once they had left the continent. The parents were being liquidated in Auschwitz and other death camps in Europe.

Chapter Twelve

Peter Faces Dilemma as Time is Running Out for Lina

Wednesday, August 16, 1939

LONDON, THE REGISTRAR GENERAL. EVERYONE will have to have an identity card number in the event of war:

The Registrar General is to announce that in order to simplify the recruitment of eligible men for the army, everyone in Britain and the Isles will have to register with the Home Office and carry an identity card.

Translated from German:
Thursday, August 17, 1939

Our great leader Adolf Hitler has decided today to close the eastern border with Poland in Upper Silesia:

Due to the unprovoked aggression of the Polish government and army, our military leaders under the guidance of our Führer have decided to station more troops in and around cities such as Leipzig and Dresden. It is thought that these cities will be the first targets of the Polish army once it gets its marching orders from the central government in Warsaw.

In order to accommodate the large number of officers, soldiers and other army personnel in these cities have taken over former Jewish houses after the Jews had abandoned them out of their own free will. The Jews have left Germany in order to re-enter their homeland (Poland), and join the Polish army. By doing so, they are betraying the Fatherland that has given them all they have. Other residents of the Jewish Homes have moved to live among their own people in the cities of Leipzig and Dresden. The Jewish people will remain in the Jewish Homes until such time that they will leave the Fatherland.

The Führer has once more made it clear that his demand for a free corridor to the German city of Danzig is a legitimate requirement of the German People to unite with their own folk, as was done in Czechoslovakia, the Rhineland and Austria. Therefore he views the pledge of France and England to come to the aid of Poland in case of war as illegal, and he sees this as interference in the internal affairs of Germany.

Wednesday, August 23, 1939

Hitler and Stalin vow not to go to war:

In a move that surprised and shocked the Western Powers, Germany and the Soviet Union signed a non-aggression pact. This makes the outbreak of a European war virtually inevitable. The signing took place in the Kremlin today. Joachim von Ribbentrop signed for Germany and Vyacheslav Molotov for the Soviet Union.

After the ceremony Joseph Stalin, the Soviet leader, proposed a toast.

"I know how much the German people love their Führer," he said, "I should therefore like to drink to his health."

It is now apparent that at the same time that the British military mission was in Moscow for negotiations concerning a pact with the Soviet Union to discourage German aggression against Poland, the Soviet Union was already engaged in secret negotiations with Hitler. It is not known which side made the first move, but it is clear that for Hitler an immediate understanding with Moscow was of prime importance.

The final article in the treaty says, "that it will come into force immediately after it has been signed and will be ratified in the shortest possible time." The two sides bind themselves to refrain from every use of force against each other and pledge themselves not to join with other powers in a hostile alliance.

For the two dictators, Hitler and Stalin, who for the past six years have been engaged in mutual vilification, it is quite a turnabout.

The pact makes German military action more likely than ever. All over Germany today, heavy transport, motorcycle, and civilian aircraft are being commandeered.

General Walther von Brauchitsch, the Army Commander-in-Chief, is to broadcast a message to all soldiers next Saturday evening.

As Peter scoured the newspapers day after day, it was becoming increasingly clear to him that the more time that elapsed, the harder it would be to get Lina out of Germany. If war broke out, all borders would be closed. Not only that, but Lina would not be able to leave. Even letters and other means of communication would be blocked.

On the same day that the Ribbentrop-Molotov Treaty was signed, two letters had arrived from Leipzig. Both had been sent a month before. It was taking longer and longer for the letters to arrive. Peter wondered how long it would be before war with Germany officially broke out.

Like all the others, the letter from Lina was written on the official headed notepaper of the insurance agency for which Peter was an agent. As always, it was written in pencil, making it all the more difficult to read. Lina used every bit of free space that was available to write her news. Peter had a hard time working out where the letter started and where it ended.

Translated from Yiddish:
Saturday, July 15, 1939
Humbold Strasse 3, Leipzig

Dear Adolf,
    It has been a long time since you wrote a letter to me. Have you forgotten that you have a trapped mother who cannot escape, has nothing to eat and no place to live?

    Write to me immediately, and tell me if Mr. Bellow can help me get out of this hell, so I can get to England as quickly as possible. He can claim that he urgently needs my services as a housemaid. Tell him that he need not worry, as I will go immediately to my niece Berta, and will not be a burden on him.

    If I do not get out by the end of the month, they will throw me out. They are preparing for war. All over town, soldiers are taking over more and more of the Jewish homes round the rail-station so they will have room for their officers. If a *milchoma* (Yiddish for war] will breakout, I will never get out of here.

Dear Adolf, help me and tell me what I should do. Tell me all will be okay!

July 17

I have just come back from the Gestapo headquarters. After a long humiliating wait, standing on my feet for over four hours, the man gave me a permit to stay here till the 1st of August. He said to me, or should I say barked at me, "If you and the other dirty Jews are not out by then, no extension on your visa will be granted. If you are not out by then, you will be sent to Poland, like all the others.

The extension cost 15 Reich Marks that I had to borrow from Witerlis. Now I do not have any more money to buy food for this week. Working in the garbage is killing me. It injures my hands and ruins my shoes. Last week I found a sock, and I put it on right away, so at least I could have one warm foot.

Dear Adolf, I am miserable and tired. I cannot last here much longer. Maybe you can send me some sort of certificate that I can show to the Gestapo. In this way, I can prove I have a permit to come to England, so it is only a question of time until I get the visa.

I heard the goyim say that they heard from Goebbels, who was in Leipzig two weeks ago, that if Poland does not allow the German unification with Danzig, and at the same time continues to be aggressive, there will be nothing left of Poland but "cemeteries." As for the Jews, he added, their worldwide net of subversion and conspiracy is pushing the two peace-loving countries to war.

Dear Adolf, if the Jews are so powerful and influential, as he said, why can't they get me out of here? Take care of yourself; do not eat what you should not. Remember you are completely on your own now. I am not there to look after you, so drink Cognac. Stay healthy and I will see you soon.

    Your loving Mama

*   *   *

On Saturday, another letter arrived from Leipzig. Peter was at a loss as to how he could stop the constant stream of letters.

Translated from Yiddish:
Thursday, July 20, 1939

Dear Adolf,

    I received your letter with the copy of the letter that you sent to David. Is there anything I can do? I cannot write to him, as I do not have the money for stamps or enough paper, but he knows what is happening here better than most people. You do not have to write to him anymore. A good man does not need a letter, and an angry letter does not help with a bad person. Dear God will help me so that I do not have to be dependent on him. It is known here that total strangers, even goyim, have helped Jews to get out, yet my own flesh and blood cannot do anything for me. Soon, I will be the only one left here; all my friends, the Haensels from Waltrbueme Strasse, Mrs. Rosenthal, the one that used to be your math teacher, and many others, have left. I just cannot remember who has gone to England, France, Palestine or even to Argentina. Ah, yes, I remember now that Jacob Stern, the one that owned the hardware shop on Kiel Strasse, had family and friends who helped him. Only I cannot find anyone one who is prepared to do anything for me. At this rate, I will be the only one left stranded. By the way, the young rabbi from the Carlebach Shul, Rabbi Bourg, left for Palestine last week. He said that they are going to be farmers in one of those new Jewish colonies in a very hot part of Palestine. I do not understand why someone with an education like his wants to be a farmer, but that is his business.

For us Jews who have not left, there is a lot of misfortune here in Leipzig. You know that all the Polish Jews that came back to sell their things have left. They did not let them stay here more than two weeks; their houses were already taken over. All of them slept on the floor of the Brody Synagogue, the one that was burnt in the Pogrom.

They say that all the stateless will be thrown out by the 1st of August, and we do not know where to go; no one will let us in. I do not know what I will do if I am forced to go once more to the Gestapo for a permit.

It is the most terrible thing that my own brother does nothing to help. It would be no problem for him to see that I get a visa to get into England. Write to him and tell him I will not become a burden on him, and, with God's help, will pay him for all his expenses once I have arrived. He should not worry; I will not even come to see him, nor sleep there for even one night. Tell him he does not have to worry, I will not even take from him one cup of coffee. Alfred Simon, the one who worked in the pharmacy that was on the corner of York Strasse, got a visa to leave to South Africa. He told me that it was a Christian, a total stranger, who vouched for him, helping him to get a visa. And me – my own brother will not lift a finger to help his own sister!

Dear Adolf, you must write to him and tell him that it is the end of us Jews. I ask God that he stays healthy and has enough to eat from today to tomorrow and will keep his wealth. One never knows what is going to happen. Write to him but do not be nasty. Dear Adolf, I do not know what I will do if they won't extend my permit, until the visa gets here from England. Dear Adolf, you tell me that I am offending you, so I will tell you something. Goyim from their mother's side do not see this as being offensive. I am totally broken. You should think from time to time about my fate, and what will happen to me. I am in despair, I am forced to jump into a stormy sea, without having learned how to swim, and there is no one to save me.

I told you once before that the things cannot be sold – they are lying about like a heap of useless sticks, so there is no point in telling me that I can live off that money. Tell Aunt to send me some money for the removal of our things, so she will not think that I need her money.

Max wrote me a very nice letter, I was very happy to receive it. He said that Aunt sent me a food parcel but it has not arrived. Maybe the *Ginnovim* [thieves] from the *Kehilla* [Jewish community] took it, or maybe even the Gestapo – who knows?

Dear Adolf, go to the Swiss consul and ask him if he can give me a permit to pass through Switzerland, so they will let me into Switzerland just until the visa arrives. They say that they have closed the borders for Jews to enter Switzerland; that includes those with money.

Love you as always,
From your lonely Mama

* * *

As yet, there were no signs of willingness from Dina to relinquish the jewelry. Peter decided the time had come to write her another letter.

Translated from German:
Tuesday, August 22, 1939
Leeds

My dear little Dina,

I received your last letter on Bank Holiday, which I spent with friends in Manchester. It will be difficult to convince my landlady to allow you to stay here overnight. I did not tell her about our relationship, nor did I tell her that you have a husband in London. You know how English women are with their double standards – I must be very careful now. We were warned by the Jewish community that as German Jewish refugees, we must be as inconspicuous as possible, and not to do anything that may anger anyone. I would much prefer that my landlady does not know your address either.

I received a letter from my mother, in which she enclosed a letter from the Leipzig police, telling her that if she has not left by August 1st, she will be forcibly deported to the East, and will have to pay a large fine and go to prison.

Could you not call Arnold, the lawyer working on Mama's case, and ask him what is happening? How long will it take? Why don't they do anything in Woburn House? If he needs money, I give you permission to sell some of the jewelry in order to pay him. The rest is to be sent to my new address in Leeds.

Mama gets only six Reich Marks from the *Kehilla* and she is hungry. I gave the Schmulewitsches her new address on Loehr Strasse – so they can send her some food parcels or money – but they have lost it. To that I can only say, "a man with a full stomach cannot understand what a hungry person grumbles about."

How are things going with the other men in your life? I hope, some day, to get a ride to London and come to see you. I would do anything to be able to see you.

Do not forget to send me the jewelry.
Peter

Chapter Thirteen

Life for Jews in Leipzig Going from Bad to Worse

Translated from German:
Wednesday, August 23, 1939

BRITISH DESTROYERS ATTACKED *PATRIA,* a French liner carrying German-Jewish refugees, members of the Bnei Akiva Zionist movement.

In the course of the battle off the northern coast of Palestine, the *Patria* was forced ashore by destroyers outside the township of Nahariya, a colony settled by former German Jewish people from Leipzig and Dresden.

Some 200 of its 1,700 passengers had drowned as a result of this criminal act committed by Chamberlain's government.

The smell of war was in the air. In Leipzig, the Wehrmacht was on full alert, while in Britain and France, there were mass call-ups of the army reserve. It was now only a question of time. When would the Wehrmacht decide to make the first move in its advance eastward? The answer would only be revealed as Germany prepared to invade Poland.

On August 25, German troops paraded in Berlin, disregarding the Versailles Treaty that forbade German armies from holding any military parades.

Wednesday, August 23, 1939

Forces on full alert as the Polish crisis deepens:

Europe's mobilization for war is almost complete. Throughout Poland, posters have gone up ordering all reservists and retired troops, as well as men up to the age of 40, to report to barracks. France has been calling up reservists for the past ten days. The call-up includes railways workers who were requisitioned in the service of the Army. Belgium announced that its aircraft defenses are fully manned. The Swiss Army is on full alert in defense of the frontiers in case of a German attack.

In Britain, the call-up continues to disrupt daily life. The Westham football club lost most of its players yesterday when they were called up for duty in the Essex Regiment.

In London, the Admiralty issued orders closing the Mediterranean and the Baltic seas to British merchant shipping. Insurance rates have doubled.

The king visited the War Office and the Air Ministry yesterday to inspect deep bomb- and gas-proof shelters.

LIFE FOR JEWS IN LEIPZIG GOING FROM BAD TO WORSE

Sunday, August 27, 1939
From Berlin, London and Stockholm correspondents

In British diplomatic circles, there is no doubt that Hitler will go on with his plans to invade Poland. This is in spite of reports that he is still hoping to somehow maneuver the British government to remit its pledge to go to Poland's aid.

Through a Swedish intermediary, the German dictator sent a message to London offering Britain a pact to defend the Empire from Bolshevism. In return, Britain should help Germany obtain Danzig and the Polish Corridor. At the same time, the pact would see to it that Germany would have its colonies in East Africa and the Pacific returned to her.

The British government has apparently declined Hitler's offer to defend the Empire. As far as Poland is concerned, the same British diplomatic circles point out that the Empire is bound by treaty to defend the Polish people if they are attacked.

* * *

In Leipzig, notices began appearing on walls in the Jewish area around Kiel Strasse and Humboldt Strasse, declaring:

August 26

All the non-Aryans (Jews) still living in the city of Leipzig illegally must bring all the aluminium or copper vessels which are in their possession (minimum 2 KG per person), to the Gestapo headquarters in Koenig Albert Allee by tomorrow, where they will be weighed and stored. Anyone failing to do so will be denied his food and fuel-rationing card for the month of September or will be deported to Poland.

The Committee for Reclaiming German Property

* * *

Meanwhile in the Reichstag – where Hitler's new headquarters were located in the quarters between Potzdammer Platz and the Brandenburg gate – Von Keitel, Chief-in-Command of the Ground Forces, Goering, Chief-in-Command of the Luftwaffe, and Goebbels, Minister of Propoganda, were summoned to a top-secret meeting with the Führer. In this meeting, the final details of the invasion were to be mapped out. Goebbels insisted that the ideal date to commence their invasion would be on the morning of Friday, September 1, when public schools in the British Isles would reopen. Goebbels made the point that attention in the media would focus primarily on this event, leaving little newspaper space to report other world events, such as the Wehrmacht's invasion into Poland. What is more, he added, on Saturday and Sunday no government meetings would be held in London. It would be Monday or Tuesday before they decided on Britain's policy, by which time the invasion into West Poland and Warsaw would be a fait accompli. Chamberlain's government would be left with no other option but to concede to Germany's plans, as they did with regards to Czechoslovakia and Austria.

An added advantage to that date would be the appearance of a full moon (coinciding with the middle of the Jewish month of *Elul*), which would help the Luftwaffe in its initial assignment to cut all railway lines from Warsaw to the front.

Now that the date for the invasion was final, all that was left was to determine the *casus belli*. It was decided by the participants at the meeting that they would round up some 20 Jews, of which five or six amongst them would be dressed up in Wehrmacht uniforms, and consequently shot in the back. In the morning, they planned to dump the bodies near the Polish-German border crossing in Lauenburg, which was the official border crossing in the Danzig Corridor. The rest of the bodies would be dressed up in Polish uniforms and thrown over the borderline into Polish territory.

Translated from German:
Der Angriff
(The Offensive was the official Nazi Party newspaper)
Monday, August 28, 1939

German border guards were attacked and killed by Polish soldiers last night:

A group of some 40 Polish criminals has attacked a small squadron of German border guards at the crossing in Lauenburg.

In the battle with the attackers, seven of our boys were shot in the back and lost their lives. More than 12 of the delinquents were killed. Most of the bandits were seen retreating with casualties across the border.

This provocative criminal act was a result of the illegal Warsaw government's policy of deterring the peace-loving German peoples' right of possession of the Danzig Corridor, which was handed over to Poland by the criminal delegates of Britain, France and the U.S.A. at the Versailles Treaty in 1919.

Our beloved Führer made it clear to the Polish ambassador in Berlin, Mr. Libzki, that under his leadership the Third Reich will no longer tolerate these unprovoked attacks on German people in Danzig and its surrounding areas. He made the point that if the Polish government will not compensate Germany for the brutal provocation, the only compensation that Germany will accept will be to allow a German railroad to cross the Corridor as part of Germany's reunification plan with the provinces of Eastern Prussia. If this condition will not be fulfilled, Germany will be left with no other choice but to declare war.

None of Them Were Heroes

Friday, September 1, 1939

Hitler bombs Polish cities.
Britain and France mobilize as Poland calls for aid.

Friday, September 1, 1939

German troops invade Poland at 5:45 this morning:

As most families in the British Isles were busy with the reopening of the new school year, the Wehrmacht crossed the border into Poland.

Shortly before 6:00 A.M. on Friday September 1, Messerschmitts, Luftwaffe bomber planes were seen violating Polish air space and dropping their bombs over Warsaw.

The Wehrmacht force, numbering some one million two hundred and fifty thousand troops, including six armored divisions, horse battalions, bike regiments and lightweight units of motorized divisions, swept into Poland today. The Luftwaffe added its contribution by knocking out the Polish railway system and shooting the Polish air force out of the sky as well as on the ground.

The pretext for this unapproved invasion was the murder staged by the Reich press office some three days ago. As part of the Reich's provocation, the press office had staged a murder of border police guards, who were allegedly killed by the Polish Army in the town of Lauenburg, while on guard duty.

Translated from German:

In a long wireless broadcast that Hitler delivered, he

LIFE FOR JEWS IN LEIPZIG GOING FROM BAD TO WORSE

blamed the Polish government for rebuffing all his efforts to reach a peaceful solution for the Danzig Corridor, leaving him with the reluctant decision to try and solve the dispute by means of force.

We, the German peace-loving people, are operating in this way neither for revenge nor because of hate. We are doing this in self-defense and to protect our rights.

Our military correspondent added that this is the first time the Wehrmacht and its top generals will have the opportunity to conclusively prove their new war tactic developed during the Spanish Civil War two years ago, known as the *"blitzkrieg."* In this sort of war affair, fast-moving armored forces operating in combination with warplanes can overcome the stalemate of trench warfare.

* * *

As the invasion continued with full force, Lina was trying to summon up every ounce of energy and willpower to survive. She was at a loss as to where she could find two kilograms of aluminium, and even if she could find some at the garbage dump or in the old pots that were left on Humboldt Strasse, how would she possibly carry it to the Gestapo headquarters in Koenig Albert Allee? If she walked through Rosenthal Park, she would be violating the rule that was signposted everywhere, *"Fuer Juden verboten,"* and would be arrested and deported to Poland. The other option would be to go along the Elsterbecken Canal, but she doubted her shoes would survive the journey, and what was more, the area was considered dangerous for Jews, who were often stopped and subjected to beatings by the Hitler Youth, who hung around that part of the city. There were rumors of people being thrown into the Canal. Lina did not know how to swim and feared she would drown if she met with that fate.

Some three days ago, Mrs. Hamburger's son, who owned the hardware shop on Berline Strasse, was taken away by soldiers dressed in Wehrmacht uniforms. This young man was one of Adolf's friends, and was always willing to offer a helping hand. Now that he was gone, there was no one to turn to for help. If only Adolf had been here, Lina thought, he would have found some sort of solution to these daily disasters that constantly haunted her.

Now that the war had begun in earnest, life for those Jews remaining in Leipzig was going from bad to worse. The room Lina occupied at the Witerlis's home was now shared with three other people, the only accessible drinking water coming from the common toilet bowl. There was no place to wash oneself or one's garments, cook, or even sit down. There was only one remaining Jewish shop that was still selling to non-Aryans. This shop was limited to foodstuffs that could no longer be sold in other stores. Although potatoes were still on the permitted list, Lina could not bite into them since her front teeth were loose, and even if she could eat them, there was no fuel for her to cook them. Bread was also on the list, but by the time Jews were permitted to buy some, it had become stale, only becoming edible after first mixing it with water from the toilet bowl.

Jews were no longer allowed to buy or obtain needles, which had to be donated to the war effort. Lina did not understand what use needles were to the Wehrmacht, but all she knew was that she could not fix her only dress, and to make things worse, the yellow star was coming off, making it dangerous for her to be seen outside. Even if she did have a needle and thread, her underpants and stockings had been in shreds for so long that there was no point trying to fix them. Lina knew that someone in the Witerlis family had a needle, but they were not prepared to lend it to her.

LIFE FOR JEWS IN LEIPZIG GOING FROM BAD TO WORSE

Her shoes that were now bound with string were stolen from the garbage dump.

The greater the Wehrmacht's success in Poland, the greater was the persecution at the hands of Hitler's hooligans in Leipzig. Rumors were spreading that the Red Army had conquered the western part of Poland, while Jews from all over Poland tried to escape to the Soviet side. Terrible stories were sweeping Leipzig about the Nazis rounding up Warsaw Jews and killing them. The Ribbentrop-Molotov Non-Aggression Pact, signed a week before the commencement of war, stipulated that the USSR would have the right to invade Poland from the East.

Every day, new rumors would circulate, and it was hard to know which of them should be believed. Lina could not believe that Jews were running away to Russia. As bad as it was for Jews under the Nazis, it could only be worse under Stalin and the Bolsheviks. If only Adolf would write her a letter, telling her what was going on with the visa, she would have a reason to survive. Even if his letter was simply a confirmation that he was alive and well, and had not forgotten her, she would derive some comfort from this knowledge. Lina knew, however, that from now on, it would no longer be possible to send or receive letters from England. The two countries were once more at war, just as they were in the Great War, the memories of which were still fresh in her mind.

Translated from German:
Thursday, September 14, 1939
Guisborough Shirt & Underwear Co
West End Guisborough
Tel Linthorpe 88249
Director S. Schmulewitsch
(Stateless, Russian Origin)

Dear Adolf,

It is Rosh Hashana [first day of the new Jewish year] today, and Yom Kippur is around the corner. Mama and I decided to take time off to try and answer all the people we still owe letters to. After all, we would like to find favor in His eyes.

There was no need to be so angry in your letter about Aunt Lina. We did not answer her as we lost the address, and she moves so frequently that it is virtually impossible to keep track of these changes. Why on earth did she not stay in Humboldt Strasse 3 till her papers arrive? You should know that we, and in particular, Mama, are doing all we can to see that our sister receives the visa to come over.

We are very happy that you like your new job at Bellows, where you will be able to earn more money than you would if you were working for us. Anyway, I always say that it is better not to work for your family – there are too many conflicting interests. Max says that working for us is no career for you.

Father and Max do not have anything against Bellow; on the contrary, they very much appreciate the fact that he did so much to get you out. I do not understand why he shows no interest in trying to get a visa for Aunt Lina. After all, it would only take one or two letters to people he knows, and the thing can be arranged. Max and Herman both think that he could have given us a better price on the sewing machines, since we are, after all, *mishpocha* [family].

LIFE FOR JEWS IN LEIPZIG GOING FROM BAD TO WORSE

I hope you finish this business with that terrible woman without going to court. I wish you *mazel* and hope you get the things soon.

From our side there is not much news. I went last night to a dance that was given by one of the synagogues in Middlesbrough. It was quite nice, but most of the men were from the Kindertransport, and are far too young for me. It seems to me that despite Father's objections, Shnoki will marry this Katz fellow after all. Father does not like Carol and his family as they look down on us *Ostjuden*. They think they are better than us because they are from the *Alrieich*. In any case, Max says that she is only 19 years old, and too young to get married. I say that if she wants to get married so much, she could find someone of her own kind.

Business could be better, especially as the winter season is coming up. Father had hoped that with the war going on, there would be a greater need for uniforms and army clothing. But one must not complain, things can always be worse.

By the way, what do you say about the little bastard attacking Poland? Do you think that will last? I think Britain should put an end to it as soon as she can.

Herman is still in London and he has been ill for some time.

Mama received a letter from this lawyer Kohn, suggesting a way to get Aunt Lina's visa, but he wants over 100 pounds for his services. Mama thinks that it is too much. In any case, she says that once the bastard breaks his neck in Poland, the whole thing will be over anyway. She was thinking of going there to see if she can get him down on the price. If not, tell him we do not need his favors, and we can manage the whole thing by ourselves. It is amazing how sly people can come out of the woodwork if they think there is money to be made from the misery of others.

If the war does not disrupt things too much, we are planning to come to Leeds on the 15th of November. If we do, we will bring the shirt you forgot in Middlesbrough, so I hope to be seeing you soon.

 Lots of love
 Dora

 P.S. Did you hear the rumor that they are starting to mobilize Jewish boys to the Wehrmacht?

* * *

Peter was annoyed and frustrated by Dora's letter. They seemed to care so little about his mother. Did they not understand that getting a visa was for Lina a matter of life and death? Their claim that they lost her address was simply an excuse for not writing. That evening, he was invited to a dance. He welcomed the distraction. His response to Dora could wait. As he left the house, he heard an announcement coming from his neighbor's wireless that the Wehrmacht had entered Warsaw.

Chapter Fourteen

Peter Discovers Newfound Freedom in Leeds

October 1939

LIFE FOR PETER IN LEEDS was better than it had ever been. For the first time in his life, he had a place of his own, had a steady job, and made friends with German refugees and even some English people. Overall, things were going very well indeed.

The Leeds Jewish community kept a polite distance from the newcomers, excluding them from their functions and social events. They did not want to be seen fraternizing with refugees, German refugees in particular. With the memories of the Great War still fresh in the minds of most gentiles, British Jews feared being associated with Germans, and did not want to stoke up any feelings of unpleasantness or anti-Semitic sentiment. On the few occasions that Peter met with any British Jews in the offices of the Jewish community, as he tried to obtain a visa for Lina, he would be asked to "talk softly," as his strong Germanic accent disturbed the goyim that worked in the building.

Since most men were called up to the army, there was no shortage of women who were eager to go out with refugees. The language barrier did not present an obstacle. Peter was keen to learn English, and although phrases like, "I love you" or "you are the only woman in my life" would not help him in finding work, he was quite happy at Bellow Engineering and at this point did not want to change. The greatest challenge was the early morning start, but waking up early was a small price to pay for the good life he had.

Peter enjoyed his freedom and independence. His only responsibility was to himself. He had no nagging mother telling him what to do, and was not surrounded by hooligans breathing down his neck. For the first time in his life, he was, or at least he felt he was, a free man. Conforming to the British etiquette and mentality was not as restrictive as he thought it would be. If by some chance, he did not send a postcard in advance to someone he intended to visit, he blamed it on the fact he was a newcomer.

Although Peter's uncle, aunt and cousins lived in Middlesbrough, he felt distant from them. Apart from an occasional letter, which he rarely answered, and sporadic visits, like the one Dora had planned for next month, Peter did not remain in close contact with them.

Soon after Peter moved to Leeds, he joined the Leeds swimming club, of which he was the only Jewish member. This would have been unheard of in Leipzig. Not only did the other members not subject him to anti-Semitic remarks, as they would have done in Leipzig, but they also considered it a privilege to have a Jew as a member of their club. They were impressed by his swimming and rigid self-discipline. Within a short time, he was part of the water polo team.

The seven pounds a week he earned at Bellow Engineering was sufficient to pay for his rent and clothes, and he was even left with enough money to take girls out to the dancing halls. The war was barely perceptible except for the fact that there were hardly any men to be seen, and food rationing was imposed, which hardly affected him at all.

The blackout was somewhat of a problem, though, making it difficult to see or be seen by traffic on the roads. Once or twice, Peter was almost hit by a car with no lights. Dancing halls and cinemas were also periodically closed during the blackouts, but the power cuts did not usually last a long time.

Peter regretted that he was unable to use some of his salary to pay the lawyer who was working on Mama's case, but unfortunately that was not possible. It would have meant working longer hours, and as a result, his social life would have suffered.

In October, he was called up for service, but was released on medical grounds due to his diabetes. Unlike many of his friends, Peter was not driven by a desire to serve in the army and take revenge against the Germans by killing as many of them as possible.

Endless streams of letters continued to arrive from Leipzig. Now that the war was in full swing, and mail was thus restricted, the letters from his mother came via Antwerp, where Lina's former neighbors, the Rosenblums, from Humbold Strasse 6 now lived. Due to this roundabout method of sending mail, it could often take up to two months for the letters to finally arrive.

Peter found it difficult to read these letters that were written with a blunt pencil on old bits of cardboard. He opened up letters from his mother with a heavy heart.

Translated from Yiddish:
Saturday, September 2, 1939

Dear Adolf,
Your letterhead paper from the insurance firm has come to an end; this is the only paper I could find, so forgive me for writing in

this way. The pencil you left me is so blunt that I can barely write with it anymore.

Dear Adolf, you must tell me, did Mrs. Kremer arrive in good health? Did you meet with her? She told me that she was going to the people that vouched for her in Aberdeen – is that far from Leeds? Can you find time to go and see her after work? She will tell you what is happening to us here, if you do not believe me.

Did you get the letter from Berta? Did she tell you that I do not have one pfening? Did she send you a package of food? Do not give anyone anything out of it. She does not send me any letters – why is she causing me so much trouble by not writing?

Adolf, I am completely in despair. I have asked for money from every person I can think of. I am entitled to five Marks from the committee, but what shall I do with it? Each time I go there, I must fill out all these forms. It is so humiliating to stand at the door with all the beggars, going from one clerk to another, just to receive money for my work in the garbage. I fall apart each time I am there, and they throw me out of there crying. These scoundrel Jews who work there, including Schmulewitsch who used to live on Loer Strasse, and is the *"Macher"* (the person in charge), to the lowest officials, are all bandits.

In my entire life, I have not taken a pfening from them, and now that I am working, they do not give me the money that is due to me. The police came the other day and told me that if I do not move my things out of Humboldt Strasse, they will deport me. I just do not know how I will do this. I cannot sell anything. After the Polish were allowed to come back last month, they sold their property and settled up their affairs for close to nothing. Now one cannot even give things away. Anyone I speak to advises me to leave my things here, and they will pick it up once I am sent to the East.

PETER DISCOVERS NEWFOUND FREEDOM IN LEEDS

Can you send me some money, even if it is only ten shillings to buy a new pencil and a postage stamp? Can you send me some soft food? Write to Uncle David and tell him to send me some butter. Adolf, I must have some fat on my bones. Tell him that if he will help me, he will not become any poorer for it.

I am enclosing an envelope so you can write your new address. You know I have trouble with English letters.

Dear Adolf, when do you think that I will get the visa? I must get out of the room, and I do not want to get another room if the permit is coming in a day or two. This room is the most terrible place to live in. I can only wish it on my worst enemies, those that have thrown me to the dogs and have no idea of my miserable existence.

I hope that by now, you have received all "the things" in one piece. Please write to me to tell me that everything is in order. In the big box, you should have all you need. The crockery is in the box with the kitchen towels: Do not open it. You must leave everything inside and lock it all up once more, so that nothing will be lost.

Rent an apartment so you can put the furniture in it. You live in one room and rent out the others with the furniture, or rent a small place for you and the furniture. If you do not have enough money for the rent, go to anyone you know, and ask them for help in finding a place to store the "things." <u>Do you understand all I write to you?</u>

Mr. Wieder from the shipping company said that because of the war, the shipment must go through Holland. It will cost more because of that. I asked him why they did not pick it up in March, as they said they would. He said that it is none of my business, and if I ask too many questions, he will have me sent to the East. He told me that someone from the agency in London will contact you about this, and if this extra sum is not paid, he will see to it that I will be deported. I just do not have any money to pay!

Once I get over there, with God's help, I will sell some of "the things" and pay back all we owe. I cannot ask Wederman for any more money. They say if I have a son in England, he can send me enough so I can live like a queen. I have enough troubles without this – do you think I will ever live through this? I do not know how to cope with all of these troubles and stay alive.

Dear Adolf, I was so excited to get your letter today, after I returned from working at the garbage, that I could not stop crying. I was astonished at what you wrote, so let me tell you once more: you do not need any money to get me out of this hell and there is no need to pawn the jewelry. You must not leave my case in someone else's hands. Do it yourself, and do all you can, or I will never get out of here. They say that children can bring over their parents and they do not have to pay for this.

My dear Adolf, I am a healthy woman and not as old as people think. I can work, and I would like to earn money. You must put an advertisement in the paper for a service girl, a cook or even a housemaid, and say that I am fifty years old, you do not need to say I am older. Call the committee and tell them I can work with old people, with children, I can even attend to sick people in the hospitals, as I did during the Great War. I am sure you will have so many job offers that you will not know what to do with them. Go over there today and tell them. You must speak with the *balerboste* (the person in charge). Adolf, you do not have to be ashamed, tell them I am your mother – they will love to have me as a worker.

Tell Aunt that she can get me out as a housemaid, and she will not have to lay out any money. If she and Uncle Zelig had wanted it, I would have been out of here long ago.

I got a letter from Berta; she told me that there is no chance of getting into Rumania! She said that they are now throwing out all the stateless Jews. It is a good thing that she and Judith have their Rumanian passports, so at least they are safe.

PETER DISCOVERS NEWFOUND FREEDOM IN LEEDS

I was thinking that I could walk to the Swiss border at Bregenz. Do think it will take me more than five days? They say that if you have an entry visa, there is no difficulty getting in. What do you think of that plan? Adolf, you must go right away to the Swiss consul in London, and see if you can get this visa for me. I do not think you will have any problem in obtaining it – you only have to see to it that there will be someone in England that will give a guarantee. Once I have this, the Swiss police will not worry that I will be staying over there too long.

Dear Adolf, you must write to Aunt Sarah today and tell her that I cannot live like this for much longer. She must send me a guarantee through the Swiss consul.

Dear Adolf, I hope you are looking after yourself. Who prepares food for you? You must not eat fatty things! Tell Aunt that I said she should cook for you and send it over. How is the work? You must not work too hard; do you understand what I am saying?

Dear Adolf, do not forget me here. I will perish if I do not get out of here soon. Dear Adolf, if you have any drop of love for your mother in you, you must see to it that I get out of here, before it is too late. You must be my protector.

Dear Adolf, with all my tensions and troubles, I have forgotten your birthday, so I bless you with health, luck and long life.

Your loving Mama

* * *

After reading that heart-wrenching letter from his mother, Peter was glad to see that he had also received a letter from his friend Walter, who was also in the Leipzig swimming team. It had taken the letter over six weeks to arrive. Peter wondered if it was delayed in Britain or in Germany.

Translated from German:
Friday, August 25, 1939
Leipzig

Dear Adolf,

    I am taking advantage of my lunch break to write to you. We have a very long day. We get up at 5:00 A.M. and finish the work at 5:00 P.M., with half an hour off for lunch. In the evening, I try to learn English. I work as a laborer for a gas company. We are building for the military outside Leipzig. I get one Mark a day. The work is very hard; we are laying a pipeline that is 20" in diameter. It will demand a lot of work till this pipe is in the place it should be. It is good to work outside.

    The dream I had about getting a driving license, going to live in Palestine, and finding work as a lorry driver, has gone out of the window. It is impossible to get a visa. We waited too long. The last boat that left with Leipzigers was stopped somewhere in the north of Palestine. Margolis and his wife from the swim team were on it, I hope he did not get killed. He was the one that told me to try and get the driving license. His brother-in-law drives a bus for the British in Palestine.

    There have been many deportations in the last month; my parents have a date for the 29th of August. I estimate that they will come for me soon too. In the meantime, I have joined a group of volunteers that work for the army somewhere in the north, by the Polish border. They say we will get better food, more pay, and will not be deported.

    I would like to know if you will ever write to me again? It is so long from one letter to the next. I am doing my best to learn English, but as we are very tired at the end of the day, my heart is not in it.

    From your mother, I hear that you are learning English easily. I meet her from time to time. She is not in a very good state, and

PETER DISCOVERS NEWFOUND FREEDOM IN LEEDS

complains bitterly that no one is doing anything to try and get her out of this place. I can understand her, but I am sure you are doing all you can to get her out.

I hope I will not have to wait two more months before I get an answer from you. Emi and my parents send their love.

Walter

* * *

After reading Walter's letter, Peter opened a letter he had received from Dina. Hopefully, she had seen sense and would return the jewelry.

Translated from German:
Thursday, September 28, 1939
The International Language Club
202 Lewisham S.E.4 East London
To Peter Rochman c/o Mrs. Alexander's house, Leeds

My dear Peter,

As yet, you have not answered my letters. Are you not answering because of your laziness? I would so much like to see you.

My husband would like to go with little Herbert to the south of France, but I would like to see you before we go on our autumn holidays. I would gladly give up my holidays just to be with you for one day.

I met Arnold the lawyer today. He said that he spent the whole day yesterday in the emigration department in Woburn House, and he cannot get them to move. They say that your mother is on a long list of people that they cannot let in. He also told me that it is the Jewish Feast of Tabernacles today, which reminded me that it was this time last year that we met in Leipzig.

Do not be so lazy and write.

P.S. What do you think of the war? I think we should have

sent soldiers to Czechoslovakia. That would have stopped the little bastard in his tracks!

Your loving Dina

28th September

I was on my way to send the letter when the postman brought this letter and parcel from you.

What a surprise and such a nice pullover! God only knows how difficult it was for you to pay for it. It must be such a big sacrifice on your part, what with times being so hard and you sending money to your mother.

I was even happier to receive your love letter that came with the parcel, so I decided to send the two letters together. I was happy to hear about your progress at work, and about your life in Leeds. No, it did not make me sad; on the contrary, it made me proud of you. After all, you are what I expected you to be, and I am happy for you. I hope that you go on enjoying your success. I cannot express how happy I am to hear that all is going well for you. You must feel like a very sick person who has recovered, and whose limbs are intact once more. So, Peterli, you must swear to me that you will go on being healthy, and that you will keep on looking after your diet.

Peterli, are you blaming me? You are wrong when you say that I have changed; I am as I have always been, and have not changed in my loyalty to you. I have changed my behavior to my husband, and other people, but that is only to your advantage. You ask me if I was offended when you said that I am like a thief if I do not return the jewelry. Peterli! Do you know the difference between offending a person and hurting someone? I will explain it to you if you wish.

It is clear that you should talk to me cordially, just as I talk to you. On the other hand, I cannot hold any secrets, and must say what is in my heart. If I did not love you, I would have no problem lying to you, as many people do, when they do not find favor in each other's eyes. Now that you have done something on your own incentive, and given me such pleasure, I will rethink my position about the jewelry, but I must wait for the right constellation of stars in the sky before I do so. Not for your sake, but rather for mine. Then, as the saying goes, "As one will call it the emptiness so will he be coming back" (as I treat other people, so will others treat me), but I do not want to lie to you, I love you too much. When you apply these methods that you talked about, that most people only use for show, you just harm yourself.

Peterli, it is better not to take steps and then be sorry about what you do. I wish you would only love me half as much as I love you, and that the whole thing with the jewelry would just blow over. You must believe me when I tell you that sometimes I am so desperate about the whole thing, because it is an agony to live in such a way. You try to hold back from me. We have often played this game, and if I could just see you as a distraction, then I would not be affected. I do hope to see you here soon – I would like to talk to you. Can you arrange it that you will not arrive here before the 25th? On the 28th, Herbert is going on holiday. When I think of my holiday last year, I immediately begin to cry and think to myself, will I ever have such a nice holiday and be in your arms once more? I hope you are not cross when I get moody from time to time, but I have never been in this situation before.

I know I cannot complain. Millions of people would die to be in my situation. Please write to me when you can, I am counting the days when I will be able to see you once more. I greet you and kiss you.

Your Dina

Chapter Fifteen

Peter Lives Life to the Full

Sunday, October 1, 1939

HELSINKI IN FLAMES AS RUSSIA INVADES. The Soviet Union invaded tiny Finland today. A "Red Army" Ilyushin aircraft savagely bombed Helsinki. Heavy fighting was reported along the 50-mile Karelian Isthmus front where the Red Army was hoping to punch holes in the Mannerheim Line.

The attack came after the Finnish Government ignored the ultimatum to come under the Soviet sphere of influence, which was part of the Molotov-Ribbentrop pact.

Saturday, October 14, 1939

The SS *Royal Oak* is sunk in its home base:
More than 830 are believed dead aboard the battleship SS *Royal Oak* after a German torpedo hit her in her home base of Scapa Flow.

The sinking has come as a shock because most

thought it impossible for a U-boat to penetrate the anchorage's defenses and that the battleship's armor would repel a torpedo. This comes in the midst of news that the U-Boat war is intensifying, and around 156,000 tons of British shipping has fallen victim to German submarines. Many servicemen's wives and their children lost their lives in another attack on the SS *Yorkshire*.

Monday, October 30, 1939

The horrors of the Nazis' dreaded concentration camps were documented in a massive Government White Paper published today.

It is a collection of reports said to be of unimpeachable authority, painstakingly collected by British diplomats in Germany over the past few years.

"The treatment of inmates is reminiscent of the darkest ages in the history of man," says the White Paper. The government explained that it was forced to make the revelations, because of "shameless and unscrupulous German propaganda accusing Britain of atrocities in South Africa, 40 years ago."

Hitler is said personally to have ordered the flogging of Jews. There are terrifying and detailed descriptions of barbarous and systematic tortures inflicted mainly by guards aged 17 to 20 in the Dachau and Buchenwald camps. Some prisoners run away in order to get shot and be released from the agony of living.

Thursday, November 2, 1939

The coldest October in 50 years:

It has been the coldest winter that Britain and the Continent have known in the last 50 years. The Rivers Thames and Tees were frozen solid. The Canal had icebergs in it to such a degree that it was dangerous for navigation.

In London, the snow was three feet high. All road traffic and most trains from the Midlands came to a halt as a result of the heavy snow.

Tuesday, November 28, 1939

There is total blackout, with the shops long since sold out of black curtain material.

Householders are urged to paint the edges of their windows black.

Road deaths have doubled, forcing the Government to ease vehicle lighting restrictions. Unlit buses cause chaos to drivers and passengers alike.

Thursday, November 30, 1939

Petrol is increased by halfpenny a gallon to 1/9p halfpenny a gallon.

Thursday, November 30, 1939

20,000 Russians Trapped, Finn Commander Reports.

Translated from German:
Sunday, October 15, 1939
Trayan St. 50, Cetata Alba, Rumania

Dear Cousin Berta,

    I am writing to you as the final resort. All the letters I have sent to Aunt Sarah and Uncle Zelig were of no use. As you well understand, I am writing about my mother. I received a letter from her the other day, which I am sending on to you, and you can judge for yourself what a poor and miserable condition she is in.

    We have done all we can from this side to try and get her out. It is just impossible – they are not letting anyone into Rumania. There are thousands of Jews trying to come in every day from Poland, Czechoslovakia, Galicia and God only knows from where else. The only ones they let in are those who have a visa to go on to Palestine. They are putting them in a concentration camp in Constantsa until a ship will come to pick them up. We had some of them come through here. The stories they are telling about what the Gestapo is doing are hair-raising. It is difficult to believe everything they say; maybe they are only saying these things to get our sympathy. But if only a quarter of what they say is true, I can only thank God we are safe here.

    Now that Judith and I got our Rumanian papers, there is no way they can deport us, like they are doing to those that came here in the last five or six years. But even here, we feel the war; it is said that the Bolshevik troops are massing on the other side of the border along the Dnjester. The Soviets are threatening to take over the whole of Rumania if the king does not give over Moldavia.

    It is not that I am afraid of these under-fed, under-clothed soldiers, who carry no decent weapons. People say that if the Germans had not helped the Red Army in Poland, they would have been chased out of there with their tails between their legs.

But the problem is that people here are saying that it is Siyoma who is encouraging them to come over. He has been arrested with some other Communists more than once by the local "Garda de Fier" (the Rumanian Iron Guard, which is the equivalent of the Blackshirts), who accused him of spying.

In any case, that is not what I am writing about. I am more concerned about Mama. I do not understand, do you not have a heart? Is she not your aunt? Do you not know how serious the situation is? Do you and your parents know what is happening over there? Would I not do more for your mother if the situation were reversed? You and I both know that if you or Uncle Zelig only put in half the effort for Mama as you did to get your parents-in-law out, Mama would be safe and well right now! Mama is your blood relative, so why do you do nothing? Do you hate us so much? Or is it because I married a Communist that you cannot forgive me? So I will tell you this, I personally need nothing from you or your family. As far as I am concerned, you can go on living your smug life in that one-horse town of yours, but if you do not see to it that my mother gets out now, I will never forgive you.

Berta

Monday, October 30, 1939
202 Lewisham s.e.4 East London

Dear Peterli,

As yet, I have not heard any sign of life from you.

I did not get the time as yet to give the money to this Rivle fellow who was supposed to deliver the money for the jewelry to your mother in Leipzig, but my feeling is that he is just a crook. How does he think he will get into Germany and pass it on to your mother? I think he will just disappear. I tell you, I have a lot of experience with these sorts of people. You do still remember, I hope, what I did when we first met? In any case, how much money are you thinking of sending? Even if I gave him the money, I do not know where to tell him to deliver it to.

There is nothing that can be done from this side anymore. I also think that you have done all you can. Yes, you could go on praying that the villain will be killed soon, that is the punishment that he deserves. You ask me what I suggest you should write to your mother in regards to the money? I would tell her to ask her brother and sister why they did not do anything in order to get her out. You yourself have done all you can. You cannot do more. In any case, we will need to keep the money from the jewelry for our marriage, and for our new start in Australia.

My husband is at work now, which gives me the chance to write to you without him poking his nose into what I am doing and asking questions. I would like to try once more and get this divorce. Maybe this time I will be able to get more money out of him.

Europe seems to be clouded over with war. It reminds me of the day before the villain's invasion into Prague. Do you remember the day we were at your mother's place, talking about the possibility of war? It did not come then, but it came this time around. Wherever we go, the villain is after us. I hope we can get to Australia before the villain gets us here.

Dear Peter, I am writing to you sooner than I was thinking of doing, because I would like to apologize or to explain myself in light of my conduct with my husband. My feelings demand that of me. As a woman and as a person, I know I have acted in the right way. This was not what I would have chosen. It was difficult for me also. That is something you will never understand; after all, I must consider the future for little Herman and me. This is the sort of dilemma I must live with. But I can assure you that you are the only man in my life. I am very sincere in my feelings for you, Peter, and the strength of my feelings have been to my disadvantage. I could not live with a misunderstanding in our friendship; it would cause me too much pain. We have both had to go through enough lately. It seems to me that you do not understand me. I have paid such a high price for my mistakes. After all, none of us are saints, Peter. We have all made mistakes.

I am telling you all this because you reproach me in such a way as if you have never done anything wrong. What is more, for weeks I have done all I can so we can meet. I do not want to tell you what price I had to pay for this sacrifice. I always say, "As one prepares his sacrifice, so God will receive it." And this is a big sacrifice I made for you.

I hope you understand. I am looking forward to the day we can be together in a faraway country.

Love Dina

Translated from German:
Tuesday, October 31, 1939
British Dolls & Toys LTD
Therpe St., W. Hartlepool, Tel 6277
Manager Carol Katz (German)

Dear Adolf,

I never know if I should call you Adolf or Peter. After all, that is the name which is still in my mind, a name that brings me such wonderful memories from back home, but I think you prefer Peter, which to me seems so strange and removed.

Is there any news concerning the whole business with your mother? The poor woman is stuck there in Leipzig – at least we succeeded in getting out. Both my older sister and her husband escaped to Brazil. Why do the Schmulewitsches not help you? They could at least pay the 100 pound bond.

Did I tell you that Yette wants to come and live with us in Hartlepool? Max and her father will not hear of it. They said that if she wants to leave home, she must get married. You know as well as I do that they oppose it, and they do not want to have anything to do with us. I wonder how all this will end.

I told my brother and Papa that I must go and see the doctor this coming Saturday. I did not want them to know that I am coming to Harrogate, as it will mean going into a long explanation why I could not go and see a doctor in Middlesbrough.

In any case, I will be coming on the 4th, on the 5:00 P.M. train. I will not be going back until Monday because of the blackout (trains no longer run at night). So that is the final date. I cannot wait to see you on the platform.

You must let me know as soon as possible if this arrangement is not convenient for you. If it is not, I have other plans for Sunday. If we miss one another, I will wait for you by the gate. If you are too busy to meet me, I suggest we meet in the same hotel as last time. Please give me an answer as soon as you can.

The toy business is very slow. We had a short spell of good sales in September, when families were sending their children to the countryside, but since then, it has been dead. I think it will pick up in the run-up to Christmas. There is talk that the whole thing will be over by then, once the bastard breaks his neck.

I am looking forward to seeing you. The desire to see you once more is so strong that I just cannot wait.

Love Lotti

Translated from German:
Thursday, November 2, 1939
15 Reginald Terrace, Chapeltown, Leeds

Dear Lotti,

I will wait for you in the station. I only hope I can get there on time – you know how it is with the fuel restriction. Buses hardly run so it may take me over two hours to walk.

The family are just not interested in my mother's case. In the few letters I get from them, they apologize for not doing anything. I would prefer they move their asses and do something instead of apologizing all the time. I think they just cannot understand how serious the situation is. They think it is a wave of anti-Semitism that will blow over once this whole thing in Poland is through, and "the criminal" gets what he wants.

On a more positive note, I got the Committee to register my mother, and send an application to Woburn House, so maybe things are moving.

People you talk to over here say that they do not see why we should send our boys to fight in a place full of Catholics and Jews. Most of them do not even know where the soldiers are fighting. One of the workers, who is a veteran of the Great War, told me that they should solve their own problems, we have a bagful with our Catholics in Ireland.

It is funny what you say about my name. My general feeling is that there is more than just an official procedure in changing a name. I feel that "Adolf" associates me with everything that has to do with home, and "Peter" with my new life. As much as I would like to disassociate myself from my former life, it is part of me and always will be – are you not the best proof of that?

I also find it bewildering that despite our efforts back home to integrate and be Germans, we were always considered as Jews, while here, in contrast, we are finally identified as Germans, yet we do all we can to disassociate ourselves from this people.

I am often tempted to tell my colleagues at work that Hitler is like a dragon, the more you feed him, the hungrier he gets. He will only learn his lesson when someone puts a stop to his plans. I refrain from sharing my thoughts in the fear that they will say, "but you are a German like him."

On a more serious note, it seems that there are many layoffs in the firm, and I could be made redundant. If that happens, I will go to live in Manchester. They say there is more work there for Germans.

I am looking forward to seeing you,
All my love,
Peter

Monday, November 26, 1939
Oak House Hotel, Leeds

My dear Peter,

It is 8:30 and I am waiting for breakfast (in bed). Until it comes up, I thought I would write you a few words. First of all, I am feeling much better today but rather weak.

I took some anti-flu powders and I will stay in bed the rest of the day.

I did not notice you leaving this morning, but I hope you had enough sleep so you will not fall asleep at work today.

I really would like to thank you for the wonderful weekend. It was worth every penny to come up from Manchester. I do hope that your plan of coming to live in Manchester will work out, and we will have the opportunity of being much closer, although I do not know what I will tell my mother if we spend the night in a hotel.

What did you think of the dance? I thought it was quite jolly, but would have been nicer if there had not been so many people. I do not think they restricted the numbers at all. I was glad that you had the chance to meet Elaine and Rolf. I did not want to tell you last night but the young man who was standing in the corner when you came in asked me to dance with him long before you came. For that matter, it was right at the beginning when they called out for the Polka. Then he stayed with me until they announced the foxtrot. Thank goodness you arrived right after that. I was glad to have an excuse to get rid of him. Between one dance and the next, he asked me to go out with him on Saturday night. I refused, of course. See how faithful I am! Perhaps you would like me to have gone with him, and then you would have had an excuse to go out with some of those girls you were dancing with, like Raina, for instance. Poor girl, sometimes I feel sorry for her that she cannot get a man to take her out, they all make fun of her.

Sheila Hofday thought that you had a very aristocratic look. (Although it was a nice thing to say, it still made me feel jealous.) She's the girl who is getting married and going out to Egypt. Her fiance, Hans Bless, is the Swiss banker I told you about, who may help get your mother out. He said if you could give him the account number and the name of the bank where the money is invested, he thinks he could have it sent to England. He told me that there is no chance that they will let your mother into Switzerland. It is known that anyone with a passport stamped "Jew" in it is immediately sent back. In any case, he thinks there are too many Jews in Switzerland as it is without those coming in from Germany. I asked him if there is any chance that you could take his place in the Egyptian Trading Company in Manchester. Sheila said she would arrange for us all to get together. Wouldn't it be nice if he could see to it that you get his job in the company?

I wanted to tell you all that last night, but you were so anxious to get back to the hotel that I thought I would tell you in the morning. But since you were not here when I got up, I thought I would write to you instead.

I feel rather tired, so I had better stop. Hope you are feeling better,

From your little rabbit,
Anne

Translated from German:
Wednesday, November 29, 1939
British Dolls & Toys LTD
Therpe St., W. Hartlepool, Tel 6277
Manager Carol Katz (German)

Dear Adolf,

It was such a wonderful visit the other week in Leeds. It brought back memories from the good old times we had back home. I thank you so much for everything you did for me, and I do appreciate the effort you went to in coming to meet me off the train, despite the blackout. It is only a pity our time together was so short.

I am sorry that the visit I was planning for next week will not work out. First of all, I cannot leave the shop so often, and second, Yette is coming. I must stay here until she gets used to the new place.

It is sad that you are leaving Leeds. It was never too far to come, if I could catch the right train, and never too complicated. With the bureaucracy, one does not need to show a permit if you are traveling within Yorkshire.

I am sorry I will not be there to help you pack before you go on your way to Manchester, but that is how things are. Could you tell me as soon as possible when you are leaving? I must try and see you before you leave. I do not know if I will get a travel permit to Manchester, but once you are in Manchester, I will do everything I can to get a permit to come and meet you there.

What you said about losing your job is very sad. I can well understand it is very unpleasant as you were just starting and now you must stop. But if we look at it on the positive side, I know you well enough to say that you are no coward, neither in your private nor business life, and you will find a new job in no time.

Once we get married, we can both work, so I do not see any

difficulty in getting by. I hope we can both earn enough so we will have some extra to get your mother out. I must say my heart is crying each time I think of her stuck somewhere with no food, shelter, clothing or money.

I can still remember the business of Dr. Konighe. I hope all will be for the best and you will not need to work so much. Keep your spirits up, and I will keep my fingers crossed for you that it will soon all be over.

Yette told me that your sister sent a very stinky letter to Middlesbrough, blaming them for not caring or doing anything about your mother. I must say that if I were in your sister's place, I would do exactly the same. I think it is such a *chutzpah* [impudence] of them to drop the whole thing on your shoulders, while they are living like kings. My father says that it is typical behavior of Ostjuden who are only interested in themselves.

I do not remember if I told you, but Carol and Yette have decided to get married. The wedding will be in Middlesbrough on the 24th, on Christmas Eve. Why they picked that date, God only knows. So what do you say to that, we will be *mishpocha* (family) in a roundabout way! I must say, I prefer to be mishpocha with you in a more direct way. I cannot describe to you the row and shouting that went on here when Carol told Mama and Papa that he is thinking of marrying Yette. You know how my father despises Galicianers, thinking that they are all lazy good-for-nothings? He forgets from time to time that it was thanks to them that he came over here, just at the last minute. Mama goes along with everything he says even though she does not agree with him. I do not want to imagine their reaction when we announce our engagement. Let them get over this first. I think it is so bad that they may not come to the wedding. Tomorrow Jane, Max and Dora will be here. They will be coming in Max's car to talk about the details of the wedding.

By the way, I forgot to tell you the big news – I am free, I have all my permits. I am out of the court's hands, and I also obtained the final papers from the Home Office in Woburn House saying that I can stay here as long as I like. I can now get a passport. So the only restriction left is a travel permit.

Moving to Manchester can only be for the better. It is a pity, though, that you must have a permit each time you want to go from one place to another. This thing with the war is terrible. The other day, when I went to the hairdresser, would you believe it but the owner told me that because of the fuel rationing I had to have my hair washed in cold water! How long will this continue?

I have a lot to tell you, so please come to the wedding. They say it will be the biggest event that Shaarei Shamayim Shul (synagogue) in Middlesbrough has ever seen.

I cannot wait to move to Manchester, if only to get out of this hole. The idea of living with you makes me very happy. Tell me if you need anything.

Yours, Lotti

December 15, 1939
The Baltimore Reporter
From our correspondent in London
Battle begins for control of Atlantic

The German success with its U-boat offensive against the British Empire and the U.S.A. merchant Navy is a disaster not only because of the loss of ships and the painful loss of human lives, but also because it is crippling the British economy and war industry mainly due to a lack of fuel.

Now that the main, if not the only, supply of fuel to the British Isle is coming from the Texan oil fields, the German U-boats try to target mostly oil ship convoys which are crossing the Atlantic. Each thirty thousand ton oil tanker that is sunk, and there have been over sixty since the beginning of the war, means no electric power for two weeks for a small city like Newcastle. Most of the electric power in Britain is generated by oil and coal unlike in the U.S.A. where it comes mostly from water.

In order to overcome the difficulty, fuel restrictions have been imposed throughout the British Isles. These include fuel restrictions for cars and electric restrictions for businesses and homes.

Translated from German:
Thursday, November 30, 1939
Guisborough Shirt & Underwear Co
West End Guisborough, Tel Linthorpe 88249
Director S. Schmulewitsch
(Stateless) Russian Origin

Dear Adolf,

We would all like to know what is happening with you. We sent a parcel with shirts for you. Did you get it? You did not even send a postcard to say thank you.

Mama and Papa would like to know what is happening. Berta got a long and nasty letter from your sister in Rumania, telling her that she and Mama have done nothing to help Aunt Lina. As you have all the papers, we do not know where the whole thing is standing. Berta said she thinks that her aunt from Switzerland can get her out, but as far as I know, they have not been on speaking terms for years.

We would appreciate it if you could somehow stop being so lazy and write a letter so we know what is happening. Papa said that he is neither a magician nor a millionaire, and cannot wave his magic wand to bring Aunt Lina here. You should tell your sister that even here, the streets are not paved with gold. Now with the war going on, we too cannot do everything we would like to. By the way, why does Uncle David not do anything? After all, he lives in London. It wouldn't hurt you to move your backside either, and instead of going to dancing halls every night, spend your time and money on your mother's case. I know it is easier to leave all the work to us.

How is life in Manchester? Have you made any new friends? Be careful with the women there, they say they are much tougher than we are here in the north! I was so upset with Berta's letter that I forgot to tell you the big news: Yette and Carol have announced their marriage. That will be the second marriage since we left home. I do not have to tell you Papa's reaction when he heard it. He was fit to be tied; you know how he hates the Germans who always think they are better than the whole world. The fact the Carol's father has a medal from the Great War does not impress him in the slightest. For him, anyone who does not speak Yiddish is at best a good-for-nothing, and at worst, a *ganif* (thief). I myself do not understand what Yette sees in this Carol. What is he after all, a doctor or lawyer? He is only a third-class merchant in the rag trade – big deal.

I will be sending you an invitation once they are printed. With the war and rationing, it is nearly impossible to get paper. You can talk to those people in the rationing office until you are blue in the face, they just do not care, as if allocating some paper for wedding invitations will change the war.

You must tell us what to answer your sister.

Love, Dora

Chapter Sixteen

Winter of Discontent – Desperation Sweeps Europe

Winter 1939

THE WINTER OF 1939/40 WAS harsh, the worst Europe had known for over 50 years. Temperatures dropped to below -22 degrees. In Leipzig, like the weather, the situation was steadily deteriorating. The unexpected military successes of the Wehrmacht in Poland encouraged the local Nazi party in Saxony to greater provocation. The Jews were even more limited in what they could do. The span of time during which the Jews were allowed on the streets was further reduced. Exceptions were made for those Jews who were on their way to and from "work," which was, in reality, slave labor. Jews were paid six Marks a day, of which two Marks were deducted in support of the war effort. They only had two hours a day to themselves, which was spent searching for food, organizing their permits and trying to find out which new restrictions had come out that day. If they were seen on the streets during the Jewish curfew, they would be arrested and sent over the border, which, for most of them, meant a certain death. New restrictions were coming out daily. These were pasted on the walls of the Jewish homes by the rail-station.

September 23, 1939

Non-Aryans are forbidden to have, wear or buy shoes with heels over two centimeters.
　The Committee for Retrieving German Property
　Non-Aryans are called to donate watches, beds, mattresses and blankets to the Volksdeutsche [German Aryans who had to leave Poland as a result of the tension].
　The Committee for Stolen German Property

October 1, 1939

Non-Aryans are strictly forbidden to have, listen to, or own a wireless. From today, all non-Aryans are required to bring such appliances to the collection center in the Jewish Committee house on Kiel Strasse 5.
　The Committee for the Internal Security of the Reich
　It is strictly forbidden for anyone who is not of pure German blood to have, own or use typewriters of any sort, including calculators or carbon paper.
　The Committee for the Internal Security of the Reich

October 15, 1939

Only Aryans and their families may have, keep and use carrier pigeons.
　The Committee for the Internal Security of the Reich
　Our great leader requires us to help our heroic soldiers fighting for the Fatherland. In order to do that, all people alike, Aryans

and non-Aryans, are asked to bring all woolen clothing including stockings to the collection center.
Der Angriff, The Offensive

October 22, 1939

Non-Aryans are not allowed to use pay phones. Anyone violating this order will be punished severely.
It is strictly forbidden by anyone who is not a member of the German race to enter or be seen near a public library.
The Committee for the Internal Security of the Reich

December 20, 1939

As a special gesture to our dear leader and the Fatherland, all people of the Jewish race who have relatives in other countries are expected to pay one week's wages for warm clothing as Christmas gifts to our brave soldiers on the Polish front.
The Committee for the Internal Security of the Reich

* * *

The so-called committees for retrieving Aryan property were nothing more than a branch of the Gestapo. The SS came up with the idea that if they could collect a certain number of pairs of high-heeled shoes, they would be able to supply the entire Aryan population of Leipzig with wood. That winter, over 15 Jewish people froze to death. Others died of thirst, after being denied access to unfrozen water.

The German high command was reorganizing the administration in the newly acquired territories of the former Poland. Poland was now divided between the Reich on the West and the USSR on the East. The decision among the policy-makers was to rename the annexed areas "*Generalgouvernement,*" which was run by Hans Frank. It took Frank, a former Leipzig lawyer, and his men until the beginning of 1940 to recreate "The New Poland." In Frank's Poland, all schools were closed, and the entire intellectual, political and financial elite was either arrested or executed.

Next came the big assignment: to concentrate all the Jews they could lay their hands on, before they escaped to the Russian-occupied zone of Poland or "Western Ukraine," as Stalin decided to rename it.

Finally the time had come that they could solve the long-standing problem of the stateless Jews (stateless Jews like Peter and Lina could not be sent to Poland before the Reich occupied it). Under the new administration, they could now ship them out of the *Altreich* (the old Germany prior to the invasion of Poland) to the newly acquired lands, although transportation was a problem, as most of the rail "rolling stock" was moving the army of occupation in the GG zone.

In the meantime, they concentrated on their next goal: rounding up the rest of the Jews in Leipzig, Dresden and Berlin. In light of the new political situation, new decrees started to appear.

January 1940

All residents of the "Jewish Homes" must report to the Local Police twice a day!

Fritz Sauckel, Commander-in-Chief of the Gestapo in Leipzig

Residents of the "The Jewish Homes" are forbidden to leave the area at any time, day or night, without a signed permit from the Gestapo Headquarters.

* * *

Although Rumania was still an independent country, it came under threat from Stalin's Soviets in the North and the Third Reich of Hitler in the West. At the same time, King Michel in

WINTER OF DISCONTENT — DESPERATION SWEEPS EUROPE

Bucharest was reluctant to sign any treaty with England or France. The king monitored the British and French reaction to the German invasion of Czechoslovakia and Poland. He was cautioned not to sign a treaty with these two governments in light of the recent history that the allies had made in Poland and Czechoslovakia. The Wehrmacht was putting pressure on the king to supply it with cheap Rumanian fuel from the oil fields in Walachei. At the same time, there was unrelenting pressure from Hitler's side not to give into Stalin's demands to annex Bessarabia and Moldavia. Stalin considered these two provinces of Rumania as part of Russia. He claimed they were handed over to Rumania after the Bolshevik Revolution of 1917. King Michel and Ion Antonescu, the Commander-in-Chief of the Garda de Fier (The Iron Guard), identified the Jews with Communism and blamed them for the impossible situation that Rumania was forced into. In Rumania and Moldavia, there was no rounding-up of Jews, but the local Fascist party, the Iron Guard, was becoming increasingly self-confident, as they witnessed the success of the Wehrmacht in Poland.

Bullying of the Jews was enforced in even harsher measures, particularly in the border areas of the USSR in towns like Cetata Alba and Kisinov. Jewish men were taken to forced labor camps where they were ordered to dig ditches and trenches on the Russian border. Confiscation of farming equipment for the 4th Rumanian Army became a daily event.

Following the example of anti-Jewish race laws in Germany, the Rumanians inflicted their own form of anti-Semitism: forcing Jews to take Rumanian partners into their business, restricting their travel and land ownership, schooling, bank accounts and government positions.

Meanwhile, in England, the newspaper headlines read:

Thursday, January 11, 1940

Equal pay for war work, say women:

The government was urged today to give women war workers the same pay and conditions as men. The call came at a special meeting in London of leading women's groups, which condemned current practices. Speaker after speaker told of wage cuts and worsening conditions as employers tried to use the high level of unemployment among women to get skilled labor at unskilled wages.

The meeting also called for the training of women as factory supervisors ready for an influx of woman in war industries. The debate follows recent allegations of prejudice against women among trade unions.

Chapter Seventeen

Schmulewitsch Family Wedding

CHRISTMAS WAS FAST APPROACHING, AND Peter could not remember it ever being so cold. He could barely leave the house; the streets were knee-deep in snow, most lakes were frozen, and pipes were cracking from the freezing temperatures.

Obtaining a permit to travel to Guisborough for Shnoki and Carol's wedding was not easy. The emigration department in Manchester harbored deep suspicions regarding German refugees traveling from inland cities, such as Manchester, to Birmingham and coastal towns like Middlesbrough and Newcastle. They were nervous that German spies would roam the docks, and indicate to German U-Boats the whereabouts of British and American merchant ships.

Sunday, December 3, 1939
Oak House Hotel, Leeds 7

Dear Peter,

Thanks for your letter that I received this morning. I suppose I must forgive you for not having responded earlier.

Mother wishes me to say that she received your letter and she will be more than pleased to see you on Saturday the 9th for the lighting of the 3rd Chanukah candle.

I am looking forward to you coming – it shall be fun. It would be nice if we could go out to the Alderly Edge dance hall. Most probably, Rolf and Elaine will come once they know you will be there.

If you do not care to come, please tell me as soon as you can by return mail, even a postcard will do. Do not forget to tell me what time the bus arrives, so I can wait for you at the bus stop. You say you never see anyone so I thought you might like to have some fun for a change.

I am disappointed that you are planning to be in Middlesbrough for the wedding, and will not be here for Christmas, but I understand that *mishpocha* comes first. I was hoping that you would be with me for the holidays – we would have had so much fun.

As for the wedding suit, I cannot advise you about getting tails or a dinner jacket, I do not know if you can even afford them. Not only is it eight pounds for the shirt but there are extras such as additional white waistcoats, ties, shorts, shoes and silk socks. Tails or a dinner jacket are only necessary if the wedding celebration is in the evening. A midday wedding can be with or without a dance reception. Then it only calls for a dark lounge suit.

I honestly cannot understand your family in Guisborough, having such an ostentatious wedding party during wartime! A party in a private house is one thing, but a lavish wedding does not look right nowadays. They are not thinking of what the goyim will say behind their backs. I see no reason to create more anti-Semitism when it is not necessary.

I have a lot of friends that got married recently before their fiances went over to join the Territorial Army in France. All their weddings were small, quiet celebrations at home. We are all sorry that you were classified as an enemy alien.

By the way my brother was recruited the day I came back from Leeds. He is attached to General Gort's 50th Armored Division. They were all sent over to France. A letter arrived the other day. He says that as yet they have not seen any action. He says that western France, where they are stationed, is beautiful, and they are having a lot of fun with the French girls. Rumor has it that by Christmas it will be all over and they will be sent home. I really envy those French girls, taking all the Jewish boys; it is just not fair leaving us here high and dry.

I told my father about the problem with your mother. His advice is to bring all the papers you have when you come, and he will see what he can do. There are one or two Czechoslovakian people that he helped get out. So maybe he could give you some advice on the matter.

Write by return mail,
Can't wait to see you getting off the bus on Saturday night,
Nothing more just now,
Love Anne

* * *

The Schmulewitsch-Katz wedding on Christmas Eve was no doubt the biggest affair that Middlesbrough had ever seen. There were over 500 guests present, many of them from the Kindertransport and other German refugees who had arrived in the last five or six years.

It reminded Peter of the Jewish Orthodox weddings back home, when one wedding would appear to be like a double celebration, one wedding for the men and another for the women. Although weddings such as those did not take place here in England, it felt as if there was a complete separation between the Ostjuden and the Germans, with the English as a sort of go-between.

Just as Anne predicted, it was ostentatious and pretentious. Peter felt that Max and Uncle Zelig were desperately trying to prove how successful they had become since they arrived. Most of the English left early; they wanted to get home for their family Christmas gatherings.

Peter restrained the urge to confront Aunt Sarah, Uncle David and Herman about his mother's situation in Leipzig. Although he knew that a wedding was neither the time nor the place for such arguments, he desperately wanted to ask them, "How is it that you have so much money to spend on an unnecessary wedding like this, when you cannot spare any pennies to help my mother escape from Germany?"

Peter could not partake of the sumptuous feast without feeling pangs of guilt at every bite, as he envisioned his mother sitting in an overcrowded room without any food to eat or water to drink. He met some old friends from back home, who had the same difficulties as him in getting their parents out of Germany. Lotti remained at this side throughout the entire wedding, constantly reminding him that their wedding would be much simpler and fun at the same time. He left Middlesbrough the following day feeling relieved. He hoped that he would never have to attend an event such as this again.

When he returned to Manchester, he decided to write his sister a letter.

Translated from German:
Thursday, December 28, 1939
3 Hardmas St.
Didsbury, Manchester 20

Dear Berta,
As you can see, I have moved to Manchester. I lost my job in

Leeds and was offered a better position here, so I think I will stay for some time. The war is going on, but we hardly feel it, except for the blackouts. Also, Germans and Austrians are restricted from travelling from one city to the next, which can be a nuisance from time to time. We need a travel permit in order to do this, but it doesn't really affect me as I do not have the money to travel. I would only like to go to London once to settle this matter with Mrs. Thorn.

From time to time, the newspapers are filled with reports about what is happening in Poland, and of course there is the rationing, and you cannot get this or that. But it is by no means as bad as it was in Germany. The stories that are coming out of Poland, about what they are doing to the population, are just hair-raising. I think that if France and England do not come to the aid of the Poles as they promised to do, there will be nothing to stop this madman from continuing in the same way.

I received a letter from a friend in Palestine the other day. Somehow he managed to get there in a roundabout sort of way. He said that before he left Leipzig, the only thing the English airplanes were doing was throwing leaflets from their aircrafts over the big cities. The leaflets contained a warning to Hitler and the German people that, "it is not a good idea to go to war, and if they do not pull out of Poland right now they will have to suffer the consequences." Apparently the people who picked them up on the streets just laughed and went on their way.

As for Mama, I am doing everything I can to see to it that she will get the visa. I must tell you that I feel as if I am sometimes talking to a brick wall. No one is interested, not even our family in Middlesbrough, and they get aggravated each time I bring up the subject of Mama. I tried to talk about it at the wedding, but Uncle David took me aside and said that it was not the time to bring up such things.

On a brighter note, I am learning English quite fast. When I have mastered the language somewhat better, I will go by myself to all these government offices.

How are things between you and Siyoma? Is he still the same austere Communist he was in Leipzig? Or is he prepared to admit that this Stalin is not the greatest leader in the world?

This Mrs. Thorn still has her hands on the jewelry, and says she will not return it unless I promise to elope with her to Australia. I myself do not know what would be worse: to have remained in Leipzig or marry this dreadful woman!

I only hope that Rumania, being so close to the Ukraine, will not be run over by the Bolsheviks, as Poland was. I hope it will all be over by the spring,
Love Adolf/Peter

* * *

Two weeks later, a reply came from Rumania:

Translated from German:
Sunday, January 7, 1940
Trayan St. 50, Cetata Alba, Rumania

Dear Adolf,

After not hearing from you for such a long time, I was glad to get your letter from the 28th December. I didn't know what to think about your long silence. I presumed it came from your complete lack of interest in our family. Mama is crying her eyes out and is waiting desperately for some sign of life from you. You should try and write to her through a neutral country, or you can send it to me and I will send it on to her.

You most probably feel insulted that I started the letter with so much criticism against you, but you go on with your roaring silence. I will not wait any longer to tell you about Mama's situation. She receives six Reich Marks a week for working in the garbage heap. From that six, three goes on rent for the room and one goes for heat so she is left with two Marks for food. The room is a hole with no kitchen or place to wash. In her letters, Mama is begging me to send her some butter and some money. There is no place here where I can get foreign money. Besides that, Jews are not allowed to buy butter or meat. Thank goodness, we have some from the farm, but we have to keep that hidden. If they find out that we have any of the restricted foods, they will nationalize the rest of the farm as they did to Siyoma's sister's farm.

Mama tells me in her letters that Leipzig Jews are being sent to Lublin, some town in former Galicia. For some reason, they now call it Generalgouvernment. They are changing the names every day; I have no idea where these places are. We hear from the Polish refugees that pass through here that they put them in open-air camps, letting them freeze to death. Of course, one does not have to believe every story that comes out of there. I know the German people better than anyone else, and I can tell you that they would never do a thing like that, in particular not to old people such as Mama. But, you know Mama's health is very bad and her heart is not good. How will she last the voyage from Leipzig to this town in a third-class compartment?

So I beg of you to do something to get her out before it is too late. I think that if she can get a visa to go to Switzerland, she could maybe stay there until the papers arrive from England. To bring her here is just not possible, I explained it in my last letter to Berta (I hope she sent it on to you). Mama came up with this preposterous idea based on some rumor that it is possible to walk to Dresden, and from there, take a train to Prague and walk the rest of the way through Vienna and Budapest to Timisoara on the Austrian-Rumanian border. She thinks that once she gets there, I can wait for her. She only needs 300 Marks to pay for a guide and a border smuggler. She was told it would not take more than a week.

What sounds ridiculous is the idea of Mama walking over 1500 kilometers! Where will she get food, shelter, and other provisions necessary for a journey such as this? What's more, how will I get to Timisoara? And even if I did have 300 Reich Marks, how could I possibly send it to her? That is not to mention the possibility that she might be caught and put in prison. I wrote to her that the whole thing is a silly idea. A week later, I got a postcard from her accusing me of not being interested in her. She added that if she would die tomorrow, I would not care.

Dear Adolf, you write in your letter that all the papers are ready and you are only waiting for a visa. Thousands of people receive help and only one poor woman, our mother, is not getting anything. The Schmulewitsches are having the time of their lives with parties and ostentatious weddings, and you, Adolf, what are you doing? In spite of the fact that you work hard, you are not prepared to move a finger for Mama. Berta writes that there is no shame in taking money from the Kehilla. She should try it and see how it feels. I cannot believe that she had the chutzpah to write that. If they (the Schmulewitsches) are against bringing Mama to England, they have definitely proved it. They do not know what is coming to them. I have never hated anyone in my life, but I curse them for doing nothing for our mother. Not only have they not done anything productive for her, they have even done everything in their power to stop her from coming.

I am at the end of my rope; my nervous system is not working anymore. If something happens to Mama, it will kill me. I am so fed up with life, I just want to die. The only thing holding me back is you, my dear brother, Mama and Judith.

Judith is beautiful and is very talented. It is a pity for her that there is no hope for this child. The political situation is so precarious; I wonder if there is any chance that we will come out of this alive.

Please answer me right away. Tell me what your plans are

regarding mother. How long do you think it will take? Maybe it is possible to do something through the Red Cross? From here, nothing works. I am asking you to write to Mama, as she is so alone.

Here we are at a dead end. We are sitting on a volcano waiting to erupt. Everything is so expensive, in particular clothing; only wine is cheap.

Judith is growing, touch wood. Soon, she will be taller than me. I cannot buy her any new clothing. She is fabulous at school and very beautiful. In my next letter, I will send you a picture of her. She looks as if she is 15 or 16 years old but she is only 12.

Siyoma was taken to a labor camp in the autumn. Now we are waiting fearfully in case they come back for him. Who knows what will happen to us? It could be that communication between us will break off. I beg of you, please do not waste time in taking action. Maybe you should try asking the Schmulewitsches to do something? Hopefully this letter will prick your conscience, and will make you wake up. Mama is 59 years old. In Lublin, there are epidemics of cholera and typhus – she could not possibly survive through these conditions.

Rosenblum's address is S. Rosenblum Antwerp, Post Restate Pelican Strasse 25. If I were you I would write a letter immediately, and if not to there, then to Zurich. Siyoma and Judith send their love.

How are things with you? What is happening with the "things?" You must see to it that nothing is stolen. Is Dora married by now? Who did she marry? How is Yetti's husband? Is her husband the German "potz" who used to come and see her in Leipzig? How was the wedding? I am really insulted they did not invite us.

Do you go to see the Schmulewitsches from time to time? What do they say about Mama? You must write and tell me everything that is happening. You must also tell me what the chances are of getting Mama out to Switzerland.

I bless you and kiss you from the bottom of my heart. I wish you the best of everything in life, and that you will be successful in everything all you do.

I hope we will see one another shortly – they say that the whole thing will be over by spring.

All the best,
Love Berta

Translated from German:
Sunday, January 14, 1939
53 Kenninghall Rd., London

Dear Adolf,

It has now been over a week since I tried to make contact with this Mrs. Thorn of yours. I was just about to give up when I got a note from her. She wrote that her son was hit by a car in the blackout, and is in hospital, but she now has time to see to your problem. She said that she will send the things to you as soon as she has a free moment. I hope that this will be the end of all our dealings with that woman.

As for you, you should try and find flowers in your own garden, and not fuck so many strange women. I hope all is good with you and you are doing well in your new job. I know you are intelligent (you lazy pig, you never did want to work). Do you think that you will succeed here without working? So, go find a hole for your prick. Here, everything is the same as usual. We are waiting for the bloody Germans, but they do not want to come.

Only one thing is worrying me, and that is Jack's father. Until now, he has had two operations and there is a third one to come. But he has no chance of staying alive. He has cancer in his small intestine and cannot digest a thing. He does not even know what is happening to him.

Keep in touch. I know it is difficult due to your laziness.
Herman

* * *

Peter found this postcard in his mailbox when he came home from work one day.

The Red Cross
Tuesday, January 16, 1940
Citizen Advice Bureau
Gaddum House, 16 Queens St., Manchester

Dear Mr. Rochman,

We would like to advise you that a telegram has arrived for you from a Mrs. Lina Rochman in Leipzig. It would be advisable to come and pick it up as soon as possible, from our office at the above address.

* * *

He rushed to the Red Cross office to get the telegram.

From Lina Rochman
Transmitted through the Red Cross of Saxony
Leipzig, January 1, 1940

My Dear Adolf,

I am still alive. I will not last much longer, no food, no clothing, no heat.

Save me, Mama

Peter was in shock. He tried to phone Guisborough but it was just impossible to get a line. He also tried to get hold of David, Herman, Lotti, but to no avail.

Still shaking from reading his mother's telegram, Peter sat down to write her an answer. The clerk told him that he would be limited to 20 words, including the address. Peter tried to explain how serious the situation was, but the man told him that these were the regulations, and they could not be broken.

Lina Rochman
C/O Leipzig Jewish Committee
Keil Strasse 5

Dear Mama,
    I am well. Good job. Doing all I can to get a visa.
    Love, Adolf

Translated from German:
Thursday, January 18, 1940
Guisborough Shirt & Underwear Co
West End Guisborough
Tel Linthorpe 88249
Director S. Schmulewitsch
(Stateless) Russian Origin

Dear Adolf,
    We got your letter today. I get the honor of answering it this time – usually it is Dora who replies.
    As far as you blaming us concerning the matter with Aunt Lina, you know the political situation as well I do. I would like to tell you that I went especially to Leeds and had a talk with Graham, our family lawyer. He told me that it would be impossible to get Aunt Lina into England.
    The only thing that we can do is to get her into a neutral country, maybe Belgium or Holland. If these stupid French would have done their job, as they promised, she could have gone there. That would have been the end of the story. Maybe we could get her

over here from one of those countries. Graham told me he would send you a letter explaining all of this.

Do you think there will be any difficulty in her getting from Leipzig to the Belgian border? There must be a train, if not daily, then at least weekly. What could be so difficult about getting a ticket and going over there? Why doesn't she do this simple thing instead of writing us these nasty letters? I think the best course of action would be for you to take care of the visa (Graham will tell you what to do) and I will take care of the financial aspect of things.

Do not think that we have nothing else to do here in Middlesbrough besides dealing with Aunt Lina's problems. With the war going on, they have taken most of the men, and we spend all our time retraining women for the job. These women are just plain stupid – it takes days to explain the simplest of jobs to them. I can tell you one thing for nothing – we do not go to dancing halls every night, acting like gigolos. We have to take care of Jack's father also. I do not know if you heard, but he has cancer.

I would say that you are an intelligent person, clever enough to find a way to get your mother out. Now that you have a job, a place to stay, and you can speak the language, there is no reason why you cannot see to it that Aunt Lina gets a visa.

As for this business with the Thorn woman, I have only this to say. My brother Herman is not the person who will get the money out of her for you. I can tell you first hand that he is just not interested in anything that is not directly related to him. On top of that, he is always ill. He hardly does what he has to do for the firm in London. You know we have endless difficulties trying to get fibers for this big order we got from the army, let alone extra fuel for the dyeing of the uniforms; buttons are also a problem. Our suppliers say that whalebone is just not coming in any longer from Japan. The ships that do get here from America without being sunk by the German U-boats bring in more important materials.

So on the one hand, they would like us to hand over thousands of uniforms each month, yet on the other hand, they do not give us any allocations. Papa and I hoped that Herman, being in London, could solve some of these problems for us, but he is like you, he likes to laze around and go out dancing every night.

This whole affair with Thorn is the biggest crime that I have ever heard of in broad daylight. I do not see why you do not go to London and straighten it out yourself.

I am waiting to hear from you that you have taken this matter into your own hands, telling us what you have done about it. I will not rest easy until I know that your mother's property is safe. I understand from Herman that she has had some problems with the police, and will be going to prison; do you know anything about that?

Hope to hear from you soon,
Max

P.S. Jane sends her love. She is now in her first month of pregnancy, and this baby will be the first Schmulewitsch to be born in England, or should I say in freedom.

Chapter Eighteen

Peter Presents Ultimatum to Dina

February 1940

WINTER 1940 WAS THE COLDEST that Europe had ever known since temperatures were first recorded. Letters stopped coming from Lina. With the two countries at war, the postal service had come to a complete standstill. In England, the population was starting to feel the effects of war, especially the presence of the German U-boats.

Tuesday, February 20, 1940

All shipping fair game for U-boats, declares Hitler:
German U-boat commanders have been ordered to attack all neutral shipping as well as Allied vessels, according to information received from Berlin.
At present, many neutral ships are passing through the Channel and calling at British ports to have their cargo checked and are granted certificates, assuring that they are free of contraband bound for Germany. Berlin now says that act makes all neutrals suspect. U-boat

commanders have been ordered to open fire without question. Any seacraft merely sailing a zigzag course is said to be grounds for immediate torpedoing.

The order will affect small neutral nations such as Holland and France. Worst hit by this situation are Norway, Sweden and Denmark, whose ships must pass through British ports for clearance, but the three nations are preparing protests to Berlin. The Norwegian foreign minister told Parliament in Oslo that 50 Norwegian ships had been sunk since the beginning of the war, all victims of Nazi U-boats or aircraft strikes.

Hitler hopes to force all neutrals to divert their exports from Britain and other overseas markets to Germany, and when the Reich itself is not the purchaser of the cargo, the German Reich will be used as a clearinghouse.

Wednesday, February 21, 1940

Two IRA men are hanged.

Wednesday, February 28, 1940

The liner Queen Elizabeth sails secretly on the first journey to the US to await the end of the war:

The liner *Queen Elizabeth* ended her secret maiden voyage today as she sailed into the anchorage off New York's Staten Island, to stay there in safety until the war is over. The 85,000-ton ship was painted in drab gray as camouflage but saw no enemy submarines as she sprinted across the Atlantic at 24 knots. Although she carries no guns or other forms of defenses, she is fitted with an anti-mine device.

PETER PRESENTS ULTIMATUM TO DINA

Friday, March 15, 1940

Six million hear Haw Haw's jaw, jaw:

William Joyce, a former factotum of the British Fascist leader, Sir Oswald Mosley, has become a popular wartime broadcaster in Germany. He has been dubbed "Lord Haw Haw" because of his nasal drawl.

Our American correspondent in Berlin reports that in Joyce's broadcasts from Germany, he seeks to undermine public confidence in the BBC and the British Press. A recent survey put his audience at an estimated six million people, one-sixth of the listening public in the British Isles.

A widespread rumor has him announcing that a certain clock in a certain town in England had stopped, and indeed it had some minutes before the broadcast! Some people have been prosecuted for passing on such rumors. What is clear is that a German, who believes that such terms as "old chap" and "my best mate" are commonly used by British working class, is writing his scripts for him.

With him in the British Union of Fascists are people like Captain A.M. Ramsay, president of the Right Club and a Conservative M.P. for Peebles and John Beckett, a former Labor M.P., also acting as secretary of the British Labor People's Party.

His public speeches are known to be full of venom, mainly towards the Jewish people of the British Isles, calling them "bloodsuckers" and "parasites" that live off the labor of the British working-class man.

None of Them Were Heroes

Translated from German:
Friday, February 23, 1940
101 Grange Road, West Hartlepool

Dear Adolf,

Please excuse me for not answering your letter before. It was simply not possible to do so earlier.

In the meantime, it seems to me that you are doing well where you are now. Do you know that it has almost been a year since you left home, and you have done better than most of us. So I do not see any reason for you to be sad, as you indicated in your letter. On the contrary, you are free, you have no one depending on you, you can do whatever you wish. So many women like you, what more do you want? Is this not what you wanted all your life? I know it is easy for me to talk, as my whole family is out although one of us is in Brazil. But we have escaped the claws of this madman, may Satan take his soul.

As things stand, it seems that it is only a question of a month or two until the whole thing will be over, although they said that by Christmas the boys will be home, and now it is nearly Passover. In any case, there is nothing to be done over there, besides running after those loose French girls. No wonder they didn't want to come home for Christmas. If "The Monster" will get what he wants in Poland, which he has already, that will be the end of the war. I think it is such a chutzpah of those IRA people attacking and leaving bombs everywhere, just now when we are putting all our efforts into fighting this animal. They really deserve what is coming to them.

I do not know if you get the news over there in Manchester. The news from the few refugees of the Kindertransport (that are still arriving from Poland) is not to be believed. The stories of what they are doing to the Jews over there are simply horrendous. Of course, one should not believe every piece of gossip coming out of

PETER PRESENTS ULTIMATUM TO DINA

there. My only hope is that it will not spill over here, and that this Oswald Mosley will not take over.

So why are you not happy? It cannot be just because of your work that you do not like. Maybe it is because you do not see any future? Maybe this is how all refugees feel. We all live in what the English call a blackout. Peter, remember, I am behind you in everything you do, and once we are together, things will work out better. I can promise you that this whole thing with your mother will work out for the best.

Now that Shnoki is living with us, I can see why her parents did not get along with her. She acts like a real princess – nothing is good enough for her. You may not believe it, but she does not get up in the morning before 9:00 A.M. and it is I who gets Carol's breakfast in the morning. About working in the shop, there is nothing to talk about. I came into the kitchen the other day, and I saw her sitting on the couch like some English lady, and you would not believe it but Carol was washing the dishes. I always thought that you Ostjuden were diligent, but maybe not all of you.

How are you health-wise? Are you careful about what you are putting into your mouth? Are you taking care of yourself? As long as we are not together, you cannot leave it to someone else.

My wish to you for the new year (a bit late) is that you will find a true friend that will be by your side at all times and he will protect you from all harm.

The photos from the wedding have not yet been developed. They say it is just impossible to get any of the material that one uses for this sort of developing.

What is happening with your mother's case? I just cannot stop thinking of her in this small musty room, all alone with nothing to wear and eat. She came into my thoughts the other day when I met someone from home who came here only two months ago. She told me that they have cleared all the Jews from the Gohlis area and around the Bahnhof. Now, all Jews must live in this triangle between Humboldt Strasse, Kill Strasse, and the Bruel. At times, 15 people are crammed into a room, with no heat or water. She also told me that every so often, they take those who cannot work, and send them to the new territories in what was formerly Poland, which is now called Generalgouvernment. There, they just disappear, like into a big hole. It gives me the shivers just thinking about it.

I must be on my way to take over from Carol in the shop. He must go before the committee today .

Love, love and love again,
Lotti

Translated from German:
Saturday, February 24, 1940
Guisborough Shirt & Underwear
West End Guisborough
Director S. Schmulewitsch

Dear Adolf,

I hope you forgive me for still calling you Adolf, but I just cannot call you Peter. To me, you will always be Adolf. It is Sabbath, thank goodness, so we do not have to go to the factory and get up at the crack of dawn.

The boys went to Shul, and left me to answer your letter. Thank you so much for your letter, it came right on time. We were starting to think that maybe you had been arrested or had left for Australia with this Horn or Thorn woman of yours.

I was glad to hear that you will be coming with Bellow next week. This friend Menashe you are bringing, is he one of us? Do you know of anyone who Papa will not have something to say about, either in front of him or after he has left? With a name like

PETER PRESENTS ULTIMATUM TO DINA

Menashe, he must be Jewish, although with you one never knows. Is he our age, or is he one of the Kinder? Why am I asking all these questions? Just bring him along and we will be glad to have him and you. Mama always says, "Where there is room for two, one can fit in three also."

In any case, your visit comes just at the right time. Max and Jane are going to Hartlepool next week to visit with Shnoki and Carol. I was not invited, so I will stay home with Mama. I wanted to ask you, when you come could you bring with you a zipper for my new dress? We cannot find these things anymore around here since the war began.

Did you know that they have started to arrest, in Middlesbrough and in Newcastle, refugees that have come from Germany and Czechoslovakia? They say that they are all spies. What a lot of rubbish, how could any of us spy for Germany? They (the Germans) did not let even us go out of the house.

I think it is all because of this Mosley, the Fascist, stirring up trouble against the Jews. In my opinion, they are arresting these people, not because they came from Germany but because they are Jews. I only hope that we will not be subjected to the Reich all over again.

Do not forget to bring your dirty laundry when you come. Hope all is well with you,
Love
Dora

* * *

The letter from Lotti made Peter think once more about his mother and her dire situation. Peter thought that at least if she could be with someone, or would have someone to turn to, that would be a source of comfort. He decided to write once more to Dina to see if he could get the money out of her, while at the same time try to find out what she had done with the jewelry.

Translated from German:
Tuesday, March 5, 1940
3 Hardmas St., Didsbury, Manchester 20

Dear Dina,

I have not heard from you for some time. My cousin Herman told me that your son had a bad accident, and I hope he is well by now.

I am writing this letter to you to find out what is happening with the jewelry that you basically stole from us. Why have you not handed it over to me? This whole story that I promised to marry you is preposterous, I never did so, and I would never marry anyone who is not Jewish, definitely not someone who is old enough to be my mother.

I would like to make it quite clear that I consider you a thief and con person, who stole our jewelry. You know very well that this jewelry was meant to help get my mother out of Germany. I can only see you as a person with no heart and no soul, knowing about my mother's situation as you do. It is you that holds the key to getting her out.

I see no other option, after I, my friends and relatives have tried to get you to hand over this property that you stole from us, but to hand the matter over to the police, informing them of your illegal trade in gold, jewelry and ornaments, smuggling them into this country for the last six years, ever since you have been a British passport holder.

Before I do so, I will give you one week, and one week only, to hand over the stolen jewelry to me. Today is Tuesday the 5th of March, 1940; I will wait till Tuesday the 12th of March, 1940.

Peter

* * *

PETER PRESENTS ULTIMATUM TO DINA

On the day he sent the letter to Dina, a letter arrived from his sister in Rumania. It was taking longer and longer for the letters to arrive.

Translated from German:
Thursday, February 1, 1940
Trayan St. 50, Cetata Alba, Rumania

Dear Adolf,

I have received a letter from Mama, which I am sending on to you. I wish there could be a way to copy the letter and send it on to the Schmulewitsches as well. They say that there is a photography shop in Bucharest that can take a photo of a letter, and give you the original back. But it costs more money than we have; what's more, Jews are not allowed to go to Bucharest anymore without a permit.

Things for the Jews here are getting worse from day to day. I do not know if I told you, but Judith cannot go to school any longer. They say school is meant only for pure Rumanians. We are no longer allowed to buy things like butter, shoes and meat. We are also restricted in sending letters. Each time I go to the post office to send a letter, I must open it and read it to the postal clerk. If it is in German, I must translate it also. They say it is because we Jews are all spying for the Bolshevik conspiracy, which is trying to take over Rumania. I am also unable to send food parcels to Mama.

What with Siyoma being a Communist, and living right on the border from the Bolsheviks, we feel the grim situation much more than others do. As the months go by, there are more and more refugees coming through on their way to Constantsa. They say that there is a ship waiting to take them to Palestine. For the refugees that managed to get here, the Kehilla tries to help them as much as it can before they go on their way. But we are also very limited and restricted in what we can do and give. My heart goes out to the women with small babies. These women have been travelling for weeks on end, with no food, water or clothing, and arrive here in rags. It makes my heart bleed. Once they arrive in the Bolshevik-occupied zone in former Poland, that the Soviets renamed "Western Ukraine," they are stripped of anything that has any value: jewelry, gold, money, watches, clothing, and even food. The barbaric Red soldiers, who serve with the Bolshevik Army, do all this.

And to make matters worse, these people still have a long way to go until they reach Palestine. How many more Red Armies of this sort will they meet on the way? They say that the British Navy does not let these boats get out of the Black Sea into the Mediterranean. Once they get there, the navy just sinks them. I must say that even with the confused situation here, I am still glad that Judith and I no longer live in Central Europe.

That is not the worst of it. These people come with stories that the Wehrmacht is rounding up all the Jews in the areas of occupation, together with the Jews coming from Germany, and sending them to camps where they are gassed to death.

I just cannot believe these stories, and I must say, they even irritate me. I think these people only tell them so that we will feel sorry for them. I have known the Germans all my life, and I know that they are not capable of doing things like that. What do they think they are, some barbaric African tribe? But I must tell you, I am so worried about Mama. If she is sent to a camp, how will she survive?

Dear Adolf, you must find a way to send her a letter or something so she will not think that she has been forgotten. I think that is what is killing her. Dear Adolf, you must find a way to get her out, you cannot let the Schmulewitsches just wash their hands of the whole thing. Maybe Uncle David can do something before it will be too late.

I hope to hear from you soon, but I know there are difficulties with the post.

Siyoma was taken again to a work camp. They are building some sort of a defense line against the Bolshevik invasion. They also took the two mules.

Now I do not know who are worse, the Nazis or the Bolsheviks.

Write soon,
Love Berta

* * *

In the envelope was the letter that Lina had sent to Berta.

Translated from Yiddish:
Sunday, January 21, 1940
C/O the Jewish Houses area, Leipzig
Kiel Strasse 5

My dear Berta,

I got a letter from you and Adolf on the same day. I think Adolf's letter arrived a long time ago, but the Gestapo gave me the two letters at the same time.

I was so worried when I did not hear from you for such a long time. Here, they say that the Luftwaffe is bombing England every day. I was scared that Adolf was killed, so you can imagine how relieved I was to get this telegram from him. It came through the Red Cross and consisted of only 20 words. He asked if I was well, and I got the Witerlises to answer in 20 words to say that I am well and he should tell Aunt Sarah that I am surviving, but not for long.

Since the time that Adolf left, which is nearly a year ago, I think I received one postcard from her and 200 grams of butter, of which the Gestapo or one of those thieves in the Kehilla took half.

If you ever write to her, tell her that I really appreciate what she did for me, and it would not kill her to send me some more. I think that living in all this luxury in that one-horse town of theirs makes her forget that she has a sister. Tell her that it is fat that I need more than anything else. I certainly do not need her letters telling me how difficult it is in the new country. Maybe send it through the Red Cross. Adolf cannot send me any money, as the customs people take it all for the war effort.

I cannot stay here much longer; we are all living on the floor of the former sports hall in the Carlebach Shul. Every day, they take people out of here, and send them to Poland. Only those who are working stay on. This woman who use to live on Gustav Adolf Strasse, the one whose husband was the editor of the *Juedischers Gemeideblat*, the local Jewish newspaper, has left for Belgium. Soon I will be the only Jew left in Leipzig. She is safe now after her son arranged a visa for her, and do you know why? If you do not know, I will tell you – because he cared for her.

I never got an answer from the Swiss Consul, but from what Mrs. Zellner, the one that owns the kosher butcher shop on Nord Strasse, tells me, one must go there with 1000 Marks as a guarantee. I just do not have that sort of money, and how, in my weak condition, will I walk all the way to Dresden? On top of that, I must get a permit from the Gestapo to go there, and I am just too scared to go over there.

Tell Adolf that he should go the Swiss Consul in England, and give them the guarantee money for me over there, and then send the paper over with the Red Cross, so I can at least get into Switzerland. Tell him that he has forgotten me here, and I am fading away, with no food to eat, no clothes to wear, no water to drink and no place to live. Tell him to tell Aunty that she should be ashamed of herself. But Adolf should see to it that he does not quarrel with her, as she is a sick woman. On second thoughts, maybe it is better if he does not say anything to her – she knows she is wrong without him telling her.

Dear Berta, you told me you have started to rent rooms in the house for people coming in from Poland. You must not let them take advantage of you. In that way, you will only lose. I know how difficult it is when you are all alone.

Dear Berta, you must see to it that you and Judith never fall into the situation that I am in. I should never have believed Adolf when he promised he would get me out of here and save me. You must buy, with all the money you have, shoes. This is the most important item. If I had better shoes, I could walk properly and my feet would not freeze. I could have been a free woman by now. Shoes are the key to your survival. If you do not buy them now, you never know when you will have the chance to buy them again. Buy them with all the money you have; in a short time your money will be worth nothing. Do not forget to buy boots too. If you do not have enough money, take it from your lodgers, or from your mother-in-law – they all have money, they are only hiding it. You must also buy fat, petroleum, butter, oil, coal and heavy material for garments. I hope you still have the sewing machine that you took from home.

Dear Berta, ask Adolf to send you things you cannot find, he works for a clothing factory. It is no problem for him to send you buttons, zippers, sewing thread. You do not have to be ashamed, as everyone does it. It was a very cold winter, the coldest I can ever remember, and not having clothing makes it all the worse.

Dear Berta, you must ask Adolf about his illness, how is he managing? Who cooks for him? You must tell him that he should not eat carbohydrates. You must also tell him not to forget to do his injection every day.

Dear Berta, tell him not to forget me here. After all, it was his idea that I should only come after he got himself organized. He cannot just leave me here – I will perish away! Do not wait – write immediately! I will not live much longer.

Out of all our friends, only Herman Uko and the Zeni family are still around. I will be the last to leave.

Write to Adolf and tell him that once he sees to my visa, he should see that you also get one for you and the child. But maybe it is better you stay where you are now that there is this anti-Semite lurking in England, what is his name, Mos... something or other, but this Rumanian Antonescu fellow is no better. I just do not know where we can all go. Maybe this idea of joining the Zionists in Palestine is our only option.

You must write to Adolf everything I tell you, and ask him what is happening with the jewelry. Did that whore give it back to him yet?

Stay healthy and I bless you and the child a thousand times. I do not know if I will ever see her again.

I hope that you, Judith and your husband are granted a long life, and that dear God will protect Adolf and you from all evil.

Lots of love,
From your lonely Mama

* * *

A letter from Dina arrived a few days later:

Thursday, March 7, 1940
The International Language Club
202 Lewisham s.e.4 East London

Mr. Adolf Rochman,

In the last letter you wrote, I did not see any affirmation about the 56 pounds and 40 pence that you owe me.

So you are trying to blackmail me now. That is your new tactic of getting out of your obligations. You suddenly feel strong. This was not the way you talked last year in Leipzig, but if you

PETER PRESENTS ULTIMATUM TO DINA

think that you can move me by blackmailing me, you are totally wrong.

I will tell you one more thing: a man who considers himself to be civilized does not write or say things like that to an honorable woman. But you, like all the people of your race, appear to be civilized on the outside, but once you take off the mask we can all see your true colors.

That is beside the point. What I would like to make clear is that after writing what you did I have nothing to add. I do not want any contact with you, and would ask you not to make contact with me in the future.

I hope you can still remember as well as I do that you did not want me to interfere in the problem of how to get your mother out of Germany. I will respect that, but you must respect the fact that I am not interested in the matter, and do not tell me about it any more. Do not get me involved in this matter.

As for the blackmailing, I would like to make the point that I never acted in such a way towards you, as you remember! I never threatened you, so don't threaten me either. What's more, I do not have a reason to threaten you.

But as an honest woman, I am prepared to reach a compromise, and wait for some time with the debt that you owe me, if only not to go on with this exchange of letters any longer.

The best thing will be if we remain in contact through your cousin Herman, as he knows the details of the matter inside out. But I will not be in contact with him by phone or letter. I will talk to him on condition that you give me back all the letters I sent you. I also want you to give me back all the other things that I gave you in the last year: a necktie, socks and the pair of brown shoes. I brought those things when I came to visit you in Leeds. All this is my property, it does not belong to you, and if you will not give them back to me, I will put a charge against you for holding stolen property and entering this country illegally.

This is my first condition before I enter into any negotiations with you or your cousin,
Dina Thorn

Peter finished reading the letter, and with a heavy heart, placed it on the table. He was at a dead end with Dina. It was clear that he could not go to the police and press charges against her, since the jewelry was brought into the country illegally and was never declared. He didn't have a leg to stand on, and Dina was too clever to be intimidated by blackmailing.

Time was running out. In the following weeks, the newspapers came out with front-page articles on what was happening in Poland.

March 25, 1940

Jews are hunted down and shot in former Poland, as the Jewish community is preparing to celebrate their Purim Jewish holiday, which commemorates the victory of the Jewish People over an oppressor in Persia some 2,500 years ago. While sales of tickets in London for the film "Gone with the Wind" have reached a record of 10,000 pounds, the news coming from the Continent is grim.

From an unconfirmed source inside the German occupied zone of the former Poland, now renamed Generalgouvernment, news is coming out that the Gestapo special police units are rounding up Jews in the big cities, and hunting them down in the countryside. Once they are captured, they are either shot on the spot, or they are loaded into livestock rail wagons and shipped to concentration camps.

Peter could no longer sleep at night, his peace disturbed by tormenting visions of Lina being treated like an animal or sent to one of those concentration camps.

The news coming from the war front was no better.

Tuesday, April 9, 1940

Norway and Denmark yield to the Nazis:

Neutrals offer only slight resistance as Nazis occupy Oslo and Copenhagen:

The British Empire has a plan to lay mines in Norwegian territorial waters in order to stop the German shipping out iron ore from the ice-free port of Narvik.

As the British Royal Navy set about its task to lay mines in the North Sea yesterday, it was confronted by an unpleasant surprise. Sailing up from the south and heading for the Fjords were flotillas of German warships escorting troopships, apparently for a full-scale invasion of Norway.

Denmark has already been overrun with only a few shots from the Royal Guard. Last night, German warships appeared off the Norwegian capital, Oslo, and the capital came under fire from the German Battle cruiser "D.S. *Bluecher*" with its 280 mm Krupp guns. Later in the night, the battle cruiser was sunk with a loss of 1,000 men, but this did not stop the Germans sending in airborne troops who eventually landed at the city airport and conquered the city.

King Haakon and his government have escaped, and are in hiding.

The Wehrmacht succeeded in getting seven divisions ashore within 48 hours, with the help of the pro-Nazi party in Norway led by Major Vidkun Quisling. There is no doubt that the British Royal Navy will have to react to this, as the British government can not allow the occupation of an allied country by German troops, posing a direct threat to the Empire's shipping.

Monday, April 22, 1940

The Chief Rabbi of England blesses the Jewish community for the Passover holidays:

This Passover feast that we are celebrating tonight – which, more than anything, should symbolize our exit from bondage to freedom – comes at a time when a fundamental part of our people are in a more modern sort of bondage.

Our people are enslaved under the boot of the Nazi animal, a sort of bondage we have never known before. As the Chief Rabbi of Great Britain, I ask each and every family not only to open your houses in order to sit one of our brothers that have come out of this most terrifying bondage among yourselves at the Passover table, but also to open your hearts and pray for those people who have been left behind. Our tradition is to keep our door open and to fill a glass of wine for Prophet Elijah. This year, we must hope that with him he will also bring one of our brethren who are still in bondage. This extra glass of wine should be on our table for someone we know who is still in slavery. As we look at this extra glass of wine, which we traditionally put on the Passover table for Prophet Elijah, each and every one of us, young and old, man and woman, child and parent, should ask himself the following question: Have we done all we can to help get this person we

PETER PRESENTS ULTIMATUM TO DINA

know out of slavery, from under the heel of the worst enemy that we the Jewish people have known in the last 3,000 years of our history?
Rabbi Joseph Hertz, Chief Rabbi of England

As the entire extended Schmulewitsch family, numbering over 15, and their 10 refugee guests from the Kindertransport, were sitting round the Passover table in Middlesbrough, Herman read the Rabbi's communal message out loud. Pointing at the full glass he asked, have we, each and every one of us, done all we can? There was silence in the room.

Tuesday, April 30, 1940

The Wehrmacht siege of Britain is tightened:
British troops being sent to try and force the Wehrmacht out of Norway are faced with heavy snow.
At the start of the war, The Royal Navy had great success on the sea front. By April, it managed to sink ten German destroyers for the loss of two British ones. The Navy also managed to get King Haakon of Norway and his cabinet out on board the cruiser "SS *Glasgow*." The Wehrmacht held its ground and the British-French Army expedition retreated with heavy losses.

With all the delays and power cuts, it took Peter over a day return to Manchester from Middlesbrough, after spending Passover with his Aunt and Uncle. Peter felt the familiar rush of relief as he left his Aunt, Uncle and cousins, and returned to his life in Manchester. Upon his return, he found a letter waiting for him from one of his lady friends, Raina.

Monday, April 15, 1940
Leeds

My dearest Peter,

    I don't know how to express my thanks to you for such a lovely letter and also the way you value my friendship, which, I hope, will always remain between us.

    Now that Jerry has been recruited, it is so quiet in the house and I do not have to sit in the pub to read your letters. They say that the situation in the front is not working in our favor. With all this naval war going on in Norway, it seems that the German Army is stronger than we thought. Jerry came home two days ago (he left today) and said that his regiment will be sent to Newcastle to prepare for a landing in Denmark.

    I have always told you, dear, that I will gladly do whatever I can for you. I hope that by now you have had a few lines from this solicitor, Mr. Graham, about your mother. How is she coping with the whole situation? It must be so difficult for her over there all alone.

    I was very sorry to hear from you that you lost your job, but never mind. Up to now, you have always managed to find your way around – you are like a cat that always lands on her feet. I am quite sure, with your personality and ability, you will never be without a job for long.

    The weather is much warmer now, and we can almost feel spring in the air, but we had more snow this winter than the last 50 years put together.

    Lotti was up here last week, she looks well, and she said she hopes to meet you when you come up north for the Jewish Passover celebration. She no doubt has a soft spot for you.

    If you want to write to me, it is always better to send the letters to Fay's house; I never know when Jerry will suddenly come home. I would not like him to find your letters in the mailbox.

Keep well and take care of yourself,
From your affectionate friend,
Raina

P.S. Peter, please always tear my letters up, you never know who will see them.

Friday, May 10, 1940

Neville Chamberlain hands over to Churchill:

Winston Churchill is now Prime Minster, but is it too late?

Neville Chamberlain, totally discredited, resigned after three days of hesitation.

In his opening speech in Parliament, Churchill said, among other things, "I have nothing to offer you but blood, toil, tears and sweat."

Tuesday, May 14, 1940

Gerard Winkleman, Commander-in-Chief of the Dutch armies, orders Dutch forces to stop fighting.

The Wehrmacht has completed the conquest of the Low Countries at the cost of 10,000 German soldiers.

The final Wehrmacht assault on the Low Countries started this morning. The 11th German army, which is under the command of Field Marshal Albert Kesselring, has scored great military successes in Holland. The Wehrmacht invasion of Holland and Belgium began two weeks ago on the 1st of May.

The relative ease with which Holland was occupied came as a result of the combined chiefs-of-staff of the Dutch Army ignoring numerous warnings and intelligence reports indicating the presence of 28 Wehrmacht divisions assembled across the eastern borders of Holland and Belgium.

The Belgian and Dutch armies were caught unprepared. This situation came about for the usual reason that they had refused to undertake resolute defense measures, coordinated with the Allies, for fear of offending the Germans.

Lord Grotto, the British Commander-in-Chief of the Territorial Army in France was too late in moving his troops north through the Ardennes. The Wehrmacht, once more, with its blitzkrieg tactic, had occupied the Low Countries before the British-French contingent had the chance to get itself on the move.

It seems the lesson of Poland was not learned.

At the same time in Britain, there was total panic as a rumor was spread. One of the Dutch generals, who came over the continent with Queen Wilhelmina of Holland, talked about a German woman spy among the Dutch people. It was a woman who worked as a nanny for a Dutch family in The Hague, who led Kesselring's 11th Army into Holland. At the same time as she was leading the army, she was stopping the Dutch army from executing its substitute plan of opening the dykes with the hope that the flooding would keep Kesselring's army at bay.

In light of this rumor, authorities in Great Britain have decided to operate against any Austrian, German or Czechoslovakian newcomer to England in order to assure that he is not operating as a fifth columnist, helping German armies to invade Britain.

Now that the siege of Britain is closing, do we

have any hope of stopping the Wehrmacht from invading the British Isles?

Friday, May 31, 1940

British troops are fighting a desperate rear-guard action on the French coast around Dunkirk, as German troops finally move in and surround them.

Yesterday the first men of the British Expeditionary Force arrived home after being picked up off the beaches. They told how they had been bombed and machine-gunned from the air as they waded out to the ships.

But dispatches from the French coast say the Allied troops are "still fighting incessantly and in good order" and covering the embarkation of their comrades.

The British and French have been driven back to the coast by a large German force of 750,000 men from the 7th and the 6th armies, under the joint command of Marshal Von Manstein and General Erwin Rommel.

The Allies have fought over every inch of territory, only giving up towns like Calais and Boulogne after terrific fights, aided by shelling from the British warships offshore.

For days, crowds have gathered along the southeast coast of Britain to catch a sight of the bombings, smoke and fire, which can easily be seen and heard from across the Channel.

Tuesday, June 4, 1940

Allied forces evacuated from Dunkirk:

Operation Dynamo, the great evacuation of Dunkirk, is complete.

335,000 rescued, Churchill reports.

Tonight men were still coming ashore from the huge fleet of destroyers, ferries, fishing vessels and even river cruisers, which have delivered the British Expeditionary Force, along with vast numbers of French and Belgian troops, from the prospect of total annihilation.

The beaches are now littered with decaying bodies and the twisted shapes of hundreds of battered vehicles. Weapons of all kinds are scattered beside the coastal lane along which the retreating army marched, still in disciplined style, despite the "junked" bombers screaming out of the sky overhead.

Friday, June 14, 1940

Nazis take Paris:

Wehrmacht parade up the Champs Elysees and on June 22, French sign an armistice with Germany.

Britain is left alone to face the German threat.

Chapter Nineteen

Berta Desperate to Leave Rumania

Friday, June 28, 1940
From correspondents in the USSR

RUMANIA: SOVIET TROOPS INVADE THE Rumanian provinces of Bukovina and Bessarabia.

It was reported today that the 3rd Russian Army, supported by the 7th Red Armored brigade, which included airborne troops and air support from Ilyushin's two bombers, crossed the border into Rumania today.

It was said that by the end of the day, King Carol of Rumania had agreed to Stalin's terms and signed over Bessarabia and Northern Bukovina to the Red Army.

Our political commentator adds that the Russians had become increasingly worried, especially since May 1940, about Rumania's "growing subservience" to Germany. Both Antonescu and King Carol, who had for a time tried to sit on the fence, are now leaning heavily over to the German side. It was in effect an ultimatum to the Rumanian Government demanding of Antonescu an "immediate solution" to the question concerning the return of Bessarabia to the USSR and the transfer of Northern Bukovina to the Ukraine. Davidescu, the Rumanian Ambassador to Moscow, declared his government's readiness to enter into negotiations with the Soviet government on the following day.

Germany, at this point, does not want to worsen her relations with the USSR, on which she depends for oil, grains, corn, steel, and other raw materials, needed urgently for the Wehrmacht's continued occupation of France, Holland, Poland and Austria.

However, there is much concern within the Reich's chancellery that the occupation of Bessarabia and the Rumanian coast of the Black Sea, by the Red Army, will threaten the Ploesti oil fields in the Walachel Plains of Southern Rumania. These oil fields are no more than an hour's flight from the town of Cetata Alba, the main airstrip in Bessarabia. This new development will create a situation whereby the Reich will have total dependence on the Soviets for oil. There is also concern for the former German citizens who had migrated to these territories in the last 50 years, who are supporters of the Nazi Party, and who would not want to live under Communist rule.

As the Wehrmacht are conquering more and more territories in the West, and Italy's conquest of Southern France, Albania and North Africa continues, the USSR does not want to be the only regional power that did not take advantage of the chaotic situation. Most Soviet commentators, including Stalin, think that now that France has surrendered, and Britain is on its

BERTA DESPERATE TO LEAVE RUMANIA

last resources, Hitler and Mussolini will start signing peace treaties with these countries, forcing them to his (their) terms. If this happens in the next few months, Stalin, as the president of the USSR, would want to sit at the negotiating table as an equal partner with Germany and Italy. This is the reason the Soviet Union is trying to grab as much territory as possible before such an event. The same sort of logic was behind the occupation of Lithuania, Latvia, Estonia, Finland and Bessarabia. All this could be done with as little risk as possible. The risk Stalin was most concerned about was a real military confrontation with the Wehrmacht. It is clear to Stalin that after the officers' military purges two years ago, the Red Army is no match for the well-trained and equipped German army, although it may be that by taking over Bessarabia with its port town of Cetata Alba, Stalin did step on Hitler's toes.

Rumor has it that Sir Stafford Cripps, the British Ambassador to Moscow, warned Stalin of Hitler's plans to instruct his Chief-of-Staff Joachim Von Keitel to prepare the Wehrmacht for an invasion of Russia in May next year.

Stalin chose the best time for his army to bring into being the first step in his desired plan since he came to power some 16 years ago, before he had a plan to turn the Black Sea into a Red Sea. What he hoped to achieve by doing so was to open a Russian gateway to the warm waters of the Mediterranean. It is clear this time around that Stalin has learned from his mistake in last year's miserable defeat in Finland.

In order to occupy Eastern Rumania with a badly trained and poorly equipped army, Stalin chose to mobilize the Red Army in the summer. By doing so, he hoped to take advantage of Germany's efforts to solidify its occupation of France, the Low Countries and Poland. Stalin also thought he could take advantage of the fact that General Rundstedt was trying to reorganize the 4th German army after the loss of 38,000 men, who were wounded, killed, or lost in action in France. Stalin was also aware of the fact that Field Marshal Kleist's 12th army had major losses during the battles in France and would be out of action for some time. What did worry the Russian generals was the reaction from Great Britain, but they know that the Empire is still licking its wounds after the Dunkirk disaster, a disaster that only occurred two weeks earlier. At the same time, Britain is doing its best to deal with a mass air attack by the Luftwaffe, the likes of which the British Isles have never experienced before, air raids that are aimed at the major industrial and population centers in Britain and Scotland.

Translated from Russian:
Monday, July 1, 1940
by Comrade Vladmir Chichanco,
our military correspondent

Our victories as the 3rd Army enter Bessarabia:
The 3rd Red Army is known for its glorious victory in Lithuania, Latvia and Estonia, where they helped the workers, teachers and farmers in these three countries, forcing their bourgeois governments to allow their working people to enjoy the great advantages of Communism.
This morning, at 3:00 A.M., led by Comrade Major General P.A. Ivan, this army crossed the River

Dnjestr south of Odessa into the Rumanian province of Bessarabia and took over the port town of Cetata Alba on the Black Sea.

Thousands of people came out to welcome our brave soldiers, who are all sons, husbands and brothers of farmers, factory workers and teachers. Among the welcomers were farm hands, stevedores, coal miners and the working people of this small port town on the Dnjestr River. They all showered the sons and daughters of our great revolution with flowers, thanking the soldiers for freeing them from the yoke of Capitalism, Fascism, and the corrupt Imperial regime of King Carol the First and his Fascist dictator, Prime Minister Ion Antonescu.

After long and fruitless negotiations with the Imperial Fascist Kingdom of Rumania, we, the peace-loving Soviets of the workers in the USSR, did not see any other way to repatriate these territories that were torn out of our beloved country by the Imperial nations, as part of the criminal act of the Versailles Treaty in 1920 after the Great War.

Our great leader Stalin could not stand idle in the face of the crying and the yearning of all the workers in these provinces to join their brothers across the border and be part of the great Soviet of the working people, which will give its people the opportunity to live under an enlightened Communist rule, and will bring the revolution to all corners of the word.

Translated from German:
Sunday, July 28, 1940
Northumberland St., Manchester

Dear Berta,

I had to cry when I read Mama's letter that you sent. I feel so helpless in trying to do whatever I can to get a visa for Mama. Uncle David is just not interested and the Schmulewitsches are doing whatever they can to avoid the subject.

Now with the war getting closer, I mean with the fall of France, no one is interested in anything else, but the big question is – will Britain survive? Everyone is running around here like headless chickens. No one will give me the time of day to talk about Mama's case.

Now that we are starting to feel the war more and more, there is enormous pressure being put on us not to be seen in the streets, not to talk German, to dress like the English, to talk like the English, and to behave like the English.

We are also restricted in our movements – we must report to the police once a day to fill in a form saying where we have been since the last visit, and with whom we met. I am starting to feel like I did back home, before I left.

Do you remember me telling you about this English girl Anne? Her brother was with the British Expeditionary Force in France and was killed last week, while trying to get on a boat in Dunkirk. Her parents said that they do not want me to meet with her any longer because I am German, as if I had anything to do with it.

We can no longer show our faces outside. We do not go to the dance halls; we do not go to the cinema. Hooligans, screaming all sorts of anti-Semitic and anti-German slogans, have now attacked the hostel that I am living in for the third time. It is really not the time to go and talk to people about a visa for Mama.

I was thinking that maybe I should move to Australia or New Zealand. I suppose the Devil will arrive there with his armies, sooner or later, but one can only hope that the Yellows (Japanese) or the Bolsheviks will get there before him. At least they are not as anti-Semitic as he is. But now, with the bombing of the Luftwaffe all day and every day, there are no boats going over there any longer. Even if there were, from where would I get the money for a ticket and visa to go there?

Do you think that it is safe where you are? I guess that every place is dangerous for the Jews. In the letters I get from my friends from the swim team in Palestine, they say that in spite of the tension between the Jewish people and the British (it is even worse with the Arabs), there is no anti-Semitism.

In this little town that they live in which is not far from Beirut, he says they work very hard, and it is very hot even in winter. They have organized a defense system and got a van and some rifles from the British Police. Every night, they go on patrol to protect the town.

In his letter he said that some of them have gone on special training missions to learn guerrilla warfare tactics from some British officers. It seems to me that Palestine is the only place where we can lift our heads without having to apologize to anyone for being Jewish. Now I am really sorry that I did not go with the Bar Kochba swim team to Palestine for the Maccabi Games in 1935, and stay there like Margolis, Herman and Hecht did.

I think that by now I would have had my own house, and I could have brought Mama out there with no problem. But there is no use crying over spilt milk. It never sounded like the Promised Land to me, even after Krystalnacht. But now I see how wrong I was.

In the letters I get from people back home who are now living in Palestine, I get the general impression that life is hard but good. There is no anti-Semitism and relations with the British are quite good. Do you still remember the "Blue Box" which we had at home? I mean the one that was on the window facing the street. What I remember is that we used to put money in it to buy land in Palestine. I always have in my mind the picture of someone plowing the land, and people walking around with camels – that was my image of Palestine, a place I could not associate with. Living there seemed to me more like going to the cinema. I see now that they were right. I have made a promise to myself that if and when I ever get out of this thing, and when this war is over, I will go and live there.

How are things with you? The newspapers here write that the Bolsheviks, led by this murderer Stalin, are talking about taking over the whole of the Black Sea, claiming it was a part of Russia before the Great War, and now they want it back. If they do come, I hope the Rumanian Army will give them a bloody nose like the Finnish people did last year.

How are things on the farm? Can you still sell the meat and wine? Who is taking care of it when Siyoma goes to the work camps?

Here, things are bad; they are evacuating the children, most of them to the villages around Manchester, some of them even to America. That is also dangerous – most of these boats do not get through and are attacked by the German U-Boats.

Do write as often as you can, we must keep in contact somehow, as long as it is possible. I am sure that one way or the other, we will get Mama out.

Maybe one day we will all meet up in Palestine.

Love

Adolf

* * *

A reply from Berta was long in coming, and did not arrive until nearly two months later.

Translated from German:
Sunday, September 1, 1940
Trayan St. 50, Cetata Alba, Rumania

Dear Adolf,

I am sorry it took me so long to answer your last letter, but there have been such big upheavals here in the last month that I just did not get around to it.

From your letter, I get the impression that you are not taking care of your health. It seems to me that you are not looking after yourself. Adolf, you must stick to your diet and not eat anything that has any sugar in it. If you do not feel well you must go to the doctor right away, you cannot neglect yourself. I think you forget from time to time that you are alone in a strange country, and there is no one there who can look after you.

I got another letter from Mama the other day. Now with the Bolshevik's occupation, letters are just not coming through (I will try to send it on to you). Mama says in her letter that she is in complete despair; she lost her job in the garbage sorting, and therefore is on the list of those who will be deported to the East with the next transport. That was six or seven weeks ago – maybe she has already been sent, there is simply no way I can find out from here.

You would not believe who I met the other day. Do you remember Hans, the son of Franke, the one who had the typewriter shop on Markt Strasse; you know the little place on the corner? Maybe you remember, he was studying Russian at the time, and came to practice his Russian by talking to Siyoma right after we got married and were still living with Mama.

I was so astonished to see him here with the Red Army, I nearly fell on my face. Apparently he was deported with the rest of the Polish Jews in October two years ago, just before the hooligans burned the Brody Synagogue. When the war started, he managed to get to the Russian zone. Now he is an officer with the Red Army, working as a translator. Who would believe such a thing? He has not heard from his parents or brother since he escaped, but he was told that they were in the Lodz Ghetto.

I asked him if he had seen Mama in one of the places where they bring the stateless Jews from Leipzig. He said that if she was put on one of those cattle trains, and transported to Poland, there is no way she could still be living. He told me that only the young, and those who manage to escape, survive this week-long voyage, with no food, water or sanitation.

I do understand what you say about the visa; what I do not understand is why the application is stuck.

I must tell you about these Bolshevik soldiers that came, so to speak, to free us from Rumanian imperialism – calling them animals would be a compliment. From the first day of their arrival, the soldiers stormed into any random house and forced people at gunpoint to bring flowers and go out to the main street by the Castle. Youngsters in police uniforms forced those that came to the town center to cheer the troops that had just entered the town (these troops were late as they were busy looting the farmers in Zataka on their way from the river to here).

Most of these soldiers come from the inner regions of Russia. They are what we call "*Muziks*" (peasants). The only thing they know how to do is loot, rape and get drunk. They are always drunk. Once they found out that we had the wine cellar, they confiscated it "for the war effort." What war are they talking about – they have not yet had one day of fighting. The day they came, our "glorious" Rumanian army just ran away and left us to live with them.

They just go into the houses whenever they feel like it, and take whatever they can find. The worst is if there are young girls or women around when they happen to be there, they will just rape them right there and then, on the spot, and take turns as the others are looting the house. This happened to Larissa's mother, and since then she has been a sick person. She tried to go and complain, and the officer told her she is a capitalist pig, and she should know better. She is pregnant now, and God only knows what will happen with that.

Ten of them came to live with us, and took over the house, and turned it into a brothel, with women coming and going at all hours of the day and night. We had to move into the servants' quarters outside and we are only allowed into the house to clean up the mess they make every night. That is not the worst of it. When Siyoma showed them his membership card from the Rumanian Communist Party and told them that he had helped the working people all his life, the officer told him that he hates Communists, "They took all we had from my family," he said. He made it clear to Siyoma that if he does not stop talking about communism and socialism, he would shoot him.

One thing I am sure of is that German soldiers would never behave in such a way. We can no longer go to the beach and the harbor. They have been declared military zones and since then have been completely closed to anyone from the town. We cannot even send letters, so I will have to give this letter to a friend who is going to Jasi and she will try and send it from there.

This week I received a letter that angered me very much. It was from Regina's son. You most probably do not know who Regina is. She is Papa's daughter from his first marriage, who left with her mother and brother to go and live in Bonn or Frankfurt after the divorce. I only met her once, when Papa was on his deathbed – that was before I met Siyoma. I was under the impression that she came to see if they were mentioned in Papa's will. What I do very clearly remember from her was a very vulgar answer to a letter that Papa sent her husband, something to do with a business proposal that he offered him. Whatever it was, he regretted it, which is okay but there was no reason to answer in such a way, blaming him for forgetting and neglecting his children and wife from his first marriage.

In any case, this letter arrived here about a week ago from someone I had never heard of before. So he explains who he is and tells me that he and his parents were deported to Poland since their grandmother (Papa's former wife) came from Warsaw. They are currently living in Suiatyn Staniscawow, which is in the Russian zone of Galicia. He asked me in the letter if I could arrange to get a visa for him and his parents to enter Rumania. He also tells me that a religious man from Manchester took in his sister Gizella. He writes about this man who had come to Germany as a soldier with the British occupational force in 1920 after the Great War and was invited by his father to religious services during the year or so that he was stationed in Bonn.

A short time before they were deported, his father wrote to this person, and asked him if he could take his daughter in, so she would not have to go with them to Poland. He agreed, but until all the papers were ready, she stayed in hiding with a German family. So she is now in England and they are in Galicia.

In any case she is now living in Manchester, working as a housemaid, and is doing everything she can to get her family out. I wrote to her, and gave her your address, so if you get a letter from her, you will know who she is.

What angered me most about the letter was that not only did he refer to me as Lieber Tante Berta, but also wrote to me in the "Du" form, as if I am a friend of his.

Dear Adolf, is there any way that you can arrange for us to get a visa to enter England? Do you think Siyoma could work there as an agronomist? After all, that is what he studied, and he has a lot of experience in this field, or maybe he can work in an office? He can speak Russian, Rumanian, German and even some English.

If there were any way that we could get a visa to Palestine, we would leave tomorrow. I am sure that he would find work there in no time; they are looking for people like him over there, but I think that we have missed the boat by now. It is ironic that when we had the opportunity to go over there, and they were prepared to lay down the red carpet for us, we did not want to go. Now that we are willing, there is no way to get there.

My mother-in-law is very sick and this thing with the Bolsheviks is only making things worse for her. Once she has gone, they will take everything away from us.

Siyoma told me that in the Communist Bolshevik system, there is no inheritance and all capitalist property must be given over to the Party or the State. Then we will all live or die in poverty.

Judith cannot go to school any longer, as she is the daughter of a capitalist who exploited the workers. Only they can send their children to school. It is just a pity that each day that we stay here is a lost day.

Siyoma's aunt from Zurich sent 200 grams of butter to Mama, but even if she is still alive, she will be so starved that a bit of butter will no longer help her.

I am working on the farm from morning till night with Siyoma and Judith. We are no longer allowed to employ workers; somehow that also runs counter to the Socialist philosophy. We barely have enough to keep us alive, as we must also provide for these hooligan soldiers that are in the house.

In terms of clothes for Judith, there is nothing to talk about – she is nearly 13 now and is growing so fast that the clothes from last year no longer fit her. God knows what will happen, I only fear that our end will be worse than Regina's.

The only thing I beg of you once more is to do something to save Mama. As for myself, I do not want anything from you or the Schmulewitsches. How is Dora? Is she married by now? How do young men and women get together in England? How do they meet?

I love getting your letters – tell me as much as you can, everything is so interesting.

Siyoma and Judith send their love,
Berta

* * *

In the envelope there was another short letter from Judith:

Dear Uncle Adolf,

It has been a long time since I have seen you, and I can hardly remember what you look like.

My German is not so good anymore. I hope you will understand what I am writing.

Life is not as good as it was. We are having a difficult time, but we hope that it will get better.

Mama is saying that maybe we will all come to England after Oma arrives there. Why are you not helping Oma to come and live with you in England?

I can no longer play with Larissa as I am a capitalist and she is a worker. When will all this be over?

Love,
Judith

Chapter Twenty

Zelig Writes in Protest Against Mosley

*An internal paper published in June 1940,
from the Ministry of Home Security*

HENRI WINKLEMAN, COMMANDER-IN-CHIEF of the Dutch armed forces (the General who was repatriated to the British Islands after the occupation of Holland two months ago), informed the MI6 that it was a German housemaid working in the city of Arnheim on the former German-Dutch border who helped the swift German victory in Holland.

A well-informed source reports that the girl, acting as a fifth Columnist for the German Upwehr, was the one who let the 17th German Army into Holland. At the same time, the Dutch High Command resolved to abandon the contingency plan of opening all dikes to help flood the Low Countries, a plan that would have held the German army at bay.

The same danger now faces the U.K., after it has

taken in some 55,000 refugees from Austria, Germany, Italy and Czechoslovakia, who are all considered enemy nationals.

His Majesty's government does not see any choice but to arrest and hold in internment all those who came to this country in the last ten years from one of the above countries on the continent.

Since not every person from the new arrivals is a potential spy or fifth Columnist, the Minister of Home Security, Sir Herbert Morrison, with the help of the MI5, has decided to divide the above-mentioned newcomers into four categories, A, B, C and D.

Category A: Considered to be the highest risk to His Majesty's Kingdom, these people are considered Fascists or Nazi supporters in their former countries. Among them is the highest potential number of spies. They will be sent to punishment colonies in the cities of Hay and Tatura in New South Wales (Australia).

Category B: Most of them are business people and intellectuals, were government workers in their former countries, and are less of a security risk. Will be sent to internment camps in the Isle of Man.

Category C: Will be redirected to inner cities, as far away as possible from harbors, ports, coal mines and industrial areas.

Category D: The least risk to His Majesty's Kingdom. These immigrants will be allowed to live anywhere, as long it is not near military installations. They will have to register with the police once a day.

Doctors, dentists and chemists will be exempt.

In order to facilitate the registration and the

categorization, a special committee has been appointed to categorize the people. This committee will be sitting in court at Northolt Park Racecourse, Butlin's holiday camp in Kent, and Kitchener camp in Dover.

Monday, August 26, 1940
The Black Code
Written by Oswald Mosley
leader of the British Union of Fascists

It is estimated that some three or four million refugees have come to Britain in the last five or six years, most of them from countries like Germany, Austria and Czechoslovakia.

It has been quite clearly established that they were sent here as part of the Bolshevik conspiracy to export the Red Revolution around the world by flooding our country with Communists.

They have no shame in taking advantage of our welfare system. At the same time they take work away from our people. Courting with our women while our boys are fighting on the front, they are flooding our beaches, cinemas and dance halls. But that is not the worst of it. Some of them have been known to spy for Germany and Italy. More than once, groups of them were caught at night, showing Luftwaffe aircrafts where to drop their bombs around the industrial centers in the Black Country. These spies, disguised as nuns, roam around the countryside and in the cities. They have been seen with flashlights indicating to the Luftwaffe pilots where to drop their bombs in order to cause the most disruption.

None of Them Were Heroes

Letter to the Editor
Monday, September 2, 1940

I would like to refer to an article that appeared last week in the new bulletin about The Black Code.

As for "three or four million refugees [who] have come to Britain in the last five or six years," it is worth pointing out that the correct number is 55,000. Allow me to add that most of them, if not all, do not live in any way off British welfare institutions, but are hard-working people who put in 16 to 20 hours of work daily. And they are mostly holding two or three jobs, trying to cover for those that have been recruited to the armed forces. Most of them are doing menial jobs that the British worker shies away from.

As for the preposterous idea that some of them go out into their backyard in order to show Luftwaffe pilots where to drop their bombs, I would like to point out to Mr. Mosley that most of those 55,000 mentioned, men and women (Mr. Mosley did not specify if those disguised nuns mentioned in the article are men or women), are Jewish refugees. I would also like to point out that very few of them, if any, are Communists. The majority are business people, doctors, technicians and respectable citizens, who are willing to take any job offered so they can help Britain at this difficult moment. These are people who have escaped from Germany, Austria and Czechoslovakia because of persecution of the worst kind in the history of man. There is no way that they will want to support these Fascist countries that they have escaped from.

All they want to do is join the British fighting forces, which many of them have done already, in the capacity of foot soldiers, translators and radio operators. They do this in order to fight the Nazi animal and help wipe this menace off the face of the earth.

On the other hand, I do understand that you, Mr. Mosley, with your party the British Union of Fascists, are a big supporter of the Nazi party in Germany. I would suggest that the Home Office put you and your people in internment camps, since the real internal threat to Great Britain comes from you and people like you.

Max Schmulewitsch, Guisborough

Translated from German:
Saturday, September 5, 1940
Northumberland St., Manchester

Dear Lotti,

Thank you for your last letter. It is not that I did not want to answer, but with the constant air raids, it is just impossible to get enough time to sit down for half an hour between coming and going from the air raid shelter. These Focke-Wulf bombers are trying to hit the Mersey dock, which is just around the corner from where we live. (I am not sure if they are trying to hit the locomotive factory, which is near there, or the docks themselves, but whatever it is, they are not very successful.) Instead of hitting their targets, they mainly hit the surrounding buildings, so we are in and out of the shelters five or six times a night. One thing I can tell you for sure, I did not see anyone with a flashlight directing them where to aim their bombs, and if there is someone like that, he is doing a very bad job of it. Maybe the nun's habits that they are wearing are stopping them from directing the flashlight to the right spot.

I was called in the other day to come and appear before the

tribunal, so they could decide if I am an enemy alien or not. You have never met a less dexterous group of clowns than those four men sitting on the other side of the table.

I knew I should have come with someone whose English is better than mine, but everything was so sudden that I did not have the chance to get hold of Joachim, my friend from Berlin, the one that got out before the Pogrom. It wasn't that I had any problem understanding what they were asking, but I could not find the right words to answer their questions. I still do not understand why they cannot bring German-speaking people to the tribunals, or at least have a translator on hand. After all, with our scant knowledge of English and their inability to understand German, it was like a conversation among the deaf.

In any case, I waited six hours in line, with people coming in and out. Each one gave advice to the next on what to say and how to behave. You could see right away, by the expressions on people's faces, which category they were put in.

So I went in, and the first question they ask me is, was I sent over from Germany to direct German aircrafts? So I ask you, if this were the case, do they really think I would come out right away and admit that I am a spy, and I simply forgot to inform the MI5? I did not say this, as it would have been too difficult for me in English. So then, they ask me to prove that I am not a spy. It was at this point that I started to despair — how could I possibly prove that I am not a spy? Even if I spoke perfect English, I would have been unable to respond. Then they said to me that I was a Hitler supporter in Leipzig because my name is "Adolf," and that I changed my name to Peter in England to cover it up.

The whole thing took no more than 10 minutes, and I was placed into category B. I was told to go home and wait till they contact me and tell me what to do. If they really suspected that I am a spy and a Hitler lover, they should have put me in category A. If not, they should have let me go. But I suspect that they have no idea of what they are doing, and decide at random who should be placed into which category. They probably devised a system whereby the first three that come in are B's, then two A's and five C's, and so on.

In any case, Friedrich, the chemistry professor I told you about, who was thrown out of Hanover University because he was Jewish, fell into category A, and was taken right away to be imprisoned in Strangeways (prison). He is now waiting for a ship that will take him, together with all the other A's, to a prison colony in Australia. Considering that my English is not so good, I did not come out too bad.

There is no news from my mother. The only information I get comes from other Leipzigers here in Manchester. They say that the Gestapo has started deporting the stateless to a place on the current border between the old Poland and the new Russia.

The Thorn whore is holding tight, and will not give over the jewelry or the money, insisting I must marry her first. If I would have had that money, I could have got Mama out long ago.

I hope to hear from you soon,
Love Adolf

Translated from German:
Sunday, September 15, 1940
British Dolls & Toys LTD
Therpe St., W. Hartlepool, Tel 6277
Manager Carol Katz (German)

Dear Adolf,
You did not have much luck. I see that the tribunal had decided that you are an enemy alien. But do not worry, the sun will shine once more. I see the letter from Bellow did not help much. He must have given out hundreds of these letters, and they just do not take any notice of them.

Dear Adolf, why do you always write to me at the last minute? If you want us to do things for you, you must tell me in advance. I only got the letter today when I was at my English lesson with Miss Bread. Every Friday, I go to her for a lesson. I was at home today and your letter was waiting for me. If I had not come, or if it would have come late, I would have only got it next Friday. I must say that I have lost my will to write to you, since you never answer my letters.

I was glad to hear that you were not imprisoned. Have you heard from your friend Miabrow? Mrs. Sholmon, your former landlady in Chapeltown, had to go before the tribunal, despite the fact that she came over here right after the Great War, and has a son in the 8th army in Egypt. They decided, though, that she is an enemy alien, and she was put into Category B. She was sent last week to the Isle of Man. I know that is small comfort to you. She made the same mistake that you did; she decided her English was good enough and she could explain her case without a translator. I told her to go with Hans, your friend from Dresden who worked with you at Bellows. He has been here for four or five years and his English is quite good. He managed with no problem to get himself into category D. She told me that she was not prepared to appear in front of the tribunal with an Ostjuden who was a Communist, as they could think that she is one of them. I did not know if she meant one of the Communists or one of the Ostjuden. Anyway, the outcome was that she fell into category B. If she had not have been so arrogant like some of those Bonn people, she could have easily fallen into category C or even D.

If I were you, I would not end my relationship with the Guisborough crowd, I would write to them in a more diplomatic way. Maybe even phone them. They say that the lines by the phone boxes in the post office are much shorter now. I guess it is because people are afraid to go too far from the air raid shelters.

I must stop here; I can hear the Dornier fighter planes coming over, I am sure the sirens will go off any minute.

Love Lotti

* * *

To his great surprise, Peter received a letter from his step-niece, Gizella, who had moved to Manchester.

Translated from German:
Sunday, September 15, 1940

Dear Uncle Adolf,

You will most probably be surprised to receive this letter from me. I received a postcard from your sister Berta living in Rumania, now under Russian occupation. In her letter she told me that she has a brother living in Manchester. When I heard that, I nearly fell off my chair.

My name is Gizella and I am the daughter of your stepsister from your father's first marriage i.e., your father is my grandfather.

I know the two families have never met; Oma used to say that Opa's new wife did not want him to meet with his former family. Somehow over the years, the contact was lost. We were brought up with the vague awareness that there was some family connection in Leipzig, but Oma never encouraged us to follow up with it.

I know that after the separation, Oma went back to Warsaw. That is where my mother Regina was born some years before in 1894. Oma came from Leipzig to Warsaw to see if she could get your father to come back home to Germany. She reminded him that he had left her there with two children and no money. She had no success. By the time she got to Poland, he had left and had gone to live in Switzerland.

Sometime at the beginning of the century, she came back to Germany and settled in Bonn with my mother and my Uncle

Joachim. She worked as a housemaid for a Jewish furrier, who she met in Leipzig, before the long search for your father. Rumor has it that it was more than work that made your father leave.

My father, who is a furrier, met my mother through this person, and they got married just after the Great War. My parents were forced to leave to Poland in October, when they deported all the Polish people out of Germany, but as I was stateless, they could not deport me.

Coming from a very Orthodox family, I was shocked to see how free life is in Manchester among Jews, even among this Orthodox family that are my guarantors.

I did not know anything about your father before I got the postcard from your sister. For that matter, I did not even dream that I had a step-uncle or step-aunt. We always thought that this Leipzig family had more to do with my grandmother's generation.

My father made a good living as a furrier. Most of his life, he volunteered to be the *Gabbai* (the synagogue's administrator and caretaker) in the Beth Shalom Synagogue in Bonn. In this capacity, he met with various English Jewish soldiers, who came with the occupational British Force after the Great War, and he would often invite some of them for Friday night meals at home.

There was a Mr. Rosenzwieg, who he still maintains contact with over the years. You know, Rosh Hashana and Yom Kippur greetings and so on. He wrote to him, asking him if he would be prepared to be my guarantor. If so, he would send me over to England, as I could not go with them to Poland. Till all the papers were ready, which took over six months, I lived with a German Communist family that protected me from the hooligans.

In any case, to cut a long story short, I am here now, and I would like to meet with you, as you are the only family I have. As tomorrow is Saturday, I will come over to see you on the 4:40 bus from Didsbury. I would be happy to find you in.

Looking forward to meeting you face to face,
Gizella

P.S. By the way, did you have to appear in front of the tribunal? It took me a long time to convince them that I am not a Communist; they did not like that fact that I lived with a Communist family in Bonn.

Chapter Twenty-One

Max Detained in Refugee Prison Camp in Isle of Man

Thursday, 17 April, 1941

THE BRAVE RESISTANCE OF OUR brothers-in-arms, most of them members of the Socialist People's Party in Yugoslavia, has been crushed by German armor striking from Hungary, Rumania, Bulgaria and Germany.

German troops freed by the collapse of Yugoslavia are advancing towards the town of Salonika in Greece to face 8th army troops that had arrived there from Egypt and the Western Desert last week.

* * *

Peter received a letter from his cousin Max who was detained in a prison camp in Port Erin, which is in the southern part of the Isle of Man. The letter was undated.

Dear Peter (like my sister, I find it difficult to call you Peter),

You lucky bastard, you managed to get out of being arrested in spite of being categorized B. We, I mean all the men, in the

Gray House fell into category C, and were still sent to the Isle of Man.

I must admit, it is quite pleasant here, the food is not bad; we are staying in an old hotel resort. The weather is good and we are as far away from the bombing as one can be. So all in all, it could be worse.

The thing that bothers us most is the boredom – there is just nothing to do all day long besides playing chess. I have improved my game considerably, but that is not the reason we were brought here. (I think the next time we play you will not be able to beat me so swiftly.)

As we are all Germans and Czechoslovakians, we are forgetting our English. With Herman, Papa and myself not being in Guisborough to oversee things, our biggest concern is the business. In the periodic letters we get from the women, it seems they are coping quite well without us. The biggest problem, according to Berta, is obtaining the raw materials. Each time one of those ships is sunk by the German submarines, there is another delay in the yarn arriving in Guisborough. I am sometimes astonished that England is known for its cloth and tweed. Even at home, before we came over from Germany, we used to buy our cloth from here. Now they have to bring it in from America. But it seems that they are coping. The funny thing is that Berta and Dora are doing a very good job of running the place, although Papa is convinced that without us men there, things cannot operate well. Herman and I are more involved with the selling side of things, and unfortunately, the big order from the Ministry of War is on hold for the moment. Berta tells me that the Ministry of War buys everything they manufacture.

The best, she says, are the R.A.F.'s uniforms. The color of the material is a very attractive blue, so if she can cut the material in the right way she can save quite a lot. If the cutters cut the armpits the right way, she can use the extra cloth for pockets. In that way, she can make another five or six pieces of clothing out of each load of 500 shirts. The shops are always glad to buy it, as there is nothing else for them to sell.

How are things with you? Have you heard anything from Aunt Lina? Some people here say that they have received postcards from their family members at home. They are sent from work camps in Poland, saying that they are healthy and are being well treated. They were also told that they were brought to the work camps to protect them from the bombings of the R.A.F. that has no mercy on children and civilians.

So, if Aunt Lina were sent to one of those work camps, she would have been treated for her teeth, and will have the chance to recuperate somewhat.

I do hope this war will be over soon. It seems to me that we will not hold out much longer, and Churchill will have to sign a peace treaty with the criminal.

I hope to hear from you soon, and, even better, to see you if we ever get out of this place,
Max

Translated from Hebrew:
Sunday, April 20, 1941

Horror stories are being told by refugees released from so-called work camps in the former Poland.

In an agreement signed by His Majesty's Government and the German Reich two months ago, there was an exchange of prisoners. The exchange was between the German Templers and former German Jews, who were taken out of what they described as "death camps" in former Poland.

First-hand evidence concerning the fate of our people in the newly-formed Poland, who are brought there from the German-conquered territories in Europe, could be only described as either hallucinations or a chapter from a horror book.

Mrs. Helga Gottschalk, a former furrier businesswoman from Leipzig, came off the boat in Haifa yesterday. She told a journalist that she was taken from the Jewish Ghetto in Leipzig just after New Year's Eve, under the illusion that she would be taken to a work camp in the Lublin area.

The journey in itself was a nightmare, with more than 100 men, women and children crammed into a small cattle car for over a week, with no food or water, besides what they brought with them. Buckets for sanitation were emptied once a day. On arrival, it appeared to her that more than 40 or 50 of the elderly and the children were dead. Once the train stopped at the small train station, they were forced out of the wagons by SS soldiers with whips and fierce dogs and walked to the nearby village of Majdanek. The guards shot those who could not make it and the others were told to carry their bodies.

Once in the camp, they were all given postcards with the stamp of the Red Cross, and were ordered to write that everything is okay, that food is plentiful and that they were being treated well. Inside the barracks, which were former stables, other prisoners told them that here is the last station, and the only way out is through the chimney. The prisoners who manage to survive over two or three weeks will be gassed and burned.

At first, she did not want to believe these stories, which she thought at the time were no more than old wive's tales. But once she was told to take part in sorting the garments of the victims, she saw the truth with her own eyes.

After being there for three weeks, the guards came and said they were looking for people from Germany. She and some others who looked healthier than the rest of the prisoners were chosen. They were taken out and housed in a hotel for two days. In the hotel, they were given civilian clothes to replace their striped prisoner shirts and trousers. At this point they were told that they were being sent to Palestine. They were warned that if they dared tell anything of what they saw or experienced, the agents of the Gestapo in Palestine would shoot them right then and there.

Translated from German:
Thursday, May 1 1941
Corporal Hans Berger
Third regiment D.M.I. (Director of Military Intelligence)
With the 8th Army of Egypt

Dear Adolf,

Thank you for your last letter. It seems that things are going well for you. I must say that I am worried about your mother. The bits and pieces of information that we get here in the Western Desert and from the *Yishuv* (Jewish settlement in Palestine) about what is happening in Germany are not very encouraging.

Since my last letter to you, which I think was over a year ago, I have been recruited to the 8th Army in Egypt. At first, I was with the Royal Artillery Corps, and we fought the 3rd Italian Army in Tobruk and El Alamein. In February we were sent to Greece and that was a calamity. I was taken prisoner.

Fortunately I speak German, so I could understand what the soldiers were planning, which gave me the opportunity to escape.

Now, back in Egypt once more, things are not going so well for us either. When I got back here, somehow they found out that I speak, read and write German. (I do not know how they did not know that before, since not only did I tell them, but I also filled in a form where I answered this question. It just shows you how much notice they take of these things.) Once they realized this, they immediately appointed me as D.M.I., and now I spend my days interrogating German and Italian P.O.W.'s, most of them from Rommel's Africa Corps. I must tell you, they do not like it when they find out that I am Jewish. One of them, a Panzer officer, said that he is not prepared to humiliate himself and be interrogated by an *Untermensch* (a derogatory term used by the German Reich to describe Jews). When he came up with this idea, he got such a beating from the officer in charge, who also happens to be an English Jew, that I am sure that is the last time that he will ever say such a thing again.

Otherwise, most of them are simple, and I would say even quite nice, young men, who in most cases do not know what they are doing in Africa, and are yearning to go back to Germany. I think it will be a long time till they see their homes again.

How are things with you? Are you thinking of joining the Royal Army? Are you still thinking of coming to live in Palestine? I am still holding this land for you in Nahariya.

Do you have a job? How much of the war do you feel over there in England?

Do you still have a chance to swim, or have you given this up? Here in Cairo we do have a swimming pool but it is only for the officers. Sometimes we swim in the Nile, but we cannot play water polo. I hope you will not be lazy and write as soon as you get the chance.

Hope to see you in Palestine some time.
Hans

* * *

Peter also received a letter from an acquaintance from Leipzig, who was exchanged for a German Templer in Palestine. The Templers were a group of around 2,500 German citizens who settled in Palestine during the second half of the 19th century. They were driven by the ideology that God had given them the task of rebuilding the Third Temple in Jerusalem. With the rise of Nazism in Germany, most of them adopted the new ideology of Nazism, abandoning the old one. In so doing, they became a potential threat to the British Mandate in Palestine and the 8th Army in Egypt. The British Ministry was glad to get rid of them in a prisoner exchange program, for Jews of German origin.

Translated from German:
Saturday, May 3, 1941

Dear Adolf,

I do not know if you still remember me. I am the son of Bamberger from the Bamberger & Hertz shoe shop on the corner of Augustusplatz and Grimmaische Strasse.

I arrived in Palestine from Leipzig two weeks ago. It became evident to me, now that I am here, that we were part of a prisoner exchange scheme between German Jews and German citizens living in Palestine called Templers.

One day, they read out eight names and told us to get into a lorry that was waiting, which drove us to the port town of Constantsa in Rumania, where we were sent by boat to Haifa. On the boat we met others that were taken from so-called "work camps" (we renamed them "death camps").

Your mother, with whom I shared a section of the floor in the old burnt-out Brody Synagogue, pleaded with me to post a letter to you if I had the chance. I know she gave letters to people who were sent to other camps. So maybe you will receive more letters.

Your mother's situation is not good. She has no food, no clothing, no shoes, no clean water, no fuel for heat, no place to live, and no one to help her. She, like the rest of us, is going around with a paper bag containing her belongings, moving from one burnt-out house to the next, with no water, heat or shelter from the rain.

I cannot tell you what to do! I am sure you are doing all you can, but if you do not get her out of there very soon, she will wither away.

Fritz

* * *

Inside the envelope was a letter from Lina. It had been a long time since Peter had received a letter from her. Besides an occasional telegram from the Red Cross, neither Peter nor the Schmulewitsch family had heard any sign of life from Lina. The letter was written on the old wallpaper of the burnt-out Brody Synagogue.

Translated from Yiddish:
No date

Dear Adolf,

I am so confused and perplexed that not only I do not know what date it is but I also do not know what day it is. I only know what time it is. I can tell the time according to when the guards come and throw food for us over the railing. It is always only the young and the strong that get to it, even before it lands on the floor. I do manage to swipe some morsels off the ground after each feeding time. That will not keep me alive. I am so hungry and thin – I cannot weigh more than 30 kilograms. It is funny to think how before this catastrophe, I would have been so happy if I had lost one or two kilograms.

MAX DETAINED IN REFUGEE PRISON CAMP IN ISLE OF MAN

Dear Adolf, we are living like dogs. No, worse! At least dogs have a master who will feed them and take care of them. But we live in the dirt and mud, with no food, water or a place to sleep. I think it is has been over six or seven months since I last had the opportunity to wash, even in cold water.

They say that in a week or two, they will take us to the new territories in the West. There, we are told, we will get food, clothes and a place to live in, with heating, water and a kitchen, and each one will work in his profession.

They said that I could work taking care of the children, while the others go to work. I must say I have not worked with children for a long time, but I am sure I will learn very quickly. The only thing I am afraid of is that I will not survive these two weeks.

Some people here have received Red Cross postcards from one of the camps in the West, a place called Majdanek or something like that. In the letters, they say that conditions are good and that they are treated well, only the journey was a bit long. I do not know what I can wear for the train journey; all I have is what I have got on. I would not like to arrive in this new place looking like someone who came out of the poor house. I do hope they will give us some new clothes before we leave.

Dear Adolf, you must try and write to me and send the letters through Rumania or even Russia, but you cannot leave me and forget me, like all the rest have done.

Do not eat things that are not good for you. Remember, till I get over there, there is no one to take care of you.

I am lonely, hungry and cold.

Your loving Mama

Chapter Twenty-Two

Hitler Invades Soviet Union

Thursday, May 29 1941

THE AFRICA CORPS LED BY Rommel have reached El Alamein. The British forces in Egypt, Palestine and Iraq are evacuating their families to India and Australia.

As the pro-German opposition is still going strong in Iraq, a new threat is facing the British army in Egypt and the Suez Canal. The Desert Corps of General Irving Rommel have arrived at the gates of Egypt. The forces are approaching from the West, and threatening to take over the Suez Canal. The canal is Britain's main lifeline to its colonies in Africa and the Far East.

In Palestine itself, there is panic among the half-million Jews, most of them European refugees, escaped from Nazi persecution. In order to protect themselves from the same fate which awaits their brothers in Europe, the Jewish government in exile in Palestine has decided to establish a guerrilla command unit named the Palmah. This new unit will take over Mt. Carmel in northern Palestine and build it as a military base, from which they will raid German concentration and death camps that are planned for Palestine once the Wehrmacht takes over.

Spring 1941
From the American press

There are numerous warnings of war against the Soviet Union. Internal and external sources are trying to alert Stalin to the possibility of war. Hitler is preparing for an all-out invasion of the Soviet Union. Stalin prefers to ignore clear signs of German invasion. He still sees Britain as his main enemy. He regards Hitler as a man of honor.

From our correspondent in the city of Bialystok, there are reports of mass army redeployment.

Wehrmacht troops from Germany, Poland and East Prussia are all mobilizing on their way eastward toward the Ukraine, Belorussia and Eastern Galicia. It seems that Stalin, with the assistance of his intelligence sources, which are spread all around Europe, is aware of these maneuvers, but prefers to ignore them.

From the European communist party members loyal to the Soviet Union, most of them dwelling in Italy, France and Germany, there is a constant flow of information. According to them, it seems that the Wehrmacht is mobilizing over 1,000,000 troops in 150 divisions for an all-out war against the Soviet Union. These troops are transported to the front line via rail, road and sea. Our correspondent, who was on a train voyage from Berlin to Moscow, reported seeing thousands of Wehrmacht troops on the new borderline with the Soviet Union.

Talking to some of the soldiers who had arrived in Warsaw by military train from France, our correspondent was told quite openly that they were on their way East towards Transcaspian in the Ukraine. It is surprising that they knew the approximate date of invasion of the "Bolshevik State," as they called it. Our military commentator in Washington adds that if this sort of top-ranking secret is common knowledge among regular soldiers, no doubt it has reached Stalin's ears too.

The British ambassador to Moscow, Sir Safford Cripps, also warned Stalin of a German invasion that could come before the 22nd of June.

Our correspondent in the Ukraine reports that Luftwaffe "Junkers" aircrafts are spotted every day flying over Russian air space, some of them up to 200 kilometers inland. These sorts of aircrafts are used by the Luftwaffe for photo and reconnaissance assignments.

Stalin, although paranoiac about imperialistic invasion, proclaims that he is impregnable. He is sure that all these warnings are nothing more than a capitalist plot to provoke him into war with Hitler. He is positive that Britain instigated these warnings in order to release the Wehrmacht pressure on the 8th Army in North Africa.

His generals and intelligence chiefs have learned that bringing him news of German activities along the frontier is not only a worthless task, but also a dangerous errand. Stalin has given strict orders that no mass preparation must be made to defend the nation against the Germans. Even reconnaissance planes violating Russian air space could not be fired upon so as not to give the Wehrmacht a pretext to attack.

Stalin is well aware that the Red Army, which mainly consists of new officers and conscripts that were enlisted only a year ago, after the purges in the army, is no rival for the well-trained and well-equipped German army. As Sir Stafford Cripps said in his report to Churchill last week: "Stalin prefers to feed the Lion with oil, grain and other raw materials necessary for the German war machine, hoping that either the Lion will be satiated and fall asleep or will seek prey in other fields."

Well-informed sources in the Kremlin report that Stalin thinks that so long as Germany receives all it needs from the Soviet Union, there is no reason for her to go to war against the Soviet Union.

Translated from German:
Wednesday, April 30, 1941
Trayan St. 50
Cetata Alba, Rumania

Dear Adolf,

It took your letter over three months to arrive. I do not know if this is because of the war, or just the inefficiency of the Soviet post system.

I cannot remember if I told you in my last letter that Siyoma has been taken with many other men of his age and younger into the Red Army. It is now over two months since he was mobilized. We have received only one letter from him. He has been stationed someplace in the Crimean peninsula, not far from the town of

Sebastopol. With Siyoma it was sort of half-volunteering. If not that, at least he was happy to go and fight with his Red brothers against the capitalists. He did not know, before he left, whether the capitalist enemy is the British, German or the American army. The rest of the men from the town who were forced to go blamed the Jews for bringing Communism to Moldavia, and hoped that one day the German or Rumanian armies would free them from this menace.

After Siyoma left, things became worse for us. That is not to say that the situation was good before he left. When Siyoma was still at home at least we, the women of the house, were protected from the Red animals. This officer and the group of pigs that have taken over our house have tried once to attack and rape me. Thank goodness Siyoma's brother Miron (the one I told you was the mayor, and acts as a sort of liaison between us and the Russian army in town) just happened to come by with the main officer of the town, and succeeded in bribing them with a pig he brought along. So they left me and went to slaughter the pig.

One of them said to me that he would get me the next time. I am more worried about Judith and Siyoma's mother and sister than about myself. I think if this ever happens again, I will know what to do. In the meantime I try to hide Judith from them, but you know it is not possible to keep her in hiding all the time.

There is some sort of rumor going around that the German Army, after its occupation of Greece and Yugoslavia, will be on its way north to Moldavia. I only hope they will get here soon to free us from Stalin's Red menace that was enforced on us. However bad they are, they cannot be worse than these Red Pigs that are here now.

Larissa's mother, the one who was raped on the first day these monsters came, had the baby two weeks ago. As bad as it is for us, it is even worse for her. Not only must she care for the child, and therefore cannot work, all her friends and relatives are accusing her of having a relationship with the Russians. We at least have some food, either from our farm or from Siyoma's sister's farm, but she does not even have that.

Our food is minimal and we have finished all the wood we collected for the winter. Those five Russian peasants living in the house took most of it.

Dear Adolf, do you think there is a way you could get Judith and me into England? Although, from the news we get here, which is not very reliable, all from *Izvestia*, the Communist newspaper (who can believe them?), we hear that that the British imperialist capitalistic army is getting a beating on all fronts, and that the Wehrmacht has driven them out of Greece, Yugoslavia, Africa and some other places. In England, the newspaper said, things are so bad that everyone is living in bomb shelters and there is no food or fuel. We never know here if these things are true, as we are only allowed to listen to news from the Soviet wireless.

Dear Adolf, how are you coping with this upheaval? Do you have enough to eat? Are you eating the right things? Have you found a woman to marry? What have you done about the visa for Mama?

I received a letter from her two or three weeks a go. I will send it on to you. I am at the end of my *koyich* (strength). At least we will all die together.

Hope you can get a letter to me.

Love,

Berta (and Judith)

* * *

Peter took out Lina's letter, which came in the same envelope. He wondered how much more wallpaper there was left in the old burnt-out synagogue if everyone there wrote letters to their relatives. It was written with a blunt pencil in a mixture of Yiddish and German. The letter was undated.

Translated from Yiddish:
No date
Leipzig

Dear Berta,

If no one will save me and get me out today, this will be my last letter. In the meantime, they will come to take me to the new place in the East. They say I will have to wait my turn. I think it is the younger and stronger ones that they take first.

We are still rotting away here in the old burnt-out synagogue. It is getting warmer, thank goodness, so at least we do not freeze at night any longer.

Now we do not have any water to drink. We can only drink from a broken pipe which drips from the ceiling.

Yesterday my only friend died and her body is still lying around. I only hope I will die soon too. If I had had the courage, I would have killed myself long ago. The tablets I brought to do it with are lost. I do not have the courage to do it any other way.

Dear Berta, Adolf has abandoned me, and Aunt Sarah has long forgotten that I exist. Dear Berta, you are the only one that can save me. Do not leave me here.

Your loving
Mama

Translated from German:
Sunday, June 1, 1941
Lance Corporal Siyoma Grusman with the 320th artillery division

To my Dearest Berta and Judith,

It is now over three months since I have been with the Red Army. The training is hard and there is much anti-Semitism among the officers.

I was recruited to this unit because of my know-how and understanding of animals. But they have me doing training like all the young soldiers. I have to clean for, and serve, the officers, as if I were some servant boy of theirs.

I complained to the *Politroc*, the political officer in charge of Communist activities in the unit. I told him that what they are doing is against the first principles of the communist brotherhood. My job should be to take care of the mules. These beasts were brought here to pull the cannons. He responded with some very nasty anti-Semitic remarks. I must say I am very disappointed. I did think that in the army of the working people, there would be no class discrimination. But I see it is no different than the capitalistic imperialistic armies anywhere else in the world. We get no clothing, no shoes; living conditions are much worse for us than for our farmhands at home. The food is scarce. Our weapons and equipment are old and outdated. The officers take all the provisions for themselves when they arrive, leaving us with the scraps of leftovers. We Jews in the platoon are always at the end of the queue. The conditions and training are very poor. I am only glad that the USSR signed a treaty with Berlin. If the Wehrmacht had launched an attack against us, there would be no chance in the world that we could hold the line against them for even one day.

The soldiers hate the officers; the officers are remorseless in their attitude to the soldiers. And they all hate the revolution and Stalin. Their only dream is to get to America one day. They do not know that there is terrible exploitation of the workers over there. That does not interest them at all.

I miss being at home and most of all I miss you, Judith. Somehow I think that the whole idea of freedom for the workers, equality for all, is not getting through to the people.

How are things on the farm? Do these soldiers still live in the house? What happened with the mules? Did the officer give them back as he promised? How are my sister Betya and her family managing? I only hope they did not touch the pigs. There is talk of the British Empirical army retreating on all fronts.

The war will come to an end by the summer, and we will be able to come home.

I love you all
Papa

Sunday, June 1, 1941

The German army has mobilized its 39th Panzer Division.

Germany is at the final stages of the war. The occupation of the Soviet Union is only a question of time, say our reporters on the Greek/Bulgarian border.

The 39th German Panzer Division, with airborne troops and the support of the 4th Rumanian Armored Division, are moving north through northern Greece and southern Bulgaria in the direction of Moldavia.

Now that there is no danger of the army being attacked from the rear, the 11th Army of Von Rundstedt is free to move north from Greece in the direction of Moldavia. This had been Hitler's intention since he came to power in 1933 – to conquer and occupy Russia.

Now that the West and South-East are in German hands, Hitler is free to move his armies in the direction of the Soviet Union. This move will be done as stage one of the final advance into Russia. From the Third Reich's point of view this is the war that will end all wars. The purpose of the invasion is to take over the raw materials, land and population of Russia, smashing Communism and its Jewish collaborators.

Chapter Twenty-Three

Peter Regrets Not Joining Friends in Palestine

Tuesday, May 27, 1941

Six warships lost in Crete Battle. German claim of 25 is refuted: Nazis dead in fighting now 18,000.

Cairo, Egypt: Britain's Mediterranean fleet has lost two cruisers and four destroyers in the raging weekend battle of Crete, but has stalled German efforts to land seaborne troops, and the epic struggle on the land now "hangs in the balance," the British announced today.

At the same time Germany has been able to broaden their major foothold at Malemi airport west of Canea, the Cretian capital. The imperial forces were forced back to new positions.

The British insisted heavy losses were still being inflicted on German troops in the fierce hand-to-hand fighting. Greek underground forces estimate the number of Nazis dead at 18,000. Of these, 5,000 were drowned in attempts to land by sea.

Monday, June 16, 1941

Surrender of Italian troops in Abyssinia:

The remnants of the Italian division shattered in the Battle of the Lake in Abyssinia have surrendered to British Forces. A communiqué from GHQ Cairo announced today that its commander, General Palermeo, has capitulated. The General is the fourth Italian divisional commander to be captured in the region of the Lake. His defeated division took to the hills, where it was being harried by Abyssinians that have run out of supplies. During the advance on Soddu, casualties and desertion effectively destroyed four Italian colonial divisions.

*Extracts from the British press
on the day of evacuation from Crete*

The rationing in the British Islands is worse:

From today, every shop window tailor's dummy will bear a sign saying how many coupons, in addition to the cost, are required to buy an article of clothing: 16 for a raincoat, seven for boots, two for gloves, and so on. Until the new coupons are printed, margarine coupons in ration books will serve to buy clothing. Despite the new law, a reporter who visited Petticoat Lane watched more than 400 articles of rationed clothing being sold with not one coupon being exchanged.

Views of the World internees
(A weekly newspaper published by the Jewish internees
in Camp Hay N.S.W. Australia)
Sunday, June 21, 1941

The internment camps policy has failed.

Heavy bombardment of the principal cities in Britain did not cease until the end of November 1940. Nightly air raids were still going on. The German air offensive went on in spite of the internment policy.

Mr. Ward Price from the *Daily Mail* called us "the enemy in our midst." Tom Harrison from the *Daily Sketch* named us "Hitler's Fifth Column in Britain." Long after we so-called "enemy aliens" had been safely interned and locked away in the Isle of Man and Camp Hay in Australia, the assaults on the British Isles by German aircraft continued. In light of this reality the Home Office, in conjunction with the War Office, has decided to abandon the policy of internment.

As the war's end is not in sight, the outcry for skilled workers has exceeded any previous demand. The Home Secretary, Herbert Morrison, has decided to release the German and Czechoslovakian Jews who were interned and imprisoned. The first to be released were industrial entrepreneurs that could help the war effort.

The Under-Secretary of the Dominions, Mr. Shakespeare, has announced that the 2,542 internees that arrived on September 6, 1940 on board the HMT *Dunera* to Australia will be let out of the camps of Hay and Tatura. These internees, being dangerous enemy aliens, will not be allowed to return to Britain.

By April of this year, most of us had left the camp. In a survey I did in May I found out that the majority of us do not want to go back to the country that has persecuted us so badly. Some 90 of us, like Doctor of Law Leonhard from the Oriental Seminary of Berlin and Hans Kronberger, a Doctor of Mathematics from Vienna University, have been asked by Flinders University in Adelaide and Melbourne University to take posts as senior lecturers.

Monday, June 22, 1941

Ancient Damascus falls to British and Free French.

Allies march into Moslem capital after two week siege.

Britain and Free France invaded Syria and Lebanon two weeks ago in a preventive move against anticipated German use of French mandated territories for attacks on the Suez Canal. Spearheads drove into Syria from Palestine, Transjordan and Iraq, but progress has not been rapid.

After two weeks of sharp fighting, British Imperial troops, which included Australian and Indian forces, took over Damascus.

Vichy France troops, under the command of General Henri Danyz, were evacuated from the Syrian capital in disarray to avoid further casualties. This comes after bitter clashes with Free France units operating with the Allies.

The British had accused Vichy of allowing the Axis powers to use air bases in French mandated territory. General de Gaulle's troops announced, "We come to wash out the shame of the Vichy capitulation."

PETER REGRETS NOT JOINING FRIENDS IN PALESTINE

The next objective of the Allies is Beirut.

* * *

Peter received a letter from his cousin Shnoki some time after her husband had been released from internment in the Isle of Man.

Translated from the German:
Thursday, June 5, 1941
British Dolls & Toys LTD
Therpe St, W. Hartlepool, Tel 6277
Manager Carol Katz (German)

Dear Adolf,

Papa came home last week. He was the last of our family to be released from the camp in Douglas. The factory in Guisborough is working 24 hours a day. It is so busy that we have opened up a new branch in town.

Berta and Dora are pulling their hair out trying to find more workers. The problem is more with the male workers. We received from the War Office an allocation of 50 Italian P.O.W.'s. Most of these workers are from the Italian division in Abyssinia.

We do have some communication problems, but three of them come from Tyrol in Italy and speak some German with a heavy Austrian accent. Most of them are nice, quiet and hard working. They work much longer hours than the English do. They do not argue, strike or drink. They appreciate anything you give or do for them. Mostly they are glad to be away from the war front. The War Office takes care of them by supplying them with food, lodging and a monthly visit by the Red Cross, and they even receive some pocket money. They arrive at every shift, chained to one another, escorted by a military policeman. Although I doubt they are trying to escape, who knows? Some of the girls on the factory floor have set their eyes on one or two of them. Most of them are not older than 23. The truth is I cannot blame them – I would do the same if I were not married. There are three of them who come from Milan. Before the war they worked as cutters, which is a great help for us. One of them is so good, that he saves us some 50 yards of material a week. We get most of it from the Board of Trade from the officers' uniform allocation yarn. With what this cutter saves, we make civilian clothing. Herman takes it down to London each time he goes. He sells it to clothing stores down Petticoat Lane. At least we can get some benefit from that good-for-nothing brother of mine.

The bombing has stopped. Only the blackouts, the rationing, the absence of men on the street and an occasional air siren remind you we are still at war.

By the way, with this whole business with the Italians, I forgot to tell you that Dora is getting married and Jane is pregnant. Do you remember the Menashe boy you brought with you before they all left for the Isle of Man? Papa, Herman and Max were in internment with him. When they were released he came to work with us, or should I say, with them (I am still in Hartlepool).

I miss not being with the family in the Gray House. Carol and Lotti who also came back are not nice to me. If I look back, Papa was right opposing my marriage to Carol. I think he and Lotti do not see me as anything more than someone who can hold the fort for them when they are away. I know that Carol, when he is away, or when he goes on his civil patrol duty, goes around with other women.

From the bits and piece of news we get from home, things seem to be very bad. They are sending more and more of the Jews to the East. People here get postcards from relatives in the work camps from time to time. In the postcards they say all is good and well, but I do not believe it is so.

A few days ago, I read an article by some Polish Jew in the *Hartlepool Gazette*. The article said he had escaped from one of

PETER REGRETS NOT JOINING FRIENDS IN PALESTINE

those camps in the East. He told the reporter that these are not work camps as they are portrayed to be. They are slaughterhouses for Jews and Gypsies, places where the Germans get rid of people they do not know what to do with. But who knows where the truth lies? To me it seems somewhat exaggerated that they slaughter people like animals.

Thank goodness the winter is over. Do you know that I nearly finished all the wood I bought before the winter? Now with all these ships being sunk by the German U-Boats, there is just not enough heating fuel to be had. I think all the time of Aunt Lina and what is happening to her in this cold. Maybe it will be better if she is taken to the East. She can wait there till the end of the war. Even if it is true that they shoot people there from time to time, I am sure they will not do such a thing to an old and harmless lady like your mother.

I hope to hear from you soon. Do not be lazy and write soon. Mama has not heard from you since they came back from Port Erin.

All my love,
Shnoki.

* * *

Peter received yet another letter from one of his swim team colleagues, Margolis, who had moved to Palestine after the Maccabi games in 1935.

Translated from German:
Sunday, June 15, 1941

Dear Adolf,

I met Hans the other day in the street. He had come on leave from the Western Desert. He told me he had received a letter from you and he gave me your address. I was really sorry to hear what is going on with your mother.

I do not know if he told you that Margeret and I from the swim team got married (maybe you remember her as Gizella). Just to remind you, it was you who introduced us. This way, it was easier for me to get the certificate. You remember that we both stayed here after the Maccabi games in 1935, but she had a visa and I did not. We live in Nahariya, the same town as Hans. Like Hans, I started with a rooster farm. Margaret's brother got out and came to live with us in Palestine. He managed to smuggle out some money. With the money, together we bought a share in a bus cooperative. It has been over a year that we have worked together as bus drivers. I just love it. Back home, we would never have dreamed of something like that, but here it is different. Here in the Yishuv, it is considered highly respectable work. Each member must put half the price of a bus into the cooperative. Once you have done that, you are a partner for life. Gedalia and I are working on the same share for the time being. (I think you know him, he used to be a reserve for the water polo team.)

My job is to drive our bus daily to Haifa and back, and once a week to Beirut. We mostly drive around the Middle East, transporting soldiers of the 8th Army from here to there. So I get to go to all those remote places that, as children, we always dreamt about – places like Baghdad, Damascus, Teheran, Jerusalem and Cairo.

During the last month, there was a war in Syria between the British 8th Army and the French that are loyal to Vichy France. I know there were some other French troops that were part of the Free French Army. They were loyal to someone called General de Gaulle. The whole thing is too complicated for me to understand. I cannot figure out who is loyal to whom, who is with the 8th Army, and who are agents. How do I know about all this? About a month ago, we started transporting large numbers of 8th Army troops north towards Damascus. On the way back we took French and German P.O.W.'s to the Acco prison. On one of those rides

PETER REGRETS NOT JOINING FRIENDS IN PALESTINE

coming back from Damascus two weeks ago, I heard one of the prisoners talking to his friend in a very clear Saxon accent.

At one of the stops, the Australian officer on guard allowed me to go and talk to him. I found out that his parents apparently live on Menekn Strasse (in Leipzig). I still remember visiting your cousin on the same street. Is it not by the lake? He tells me that he has been in the army for the last six months, as a wireless operator. Until he was sent to Syria, he was stationed in Leipzig and could go home frequently. When I asked him what was happening with the Jews, he says that there are very few Jews that are left in Leipzig. Most of those Jews who are still living in the city congregate around or in the old Brody Synagogue. The few who walk around town look as if they were pulled out of the sewer canals. They are dirty, scruffy and hungry looking. They look as if they have not changed out of their clothes for months. On top of that, he says that you can smell them a mile away, and most likely they have not washed or shaved in months. He mentioned being shocked to see the transformation in his Jewish neighbors from Gohlis, who had always dressed in the fanciest clothing. He could not understand what had happened to them in the last year. The father, who works as a clerk for the Gestapo administration, told him that there were only very few Jews left in Leipzig. He told me that in a short time, they will all be sent to work camps in the East. He did not like the army and was glad to be out of the battlefront. He was worried that his parents would not know where he was. He thought he could send them a message through the Red Cross. This Leipzig boy was told by his superiors that it will only be a matter of months before the British forces all over the world will collapse and surrender. Russia will not last more than two months, maximum, until the autumn. Their information officers told them that by Christmas all the boys would be home, so he thinks that being a P.O.W. is better than being a soldier. With the way things are over here, who knows, maybe he is right?

Hans told me that you were having real problems getting your mother out of Germany – I trust this has been solved by now.

Here in Palestine, wherever you go, it is very hot. We only have rain two or three months of the year, so we can swim in the sea, which is just down the road, all year round. It is funny to see the local Arab people come out and dance when the first rain starts in October or November. I would say that in Leipzig, it was the other way around – we would celebrate when the rain stopped and the sun came out!

In the few years I have been here, I have managed to learn Arabic and some Hebrew, which is the modern biblical language. The Hebrew is not difficult, if you know some of the Jewish prayers we learned in school. I just cannot master English. It takes me a long time to find the right words in English for what the p.o.w. is saying in German. I hope that after the war ends, I will know more because of my work in translation.

The town we are living in is about halfway between Beirut and Haifa. It is on the sea and we can go swimming nearly every day of the year. I am only sorry that you are not here. We miss your training. I am sure you that by now, you will have improved your swimming tenfold.

Margaret sends her love.

We both miss you,

Margolis

* * *

Peter did not know whether to envy his former swim team colleagues, or pity them. It seemed they had a better and freer life than he had here in Manchester. He promised himself that when all this would be over, he would go and visit them over there and maybe also buy that plot of land Hans was talking about.

Chapter Twenty-Four

Liquidation of Cetata Alba – Berta and Judith Meet a Tragic Death

O**N SATURDAY JUNE 12, 1941**, the 11th Wehrmacht Army, under the command of Field-Marshal Rundstet, accompanied by the 4th Rumanian armored division, under the same command, entered the town of Cetata Alba. From the German strategic point of view, it was no more than a preparatory move. The main objective was the invasion of the Soviet Union, which came two weeks later. Von Rundstedt's plan was to cross the Ukraine and take over the rich oil fields in Tashkent and those along the Caspian Sea. In a later stage, he planned to join forces with the 6th Army of Von Paulus. Both armies were preparing to cut the Red Army off from its supply route on the River Volga. This, they thought, would enable them to get to Moscow before the winter.

On the other hand, the Rumanians considered the entry to Moldavia and the takeover of Cetata Alba as a reoccupation of the province they were thrown out of a year earlier. Like many towns and villages taken over by the Wehrmacht, Cetata Alba was occupied by the Gestapo, with its liquidation squads, known as the *Einsatzgruppen*.

Most of the Jews and Communists living in Cetata Alba and the surrounding villages took their belongings and fled over the Dnjestr River, north to Odessa, when they realized what was coming. Accompanying the fleeing refugees were hundreds of Red Army deserters.

There was a small number of German-speaking Jews who stayed. They thought that the German soldiers would not harm them. On the contrary, the Wehrmacht would seek their help, they thought. They knew that the officers would need translators and liaison personnel, people who could communicate with the Rumanian population and the Russian p.o.w.'s.

Within a short time, the Rumanian Greenshirts had rounded up all the remaining Jews in Cetata Alba. As a first step, they concentrated them in the old synagogue by the Castle. The second stage came sometime at the beginning of August 1941. In this stage, the Greenshirts burned the place down with the people in it. This was the end of a glorious Jewish community, a community that had dwelled on the shores of the Black Sea since the Byzantine period.

Translated from Russian:
Friday, August 15, 1941

Dear Mr. Adolf Rochman,

I am writing this letter with the help of my neighbor. He does not know German, so I hope you can find someone who can translate this letter for you. My husband, Miron, is not here. He is in hiding in one of the neighboring villages. My name is Marissa. I am Berta's sister-in-law. Miron is Siyoma's older brother.

I found your address among the scattered papers that were left behind by your sister. They have been stored in the servants' quarters of their farm since the Russian occupation last year. The Germans, who came into our area about two months ago, chased the Red Army out. Berta, who was always so pragmatic, did not escape across the Dnjestr with the rest of the Jews. She thought the Germans would be seeking people like her, people with whom they have a common language and culture. Someone like her could help communicate with the local population.

For some time, the plunder, looting and rape that accompanied the Communist occupation had stopped. The Germans seemed to be in control, and things returned to normal, if one can call this whole situation normal. All the stories about killings, detention, expulsion, and the other horrible acts that the Germans were supposed to inflict on us, just did not happen.

Berta decided to go to the Castle. She planned to work for them as a nurse, secretary or translator. After being there for a while she thought she would go to the Commandant. Berta knew that if she told him what the Bolsheviks had done to them and to other German families, the Commandant would see to it that she and her family would get back all of the property that had been confiscated from them.

I warned her not to go. "Let sleeping dogs lie," I said. Fortunately, at the gate, she met this soldier she knew. Apparently he was a student of hers in the Leipzig Musical Conservatory. He told her not to dare to go in. "That will be the end for you and Judith," he said. He told her she should immediately go into hiding. He would see if he could use his connection with the secretarial staff of the Commandant to get her a permit to cross the river. In the meantime, she should do everything possible to obtain a certificate as a Rumanian peasant. As a Rumanian she could claim that she had a husband and farm waiting for her across the river. Until then, she must stay out of sight. He would do all he could to bribe the Rumanian Police Legionnaires search parties. Hopefully, he could keep them away from the farm. He made it clear that time was short. He knew of German plans to liquidate all the Jews and the Communists in the town.

Berta came home, picked up Judith and came to our place. She was in complete shock. I had never seen her in such a state. We could not keep them here. Informers are everywhere; it could be very dangerous. At night, the three of us sneaked into the wine cellar on their farm. By moving bottles, we managed to create a small hiding niche behind the wine vat for Berta and Judith. At night, I would come with food and leave it at the old stable. Later, one of them would come out and take it.

Berta's student from the Musical College kept his promise. The search parties visited all the houses where they suspected that Jews or Communists might be hiding. They never came to Trayan 50. I would have seen if they had, as we live just across the street from their farm.

For a while, the Wehrmacht and the Rumanian Army stopped all other activities. People in the market said they were preparing for war against the Soviets. During this time, I tried to get forged Rumanian papers. It was not possible. No one would help me. I cannot read or write. I did not have the money the forgers wanted for counterfeit papers.

About a month ago, Berta's former student moved on with the German Army into Russia. There was no one left who could protect them. One morning, about two or three weeks ago, I saw from my window that Greenshirts were entering the farm. They went straight to the wine cellar. They had an informer with them.

There was nothing I could do to stop them. I ran out to the street, and gathered together with the other neighbors outside the house. The Legionnaires came out of the cellar dragging the two of them across the yard. They pulled Berta by her hair. While being dragged backwards, Berta tried to pick herself up. Each time she did so, one of the Garda de Fier thugs would clobber her with his baton. The whole thing only took a few minutes. To me, it felt like an eternity. Once they got to their lorry that was parked on the street, they threw the two of them inside. Other Jews and Bolshevik supporters were already inside the van. Then they drove off. Our eyes met for a second, but I dropped my face immediately. I was afraid that one of the Legionnaires would suspect that I was associated with them. Since then, I cannot sleep at night. I feel like Peter betraying our lord.

They were driven to the old synagogue, where the Rumanian police gather all the Jews that they arrest. I do not know what happened to them after that. I walk by there nearly everyday, hoping to see one of them from the windows or in the courtyard. Each time someone comes close, the Garda de Fier chase them away. I overheard in the market today that the guards take groups of them out each night to the forests and shoot them. I hope this is not true.

The Germans and Antonescu people take food from us. We are only allowed to have one loaf of bread in the house. They even take what we grow in the garden. If anyone is caught smuggling food, he is taken to the Castle. Most people do not come back from there. They say that they take them to work in Germany.

I do not know how much longer we will survive. No one has any idea how long they will stay alive in the synagogue, with no food or water.

I do not know if you will receive this letter, but I am sending it through people who can get this sort of letter through.

I ask of you please not to answer me. It is dangerous to receive letters. In any case, I cannot read.

Love, Marissa

* * *

This letter from Marissa to Peter was smuggled across the river, where it then found its way to the Ukrainian partisans. It was never delivered to its destination. After the war, it was kept in the Red Army's archives in the city of Ismail (Moldavia). It was used as evidence in the Mihai Antonescu war crime trials. After Glasnost in 1990, it was returned to Marissa.

Monday, June 23, 1941

Germany Declares War on Russians.
    Hitler assails Soviets as armies move.
    Nazis break pact and invade Russia.
    German Panzer divisions are smashing their way into Russia.
    The Russian army numbering over seven million was caught unprepared.
    At dawn on June 22nd, the Wehrmacht, together with its allies, opened a 1,800-mile front against the Soviet Union. This invasion came in spite of obvious indications that Hitler was about to break his non-aggression pact with Stalin.
    The Germans who had massed 100 army divisions, together with their Finnish and Rumanian allies, rolled over the 1,800 mile border from the Arctic Circle to the Black Sea.
    Mr. Molotov, the Commissar for Foreign Affairs, broke the news to the Russian people over the wireless today. In his broadcast, he described the German action as, "This unheard-of attack on our country, which is without example in the history of civilized nations."
    Mr. Churchill responded to the invasion by promising Russia "We will offer any technical or economic assistance within our power or capability." He went on to say: "We are resolved to destroy Hitler and every vestige of the Nazi regime. Nothing will turn us from this. We will never parley, never. I gave clear and precise

warnings to Stalin of what was coming. I can only hope these warnings did not go unheeded.

In Moscow, military music is being played over the wireless, interspersed with news of the fighting. Programs featuring the heroic deeds of the Russian forces can also be heard. There are also reports of meetings at factories all over the country. In these meetings workers are vowing to "smash to smithereens the hordes of bloodthirsty Fascist German dogs."

On the battlefield, it is obvious that the Germans have made huge gains in territory. But observers point out that Russia is a vast country, which Napoleon found out to his cost. The mere possession of territory does not ensure victory.

It is apparent that the Germans are attempting to score another blitzkrieg victory, designed to knock the Russians out of the war before an ever-lengthening chain of supply becomes a major problem.

It is felt in military circles that if the Russian Army can hold on until the first heavy snow falls, they may win the war. If snow does fall, the German Panzers and crews will run into difficulties, due to the fact that the Panzer Corp is unsuited to the intense cold of the Russian winter.

Meanwhile, the Russians are striking back. The Red Air Force, with its Ilyushin 4-11's, is bombing targets in Finland, East Prussia and Constantsa. Constantsa is the main oil port on the Danube, on which the German Panzers are dependent for fuel. German Panzer forces, often operating far in advance of their supporting infantry, have driven a great wedge between the 18th and 51st Armies defending Moscow.

None of Them Were Heroes

Last night Russian soldiers were retreating on all fronts, from the Baltic to the Black Sea. As a mark of how serious the danger to Moscow is, Stalin has taken over the post of Commissar for Defense and is now in command of Russia's defenses. Reports from the front suggest that the Germans are also making progress in their advance towards Leningrad, Smolensk and Kiev.

A German military bulletin suggests that two Russian armies have been encircled and would "in a few days be forced to capitulate or be annihilated in one or two days."

Chapter Twenty-Five

Peter Announces Marriage

Not yet aware that his wife and daughter had been killed, Siyoma sent a letter to Berta and Judith:

Translated from Russian:
Monday, September 15, 1941
Sergeant Siyoma Grusman, 56th Army, 320th infantry division

My Dearest Berta and Judith,
 It has been over a month since I have heard from you. I do hope all is going well. We have been fighting against the German Army for the last month in the city of Kerch. Many soldiers have been killed. We do not know what will happen. We are on the move all the time, so there is not much time to write.
 Write as soon as you can.
 Your loving father

BBC Broadcast
Monday, September 1, 1941

At midnight zero hour – for Britain's new V Victory

campaign – the BBC started its broadcasting in occupied Europe with the familiar opening notes of Beethoven's Fifth Symphony, which is similar to the Morse code for "V," and these were repeatedly broadcasted on all the overseas services.

Mr. Churchill explained: "The 'V' sign is the symbol of the unconquerable will of the occupied territories and portent of the fate awaiting the Nazi Tyranny."

At the same time the BBC urged listeners in Europe to go during darkness and chalk the V sign on doors, walls and pavements in order to rattle the Germans.

* * *

Major General Fedor von Bock, Commander-in-Chief of Operation Barbarossa (code name for the invasion of the Soviet Union) was convinced that the entire occupation of the Soviet Union would take no longer than four to six weeks. The invasion began on June 22, 1941. If this were the case, he figured there would be no necessity for winter equipment. Supplementing the army with special winter clothing to protect the soldiers from the harsh Russian winter would only slow down the operation.

The winter of 1941 came early. In areas such as the Ukraine and Odessa, temperatures drooped to 3 to 4 degrees below zero in September. This unexpected change in temperature forced a total reorganization of the Quartermaster Corps. The situation called for a swift collection of winter clothing and blankets. In Leipzig, like other cities, the easiest way to collect these items was from the few Jews still living in Germany.

The Leipzig "Committee" (abridged name for The Committee for Restoring Stolen German Property) decided to transfer the remaining Jews from the burnt-out Brody Synagogue on Kiel Strasse to the remains of the burnt-out Luebecker Synagogue on Gustav Adolf Strasse. (The synagogue was demolished on Krystalnacht.) In this way, the Committee was able to store the clothing and blankets it had collected. The Brody Synagogue still had a roof and served as a better storage place. Once this was achieved, the Leipzig Jews were imprisoned in the former synagogue's cellar. The only thing remaining from this grandiose building was a cemented hole in the ground, which was enclosed by a barbed-wire fence. At night, the guards covered the hole, with the prisoners inside, with tarpaulin. Thus, the Committee simply stripped the Jews of their last possessions.

The property was taken either by force or in exchange for a loaf of bread. In Lina's case, her blanket and the dress she had on her back were all she had. In return, the Committee gave her a certificate, acknowledging that she gave her blanket to the Reich for the war effort. Unfortunately, she could not keep warm with this certificate.

Translated from German:
Die Rote Fahne
(*The Red Flag* was an underground Communist newspaper in Germany. *The Red Flag* was printed outside of Germany and was smuggled into the Reich, and distributed to members of the Communist party. By 1933–34, the security police executed the editors.)

> Only 131,823 Jews are still estimated to be living in Germany. There is talk of a "final solution" to the Jewish problem.
>
> Out of a community of over 550,000 Jews living in our country in 1933, there are only 132,000 left.
>
> The majority of the Jewish community first settled in Germany over 1000 years ago. Some of them arrived even earlier, with the Roman Legions in the first century.

Once the Third Reich started to implement its policies of persecution, pillaging, and robbery against the Jews and Communists, it started on its pathway to destruction. These policies have finally ended with the expulsion of all Jewish people from this country. These acts of oppression will bring the downfall of the 1000-year Fascist Reich of Hitler in two or three years.

This Jewish community, which has contributed so much to German cultural development, science and politics, is now in its most difficult hour. We members of the Communist party should not turn our backs on them at this ebbing hour in our history.

Two-thirds of the community has left in the last eight years. They have migrated to any country prepared to open their doors to them. In newly conquered territories, the Nazis are implementing their "Final Solution."

From reliable sources we hear that Goebbels was heard to let slip the remark that such and such was the "Final Solution to the Jewish problem." Many ears pricked up. Goebbels was apparently referring to the provision of brothels for foreign workers. The fact is that the words "final solution" are also being used by Nazi leaders, following a secret meeting called by Heydrich.

Heydrich, speaking to officials of government departments, is said to have been obliged to admit that the "final solution" refers to "the Jewish problem," a plan that calls for the total extermination of an estimated 11,000,000 Jews living in Europe.

Many thousands of Jews are believed to have been killed. Most of the victims have perished by haphazard shootings, beatings or in transport. As part of Heydrich's plan, the task will be carried out more systematically. It will be organized in special camps with facilities for mass extermination.

* * *

Peter, not knowing that his sister Berta had been killed, continued to write letters to her, in the hope that she would read them and send them on to his mother in Leipzig. The letter was delivered to Miron's wife, Marissa, who was afraid to tell anyone that she received letters from capitalistic countries.

Translated from German:
Thursday, November 13, 1941
Manchester

Dear Berta,

It has been some time since I have received a letter from you. I have not heard anything from Mama either. I only hope that you and she are still well and that the war has not interrupted your life too much.

The last letter I received from you was over six months ago, in which you told me about the Red soldiers and how they are treating you. Now that Germans are there, it must be better.

I must tell you the big news. On Yom Kippur, I decided not only to fast but to also go to *Shul*, something I have not done for years. Somehow, the war and all that is going on is making me more religious. Maybe it's because I think we must depend on God more. As I am not a member of any specific synagogue, I chose to go to the Rumanian Shul on Cheetham Hill Road. I hoped to meet someone that had recently come from there, who could shed some light on what had happened to you and Judith in Cetata Alba. I met no one who even knew where Cetata Alba is, let alone anyone who had met you or Siyoma.

But I did meet this small manufacturer, who is a producer of bolts and nuts for the War Ministry. He offered me a job in his four-man factory, where I started working just after *Neilah* [the closing prayer of the Yom Kippur service]. He also arranged for me to rent a room in one of the bedsits they have on Northumberland Street that he and his wife are running for German refugees.

The other day, his daughter came home on leave from the army. Her beauty stunned me, a sort of healthy look that one does not see in Jewish women. The uniform she was wearing, from the Women's Royal Air Force, only enhanced her beauty. She looks so much like her father: tall, slim, with a kind-looking face. She has enlisted in the W.R.A.F. Her job is to drive a lorry with airplane parts. Everyone calls her Mike, but her real name is Myrtle. Her father and mother are cousins and they are both second generation Rumanians. The two families come from central Rumania. When I looked it up on the map, I saw it is about halfway between your town and Bucharest. I wonder if you know of this town.

Anyway, one thing led to another and we started going out each time she had leave from the Air Force. Mostly we go to the dance halls. (It is impossible now to go to the cinema; there are too many power cuts.)

This relationship seems to be much more serious than any other I have had. The funny thing is that she was a member of the British Communist Party until she joined the W.R.A.F., just as Siyoma was when you met him.

I am going to send a telegram to Mama via the Red Cross with the news.

I hope you will receive this letter in spite of the war.

Love Adolf

* * *

The following day Peter went to the offices of the Red Cross in Manchester to send a telegram to Lina.

LIQUIDATION OF CETATA ALBA

Friday, November 14, 1941

Dear Mama,
   I have found a girl from a good English family to marry.
   All is well with me.
   Adolf.

* * *

Peter received a telegram in response from Lina one week later:

Thursday, November 20, 1941

Dear Adolf,
   Wonderful news. May you have a long life, *iy"h* (with God's help). I will be sent to the East in a week or two. Is she Jewish?
   We will meet after the war.
   I am hungry.
   Mama.

* * *

On the same day, Peter also received a letter from a person in the U.S. that he had never heard of before:

Translated from German:
Wednesday, October 15, 1941
Des Moines, Iowa

Dear Mr. Adolf Rochman,
   You most probably do not remember me. I am the son of Max Bloedel who had the auto-repair shop on Bornaische Strasse. You would not know me as I am only 17 and did not go to the Carlebach Shul. My mother not being Jewish, I was considered a *Mischlinge* (child of a mixed marriage). My mother and I got a permit to leave, and she was told that she must denounce her

marriage to my father. This involved admitting in front of a judge that she made a mistake by marrying a Jew, admitting to *Rassenschande* (polluting the race). She could have done it when my father was deported with the Polish Jews, but she did not want to. She thought it would be shameful. We had to stay with the rest of the Jews in the burnt-out synagogue. About two months ago, just before the Russian campaign, they transferred us all to the former cellar of the Luebecker Synagogue on Gustav Adolf Strasse. Over 400 people were shoved into this hole in the ground. We had no protection from the rain or the sun, men, women and children all crammed together. Supervising us were guards and SS people.

From time to time, they took people away to work camps in the East. This was just too much for my mother. So she gave in, and a short time after we got a permit to come to N.Y. where my aunt lives. From there I was sent to boarding school in Des Moines, Iowa.

Your mother gave me your address and asked if I could somehow contact you when I was free. She looks bad, like all of us. I do not see how she will last. She was hoping that she would be sent to the work camps in the East. She thought there would be better food and conditions there. I think that was the only hope that was keeping her alive. We all lived with this hope. Now I know that anyone sent there is killed and burnt. She has no clothes, no food, and no place to sleep. Just before we left, the Committee took away our blankets from us. They told us it was "for the war effort." She can only get food from what is left on the floor after the guards throw bread into the hole once a day. That is not enough to live on.

I do not want to tell you what to do. I am sure that you are doing your best to get her out, but I would like to point out that if she is not released shortly, it could be the end of her. Either she will be sent to the East or just die from hunger, exposure or exhaustion. I am astonished that she has held out so long.

I do not know what to advise you. I hope you will find a way.
Fritz

* * *

The following day a message arrived from the Home Office:

Friday, November 21, 1941

Dear Mr. Adolf Rochman,
I am glad to inform you that the entry visa you applied for in the name of Mrs. Lina Rochman from Leipzig, Germany has been granted.
You are kindly requested to come to our office on 97 Kings Road to see to the formalities.
Morrison Herbert
Undersecretary for Immigrations

* * *

By the time Peter got this message, informing him he could go and fill in the necessary forms, it was already too late. Lina had been sent to the central prison in Leipzig. By that time, the Gestapo was interested in holding onto every Jew they could lay their hands on, as they were paid six Reich Marks daily from the state for each prisoner they held. Once they had obtained the legal papers, which allowed them to move Lina from her "permanent address" to their installations, there would be no way they would let her go. The legal justification for Lina's detention was that she had over-extended the residency permit that each non-Aryan had to renew every month, or sometimes every week.

By August of 1941, the 11th Army of Field-Marshal von Rundstedt had stormed into southern Russia, in and out of Odessa, with little resistance. The 11th Army was able to conquer the city of Kerch in the Crimean peninsula. However, for the first time, after a series of easy victories, Field Marshal von Rundstedt came up against stiff resistance, mainly from Major General Koslov's

56th army. Siyoma was a veterinarian in the 320th regiment of this army. He was badly wounded in the battle for the city on 25th October, 1941. A short time after his injury, Siyoma was taken by boat across the Ketcenskij straits and rushed to hospital in the city of Rostov.

Siyoma moved on, this time as a civilian veterinarian and a doctor in the inner parts of the Soviet Union. He ended up in the city of Tashkent in Mongolia. The last letter he wrote to his wife was in September of 1941. Whilst writing this last letter, he was still on the move (in battle) and was unaware of her death. All letters that arrived through the Red Cross reached his sister-in-law's house in Cetata Alba, but since she could not read, she simply ignored them.

September 4th, 1941
Sergeant Siyoma Gursman 56th Army 320th Infantry division
On the outskirts of Kerch

To my dearest of all,

I am writing this letter in Yiddish for obvious reasons. I know my Yiddish is not the best and I know Judith will not understand, but I am sure Mama will translate for you.

It is a long time since I have received a letter from you. I do hope that all is well at home. I assume that no letters arrived from you because of the difficulty of sending mail between the lines. I am convinced that a letter will arrive in a day or two.

I am only encouraged by the old saying "No news is good news."

Here we get bits and pieces of news about what is going on back home. The rumor is that the Wehrmacht has taken over Cetata Alba and the area right up to Odessa. We hear that they are very stern but fair with the populations, particularly with those of German origin who are helping them with logistics. But who can know? Every one here has a different story, all depending on where he comes from, what his rank is, what his function is and what his hopes are. The confusion, disorder, cruelty, and savageness here, and I would presume in the whole of the Red Army, is some thing that is not only beyond my belief, it has shaken my whole belief in the Communist system and talk of brotherhood and equality. It is nothing more than the worst sort of capitalism; every man for himself, with none of the rewards of the capitalistic system. The privileges that are given to the party officials – cars, clothes, and the best of foods – we in the field see nothing of. They come from time to time from Moscow and give us talks about what a privilege it is to fight for the Motherland and for its leader Stalin. Then they go back to their comfortable homes at the end of the day, leaving us to get killed and wounded in the name of the world workers' solidarity. But the worst are the lies. It is forbidden to talk or ask questions about the German Soviet pact from two year ago. A soldier in my command who asked one the party officials about this was court-martialed and shot the following day for treason against the Motherland. No explanation why all the officers were killed just a short time before then and no one will tell us why the army was so ill prepared for the Wehrmacht invasion. The only thing these fat over-fed officials talk about is the great wisdom of our beloved leader Stalin. Motivation to fight is close to zero, including for me. There are many deserters who join the other side.

I may think…

The fighting is bitter, and the only thing that keeps the men going on is the fear of being court-martialed. I have been wounded twice but was forced back to the battlefield. The only thing that is keeping me alive is the hope of seeing both of you once again. There is no way we can win this war against the Wehrmacht, which is so well prepared and has such high morale.

In the long hours of guard duty I do every night after the days treating the mules and horses I ask myself again and again, how

None of Them Were Heroes

did I believe, preach and fight for all these empty slogans? How did Stalin and his gang manage to blind me for so many years?

I can only hope the Wehrmacht will win this war as quickly as possible and I will be free once more to come home and live a true life for the first time.

Your loving father,
Siyoma

Chapter Twenty-Six

Too Little, Too Late –
Peter Finally Receives Visa for Lina

Friday, December 5, 1941

Reds push Nazis back up to Kharov. Russian armies broke a new German offensive in the Upper Done basin, scored new successes at each end of the Moscow defenses and continued the pursuit of the beaten Nazi forces on the Azov coast Thursday. But a powerful German thrust at Moscow from the southwest admittedly drove a Panzer wedge into the Red's defense lines and forced the Soviet withdrawal.

The early arrival of the Russian winter and the heavy autumn rains caused the Wehrmacht's provision units delays in the resupplying of ammunition, food, fuel and clothing to the Panzer troops on the front lines. There is talk among Wehrmacht generals of retreating south to the warmer parts of Russia before the harsh Russian winter will close and set in on the troops.

Sunday, December 7, 1941

War Oahu bombed by Japanese planes:
President Roosevelt announced this morning that Japanese planes had attacked Manila and Pearl Harbor.
Six dead, 21 injured, at emergency hospital.

* * *

At the end of November 1941, Lina, together with the remainder of the Jewish "prisoners," was taken from the former cellar of the burnt-out Luebecker Synagogue on Gustav Adolf Strasse to the Gestapo prisons just two streets away. In the Gestapo prison, sanitation, food and dwelling were somewhat better. There were daily meals of 200 grams of bread and soup; there was also a water tap where they could wash and there were straw mattresses and blankets, allowing them to rest during the day. This was the method the Gestapo adopted to break the resistance of the victim, who was to be transported at a later stage.

Upon arrival, they were told that in a short time they would receive new clothes, train tickets and certificates before being transferred to the other non-Aryan work camps in the East.

What delayed the move was the Wehrmacht's use of the railway lines, as it transported its troops to the Eastern front, where they fought against the Communists and the Bolshevik menace. Lina was promised a room to herself, and was told that she would be responsible for taking care of the children while their parents were at work. Lina was worried that she would not have enough money to pay for the journey, as she only had 15 Reich Marks, which covered just a quarter of the fare.

Rumors were circulating among the prisoners that Japan had attacked and conquered the u.s. There was other talk here and there that the Wehrmacht were not doing as well as expected on the Russian front.

As the remaining Jews were being imprisoned in Leipzig,

there was an unrelenting effort by the Reich functionaries in Berlin, such as Eichmann and Burman, to develop an extermination system. This system had to enable the liquidation of the entire European Jewry, in a quick, clean, cheap and discreet way. All the Reich's appropriate councils and authorities, including the chemical and steel industries, the Railway Board, the Reich's Department for Jewish Affairs, the Treasury and Wehrmacht, were at work to achieve this aim. Each department concentrated on developing an apparatus that would gather (with as little protest as possible from the inmates themselves and from the surrounding population) and eventually destroy this undesirable element within Europe.

By February of 1942, the system was up and running. The concern was that the transports would be delayed on the way, and the inmates would take advantage of the weak links in the chain and escape. It was easier, more efficient and cheaper to detain Lina and the rest of the Jewish inmates in Leipzig until such time that the system would prove to be in perfect running order.

By mid-January 1942, Lina and the others were given postcards and ordered to write to their relatives and friends about their living conditions. Lina wrote to Berta, not knowing that she had been liquidated some six months before, and to Peter.

Written on a Red Cross postcard:
Thursday, January 15, 1942

Dear Adolf,
I am feeling a bit better, the food is good here, and they are treating us well. They promised that in a week or two they would be sending us to the family work camps in the East. They told us they are doing this so we will not suffer from the shortage of food and exposure to air bombings that are inflicted on us by the British.
Dear Adolf, can you send me the value of 60 Reich Marks

through the Red Cross so I can pay for the train? Will meet after the war. I will send you my new address once I get there so you will be able to find me when the war ends.

Love Mama

* * *

The Reich Train authority was one of the largest government agencies operating within the Reich. It employed some 900,000 workers and provided an important service to the army and civilians. It was the eastern department, known as the GBL department, that was in charge of transporting the Jews to the liquidation camps. Although the Jews were transported in cattle wagons, they were charged as if they were passengers traveling in third class. As for children under the age of ten, they were charged half-price, and any child under the age of four travelled for free. If the Gestapo managed to organize groups of over 400, they would get a fifty percent discount.

The person in charge of the transportation of Jews, which was known as *Sonterzuge* (special trains), was Franz Novak, who was imprisoned for six years after the war on charges of war crimes.

In the trial listings, the transport of Jews was written down as people transport, but in reality they were mobilized as cattle. In order to save money on trains and locomotives, the Jews were transported in wagons that in 1940/41 took 1,000 people at a time, but later in the same capacity carried 2,000 and sometimes even 5,000 people. The space allocated to each person was 20 square centimeters (about the size of two airmail envelopes). The excess weight of the train slowed it down to less than 50 kilometers per hour, and forced them to use two locomotives instead of one. Jewish trains were shunted to the side to allow trains with higher priority to move on the main lines.

In the better cases, the human freight was locked inside the wagons for hours and days while the guards and rail workers went to the nearby town to eat, sleep and entertain themselves. In the worst cases, they were abandoned and left to die. This often happened if the rail was bombed and the guards ran away. Compressed into sealed train wagons with no air, food or water for hours on end in rail-stations or in open fields, most of the survivors remember the train rides as the worst experience that they suffered in the Holocaust.

It was so hot in the summer that one would get burnt touching one of the metal parts of the wagon. In winter, they were so cold that most of the deaths of the young and elderly were attributed to freezing conditions. It is estimated that over forty to fifty percent of the human freight died before the train reached its final destination.

There is no evidence to suggest that the train workers were aware of the fate of the human freight that they transported, but there is no doubt that the officials directed the trains to remote train stations, where there was no industry or people living nearby. At the end of the war, some of the officials were accused of war crimes and put on trial, but none of them were convicted.

The Gestapo kept an administrative ledger of each person, enabling them to trace a person at any given moment of their life. By the end of 1941, Lina, along with the other Jewish residents held in the Luebecker Synagogue, was imprisoned by the Gestapo. Although they knew where she was, they deliberately did not note it down. In this way, they were not required to fill out any police record explaining their arrest.

Translated from a handwritten Gestapo document:

February 6, 1942

Whereabouts of Lina Rochman:
    September 24 – moved from her residence on Keil Strasse 5

first floor to Luebecker Synagogue Gustav Adolf Strasse bottom floor. Left to an unknown destination 30 November 1941. Was last seen on the train leaving for Riga in the new territories on 5 February 1942.

The Gestapo did not provide an explanation of why Lina was travelling to Riga. The 200 surviving "prisoners" were marched in the early hours of February 2, 1942, from the prison camp of the Gestapo to the rail-station. The sight of this pitiful group of people marching through the streets of Leipzig at that early hour of the morning was not pleasant to the eye. Dressed in rags and wearing broken shoes, hungry and humiliated, as they wrapped blankets tightly around their bodies to protect themselves from the bitter February cold, they were escorted by young healthy-looking SS soldiers, each holding a dog leash in one hand and a whip in the other. The Alsatians were barking furiously while the SS guards were shouting *"Schnell, schnell verfehluten Jude"* (Quick, quick, you damn Jews), whipping those like Lina who could not keep up.

Although it was only a three-kilometer walk to the station, Lina thought she would never make it. There was blood oozing from her back, where she was viciously whipped by one of the soldiers. She also had a bleeding foot where one of the Alsatians had bitten her.

Amidst the barking of the dogs and the shouts of the SS guards, one could hear the heavy breathing of the people and the cries of the children. From the few windows of the early risers, one could hear shouting and cursing, "You damn Jews, our boys are getting killed in Russia because of you – our Führer will see that you will all pay for it."

Along the way, the onlookers would throw rotten vegetables at the Jews. There was the occasional bypasser, who put his life, and that of the hungry recipient, at risk by pushing half a loaf of bread, or even their whole lunchbox, into the hands of some of the prisoners. Helga, the former mathematics teacher from the Carlebach Shul, helped and supported Lina along the way, as she had done for the last two months. In spite of the short distance from the police station to the rail-station, it seemed to Lina that this was the longest journey she had ever endured.

It was around 6:30 A.M. when they finally arrived at the loading bays, which were located just outside the Haupt Bahnhof, the main rail-station. The prisoners were ordered to sit down on the platform, which was covered by a thick layer of snow and cattle dung. They were warned to put their heads down and not dare look at the soldiers. They waited patiently for six hours while herds of cattle were unloaded and taken away. It was midday by the time the wagons, which had carried the cattle, were emptied. So intense was the bitter cold that five of the prisoners died from exposure.

Three of the younger men were ordered to take straw from the stacks of hay that were put there for the cattle, and to spread it on the floor of the wagons that by that time had been emptied. The wind and cold seeped through Lina's clothes and blanket. Her hand and legs were frozen; she could no longer move them. She kept asking Helga when they would let them into the station, so they could at least be under shelter until their train arrived. Helga reassured Lina, who by that time was half-demented from exhaustion, hunger and cold, that they did not want them to go into the station so the Aryans would not hurt them.

A short time later, the guards with their Alsatians arrived once again. While the Jews were freezing to death, they were ensconced in the warm comfort of the bar in the station. Waiting for the train to be cleared of its animal freight, so it could be reloaded with human freight, was their time to rest.

The growling, barking, whipping and shouting resumed once more. They were ordered to stand up. Those who could not were whipped mercilessly. The rest hurried to get up. A ramp was laid down from the platform to the cattle carriages. They were forced to enter the wagons. One or two hesitated for a moment in protest, trying to show the soldiers the tickets they had bought. The dogs and the soldiers saw to it that the protest was over in a flash. The prisoners started to trample on one another in their attempt to get a better place in the wagon. Lina and Helga were pushed in with the rest of the group. Lina found a place in the corner. More and more people were coming in, each one pushing Lina and Helga closer to the wall. The last to enter were pushed in by the soldiers with whips, clubs and rifle bayonets.

They were still some twenty children outside. The SS men lifted them up and threw them over the heads of their parents. People started to shout and scream that they must go to the toilet; others asked for water. It was so crowded that those who had lifted their hands to maneuver themselves in had no room to put them down once more. Others had to stand in the same position without being able to move the whole duration of the voyage; they could not even turn around. The situation worsened when the guards slammed the doors shut.

The one person squeezed by the door got his hand wedged in the hinge and could not get it out. Others urinated in their clothes. It was impossible to know how many people had fainted or died as a result of the gruesome conditions. Each one tried to push and shove the person standing next to him so he could find a more comfortable position. The Gestapo had managed to squeeze some 50 to 60 people in a carriage that was used to transport ten heads of cattle. After 3:00 p.m. the train started on its journey.

The Gestapo was under strict orders not to allow Jewish prisoners into the station. This policy was implemented in order not to shock any Aryans who happened to be in the station. The general policy of the Reich was to disrupt as little as possible the lives of whom they called the decent hard working Germans. In any case, they were to be transported in cattle wagons, although they had paid the full train fare to be transported in third class.

Furthermore, they considered it a waste of time allowing them entrance into the station when they would be taken out again anyway. The rail board did not permit cattle wagons into the passenger side of the station.

After about three hours, they arrived in Dresden; Lina could discern the name of the station through the crack in the wooden wall just beside the corner where she was sitting. Once again there were Jewish people on the platform. They had also been waiting since the early hours of the morning. Frozen, hungry and humiliated, they were shoved into the next three wagons behind. Once again, they waited many hours until the train was loaded, and the SS men had finished their supper and rested before the night voyage to Berlin. In the early hours of the following day the train got to Sachenhausen rail-station where it loaded the prisoners of the camp who had been imprisoned there since Krystalnacht in November 1938. By the afternoon, the train continued to Breslau and the same procedure repeated itself there.

After leaving Breslau station, travelling east in the direction of Riga, the train stopped. The doors were opened, and ten of the younger men were ordered out. These young men were told to clear the dead bodies, and the straw that was covered in lice, excrement and vomit of the dead people. They were ordered to bury the dead and bring water from a nearby well to wash the carriage. The fresh air that came in when the door was opened, the new straw, and the bucket of water that was brought in, helped Lina to revive somewhat. By this time Lina had lost her mind and started to behave like an animal. She, like others from the train in her predicament, was brought out to the field by the side of the train. The guards from the SS personnel entertained themselves by throwing morsels of bread onto the ground, and watching gleefully as the frenzied people squabbled and fought amongst themselves to reach the bread.

After the carriage was cleaned and emptied of the twenty dead bodies, there was more space for Lina and Helga to sit together. The continuation of their journey was once more delayed as the wagon had to be shunted to the sidelines for over five hours in order to let an L train, used to transport soldiers, pass by. After a nightmarish week of travel with no food, water or fresh air, the train pulled into the Riga railway station in Latvia. The Latvian Gendarmerie was waiting for them there, as well as funny-looking people in striped pajamas. With whips and dogs, the Gendarmes ordered the people that were still alive to jump out of the carriages.

Once they were out, and all standing in line on the platform alongside the train, the pajama people went in, pulled out the dead bodies and piled them up on trolleys. They were to be burned in the crematorium inside the camp. Lina's body was the last to be taken out of the carriage and was thrown on top of the pile. Upon arriving at the camp, the pajama people opened Lina's mouth, and pulled out a golden tooth. They quickly looked through her ragged clothes to see if she had hidden any valuables in them. After being satisfied that there was no more value in the body, Lina's body was casually tossed into the crematorium to be burnt.

Family Photos

None of Them Were Heroes

3 Humboldt Strasse

Judith

Berta and daughter, Judith

FAMILY PHOTOS

(Left to Right) Berta, Lina and Adolf

Myrtle and Adolf/Peter

Memorial of Leipzig shul destroyed on Krystalnacht (chapter 25)

Zelig

Leipzig Train Station